PATER'S PORTRAITS

Mythic Pattern in the Fiction of Walter Pater

"All art is dream, and what the day is done with is dreaming-ripe, and what art has moulded religion accepts, and in the end all is in the wine-cup, all is in the drunken fantasy, and the grapes begin to stammer."
W. B. Yeats

PATER'S PORTRAITS

Mythic Pattern in the Fiction of Walter Pater

by Gerald Cornelius Monsman

The Johns Hopkins Press, Baltimore

To my Parents

 PREFACE

Throughout this study I have used certain basic abbreviations in quotations from the works of Pater. The ten volumes of the standard Macmillan edition are abbreviated in the text as follows: *The Renaissance: R; Marius the Epicurean: ME,* I or II; *Imaginary Portraits: IP; Appreciations: Ap; Plato and Platonism: PP; Greek Studies: GS; Miscellaneous Studies: MS; Gaston de Latour: GdL;* and *Essays from the "Guardian": EG.* The 1889 edition of *Appreciations* is cited as *Ap* (1889), the *Uncollected Essays* I have abbreviated *UE,* and the *Imaginary Portraits* edited by Eugene Brzenk is rendered *IP*B. The numbers following the abbreviations refer to the page numbers. For the remainder of the quotations, I have used footnotes.

In the writing of this study, I have many people to thank, in particular the English faculty at The Johns Hopkins University. I am deeply in debt to J. Hillis Miller and Charles Anderson, who have given me great help in their comments on my rough drafts, and to Earl Wasserman and Don Cameron Allen for taking the time to give advice. I wish also especially to thank John Sparrow and Lawrence Evans, who have gone out of their way to render substantial help. There are others, certainly, who should also be thanked: all those, for example, whose written or spoken ideas have long since sunk into the matrix of my own thought and are no longer separable from it. Indeed, even what I owe to such writers as Friedrich Staub and R. T. Lenaghan I can no longer adequately assess—that I leave to other scholars to judge. Finally, I acknowledge my indebtedness to the late A. O. Lovejoy, who during my undergraduate years suggested I read *Plato and Platonism* in connection with a paper with which I was then struggling. This was, I believe, my first introduction to Walter Pater.

It is, however, to my parents that I dedicate this study, for I, too, as a child in the house of life lived in a perfect summertime where no winter came. Such happiness one may be fortunate enough to pass on, but can never pay back.

Durham, North Carolina   G. C. M.
June, 1966

CONTENTS

✒ INTRODUCTION

Despite the recent growth of interest in the literature of the Victorian period, little has been written about one of the greatest of Victorian prose masters, Walter Horatio Pater. In one area particularly there is a gap: Pater's fiction clearly needs fuller and better critical analysis than it has had so far. Only his novel *Marius the Epicurean* can be said to have drawn a fair share of attention, yet only rarely has it been considered within the broader framework of Pater's other writings and certainly not in detail. Perhaps this absence of adequate studies stems from an acute critical embarrassment as to which of Pater's varied writings are legitimately fictive and worthy of the attention of the literary critic and which ones should be left to the art critics, the philosophers, and the historians. Iain Fletcher, in an excellent monograph, has described the problem well: Pater's work, says Fletcher, "seems to lie in a twilight of categories between criticism and creation; between art and literary criticism, belles lettres, classical scholarship, the journal intime and the philosophic novel."[1] Perhaps what is needed is a more flexible understanding of the nature of fiction and a corresponding willingness to read many of the portraits in *The Renaissance* and *Appreciations*, for example, as contributing toward the imaginative universe of the writer. But since there are differences between these historical portraits and those fictional portraits which Pater calls "imaginary"—the poetic latitude that Pater permits himself in the imaginary portraits being far greater than in the historical portraits—this study will limit itself to the general area of the so-called imaginary portraits, using the other writings as the occasion warrants.

From the start Pater's fiction presents the prospective critic with numerous causes of frustration, not the least of which is a marked lack of both dramatic narration and description. How does the

[1] *Walter Pater* (London, 1959), p. 5.

hero really look? How does he sound? What are his specific emotions? What are the details of his actions? Such questions are usually unanswered by Pater, for he is rarely vivid and first-hand, and his fiction always tends toward exposition. Pater talks *about* sensations and ideas—he summarizes them, one may say—but he never presents them realistically. Like the deaths which in Greek drama take place off-stage, so in Pater we are told, rather than shown, what has happend. When Percy Lubbock says there is little drama in Pater's fiction,[2] he points to a real problem, I think.

The style, about which I will have more to say in Chapter II, contributes to this tendency toward non-dramatic exposition. Syntactically, Pater's sentences are often exceedingly involuted, and the antecedents are frustratingly vague; there are times when Pater completely fails to sum up the heart of the matter in language that does not annihilate the thought. Further, because the diction is so abstract, there appears to be little connection between individual words. Only concrete words can explode against each other, and Pater persistently tends to choose vague words, generalizations such as *life, death, love,* and ignore the specifics which give body to a work. These stylistic features make it difficult to focus on a passage and give it the sort of intensive explication one might give, for example, to a passage of poetry. But, of course, this quality of abstraction is typical of much Symbolist writing; it is not unique with Pater. Since the good prose wine of the last century is not generally in very great demand, the twentieth-century reader may simply be prejudiced, but it is well to remember that there can be no appreciation of the literary style of, for example, Yeats without a genuine liking for Pater. Just as Spenser is the real test of one's palate for the sixteenth century, so Pater, perhaps, is much the same for the late nineteenth.

At any rate, for all his obvious failings in narration and description, Pater is one of the prose masters of his time. Judged by his own standards, his fiction achieves real success, for every portrait reflects just that sort of careful artistic structure which he demanded in the best work. Considering "the effects of conscious art" in the telling of a story, Pater wrote in "Style" that "one of the greatest pleasures of really good prose literature is in the critical tracing out of that conscious artistic structure, and the pervading sense of it as we read" (*Ap,* 24–25). By using ellipses and cutting quotations to the bone, by juxtaposing widely separated passages and so bridging the expansiveness of the prose, one can

---

[2] *The Craft of Fiction* (New York, 1945), p. 195.

show exactly this sort of conscious art at the heart of every one of Pater's portraits, all of which, whether historical or imaginary, are philosophic apologues of the relation between the universal and its particular expression, their dialectical structure a reflection of his concern with this relationship.

Some readers may deem it a serious flaw that the subject and structure of Pater's stories are identical; I think, however, that this is a mistake. Pater expresses the abstract contrast of the universal and the particular through myth, in which ideology has become poetry and the theoretical has been given the concrete immediacy of drama. Of course, the drama which we have here is of a unique kind, not at all the sort of drama which Percy Lubbock demanded from Pater. Myths usually preserve only the bare minimum of narrative and descriptive elements, for the elaboration of action by symbolic means requires simplicity. Like the old Bible stories, myths can more easily dispense with the accidental and the transient, with characterization or motivation, for example, because they deal with universal patterns of reality. It has sometimes been said that Pater does not really convincingly prepare for the denouement within the context of his story and that the climax tends to be melodramatic. But this is true of myth, too, which so often seems to lack justifiable motivation; and if, as U. C. Knoepflmacher asserts, "the quality of Pater's fiction is nondramatic, derivative, almost static,"[3] much the same could be said of Ovid; his stories, too, are only motionless pictures in a gallery.

Mythic pattern is far from being a defect in Pater's fiction; on the contrary, it is a striking anticipation of the twentieth century. We recall the great interest of the Cambridge anthropologists in the Dionysiac side of Greek civilization, an interest which revised the idea that the Greeks had dismissed the dark and irrational qualities of existence in their dedication to reason and their commitment to life on this earth. This concern with the mystery cults and their relation to primitive religious ritual and myth, best exemplified by Sir James Frazer's influential *The Golden Bough*, is anticipated several years by Pater.[4] Further, the way in which Pater employs myth in his fiction resembles the use of it by such

---

[3] *Religious Humanism and the Victorian Novel* (Princeton, 1965), p. 159.

[4] Pater himself was anticipated by the syncretic or comparative mythographers of an earlier generation. And if one defines *myth* not in terms of the broad modern conception of archetypes (as does Mircea Eliade) but rather after the fashion of simple stories (as does Douglas Bush), then the whole of English literature from before the Renaissance until Pater's day is replete with examples.

modern writers as T. S. Eliot and James Joyce. The significance of the impressive amount of meek scholarship which went into each portrait and tied it so closely to cultural history is that Pater did not approach his stories with the idea of imposing some fabricated pattern on reality from the outside; but, rather, like Joyce, that he sought such a mythic pattern in reality, even in his own biography, as he shows us in "The Child in the House."

In Pater's fiction myth begins with the theme of "renaissance"—the artistic and cultural awakening which occurs when the universal and its particular are reconciled. This awakening is described by Pater in terms of the two divine brothers Apollo and Dionysus, whose legend, like that of Demeter and Persephone, is merely another version of the myth of the *Magna Mater* and her year-daimon. Apollo is the older and the immortal god; Dionysus "comes of the marriage of a god with a mortal woman; and from the first, like merely mortal heroes, he falls within the sphere of human chances" (*GS*, 44). Apollo corresponds to the universal, the *Magna Mater*; Dionysus, to the daimon which dies to make way for the new year, revitalizing the creative powers of the earth goddess. The Apollo-Dionysus myth is not, however, used by Pater as merely a story of seasonal flux; rather, Apollo is the embodiment of the spirit of humanity, and Pater's Dionysian year-daimon hero is the divine consort of humanity, one who loves both the individual and all men supremely well. In Pater's first essay, "Diaphaneitè," a sort of *Ur*-portrait, the ideal personality is presented in nature and function as the distinct counterpart of Apollo. That the Paterian hero should be conceived of as the divine priest of Apollo is wholly fitting, for just as Apollo was the greatest patron of art, the leader of the nine Muses, so the hero in Pater's fiction is a bearer of artistic and cultural awakening to his age. The daimon hero is not the primitive Dionysian god whose virility fructifies nature, but the modern god whose virility fructifies culture, for just as Dionysus by life and death heralds the birth of the plant kingdom, so the life and death of the Paterian hero heralds the awakening of intellectual vitality.

All of these ideas will be examined in greater detail in the following pages. In my initial chapter, "Art and the Gods of Art," I use Pater's first book, *The Renaissance*, as the basis for my discussion of the relation of the gods Dionysus and Apollo to cultural rebirth, while in the second chapter, "Portraiture and the Early Portraits," I begin my discussion of the fiction proper, relating the genre of imaginary portraiture to the mythic pattern of Apollo and Dionysus. In Chapters III, IV, V, and VI, I continue the chronological sequence begun in Chapter II, identifying in each of the portraits the essential mythic pattern lying beneath external form and subject. Finally, in Chapter VII, I attempt to view my thesis from a new perspective, seeing all of Pater's writings in terms of the ultimate image of the circle. Since I am discussing a single theme, not several which could be treated separately, I have selected an essentially chronological organization. Such an approach frees one from the impossibility of having to talk about all of the fiction simultaneously while allowing one to demonstrate Pater's remarkable stability of thought over a period of thirty years.

Since there has been as yet no book-length study of the mythic core of Pater's work, the call for a new and complete study of his fiction is obvious. It is not the primary purpose of this study to relate Pater to the English, French, or German thinkers and novelists of his time. Neither do I wish to analyze Pater's psychological make-up, to interpret his fiction in the light of his supposedly warped psyche. Aside from the fact that he was terribly shy, that he impressed acquaintances such as Violet Paget and George Moore as staid and dull, there is little evidence to indicate abnormality. Pater's philosophy certainly was not incompatible with existence, nor singularly morbid, as some allege. His noted celibacy was of the monastic kind, for he was, in Joyce's words, "a priest of eternal imagination" and would take for his mistresses none but the Ausonian Sisters.

In the chapters which follow, the emphasis will be upon that pleasurable "tracing out" of the conscious, artistic structure of Pater's fiction. The scope of his writings comprises nothing less than Western culture itself; its subject is all that man has written, thought, said, sung, hoped, or prayed as a civilized creature in the last two and one-half millennia. The author's success in handling such a vast subject in an age when talents were not those of a Dante is undoubtedly attributable to his discovery of a coherent pattern by which art, religion, and life can be organized.

Art, religion, and life—these, surely, were in desperate need of organization, for the repercussions of the "new philosophy" of the Renaissance, the so-called crisis of European consciousness, had not subsided in Pater's time any more than it has in our own. Accordingly, Pater wistfully contrasts the universe of Pico with that of Pascal: "For Pico," says Pater,

the world is a limited place, bounded by actual crystal walls, and a material firmament; it is like a painted toy, like that map or system of the world, held, as a great target or shield, in the hands of the creative *Logos*, by whom the Father made all things, in one of the earlier frescoes of the *Campo Santo* at Pisa. How different from this childish dream is our own conception of nature, with its unlimited space, its innumerable suns, and the earth but a mote in the beam; how different the strange new awe, or superstition, with which it fills our minds! "The silence of those infinite spaces," says Pascal, contemplating a starlight night, "the silence of those infinite spaces terrifies me." (*R*, 41–42)

Pater, too, was terrified, for he himself seemed caught in the antinomy of the relativism of the modern consciousness and the need for some normative aesthetic, religious, and metaphysical system of values.

But his sensitivity to the problem was also a measure of the great extent to which he accepted the scientific world of relative, finite realities; and when he exhorted the young men of Oxford to burn with a "hard, gemlike flame," he called them to live life not less in the spirit of the Bunsen burner than in the spirit of the waxen candle in a holy place. Happily, Pater believed that the antinomy was only apparent, that the material world of "perpetual flux" and the world of eternal rest, which is God, are not forever divided. He effected his reconciliation by a mental pilgrimage back to that early time in civilization when science and religion were not divorced, to those old mythical patterns and that almost animistic consciousness which accepted nature as the "visible vesture and expression of God." The aim of this study is to discover in Pater's fiction the use of these old scientific-religious patterns of myth to explain moments of religious and cultural awakening, to reveal the way in which one man arrived at a *credo* that would answer to the desolation of life and culture. "And so I penn'd it down," says Bunyan, "until it came at last to be, for length and breadth, the bigness which you see."

PATER'S PORTRAITS

Mythic Pattern in the Fiction of Walter Pater

 ART AND THE GODS OF ART

ART

In 1873 Walter Pater published his first volume, a modest, blue-green book entitled *Studies in the History of the Renaissance*.[1] It embodied a philosophy of art and life that had been circulating within the walls of Oxford for some time, for a graduate of Brasenose, Pater's college, tells us that by 1864 Pater was already "vaguely celebrated," rumored "to have a new and daring philosophy of his own, and a wonderful gift of style, owing his Fellowship to these two, for he was no scholar, as the Universities understand the word."[2] Arthur Symons, Pater's admiring protégé, records that from the very first the book was "taken as the manifesto of the so-called 'aesthetic' school,"[3] and, indeed, T. S. Eliot has gone so far as to attribute directly to Pater's influence a number of "untidy lives" among these *fin-de-siècle* rebels devoted to the cult of sensation.[4] No doubt part of the younger generation's enchantment with the book lay precisely in the older generation's somewhat indignant reaction to it, for the volume—more particularly, its Conclusion—raised numerous conservative eyebrows, notably those of the imposing Benjamin Jowett, Master of Balliol.[5]

Needless to say, Pater himself was greatly pained both by the attacks of the moralists, such as Jowett, and the misunderstandings of his would-be disciples. He suppressed the supposedly hedonistic Conclusion in the second edition of *The Renaissance* because, as he said, "I conceived it might possibly mislead some

[1] Later (in the second edition) it was entitled *The Renaissance: Studies in Art and Poetry*. The essay on Giorgione was added in the third edition.

[2] Arthur Benson, *Walter Pater* (London, 1906), p. 22.

[3] *Studies in Prose and Verse* (London, 1904), p. 64.

[4] *Selected Essays* (New York, 1950), p. 392.

[5] See Benson, *Pater*, p. 55. The Conclusion had first appeared in 1868 as part of "Poems by William Morris" in the October edition of *The Westminster Review*, but since the review was unsigned, Pater remained for the nonce only "vaguely celebrated."

of those young men into whose hands it might fall" (*R*, 233), and he only reintroduced it in the third edition after he had "dealt more fully in *Marius the Epicurean* with the thoughts suggested by it" (*R*. 233). Although Pater never expanded the brief pages of the Conclusion, almost every idea there formulated can be amplified by reference to his later writings, for although he translated his basic ideas into the materials of fiction, he never abandoned his original belief in "experience":

> Every moment some form grows perfect in hand or face; some tone on the hills or the sea is choicer than the rest; some mood of passion or insight or intellectual excitement is irresistibly real and attractive to us,—for that moment only. Not the fruit of experience, but experience itself, is the end. A counted number of pulses only is given to us of a variegated, dramatic life. How may we see in them all that is to be seen in them by the finest senses? How shall we pass most swiftly from point to point, and be present always at the focus where the greatest number of vital forces unite in their purest energy? To burn always with this hard, gemlike flame, to maintain this ecstasy, is success in life. (*R*, 236)

Certainly, in the urgent tone and seductive beauty of a passage such as this, there is much which could be misinterpreted.

Behind the hortatory mood of the Conclusion lies the message of modern science. Indeed, Pater had prefaced his Conclusion with an epigraph from Plato's *Cratylus:* "Heraclitus somewhere says that all things are moving along and that nothing stands still."[6] The world, says Pater, following Heraclitus, the "father" of the scientific spirit, is in perpetual flux, the seemingly solid is only a loose "group of impressions—colour, odour, texture—in the mind of the observer" (*R*, 235). The real world of facts, then, seems to dissolve into psychological atomism, a hopeless solipsism. "The whole scope of observation," says Pater,

> is dwarfed into the narrow chamber of the individual mind. Experience, already reduced to a group of impressions, is ringed round for each one of us by that thick wall of personality through which no real voice has ever pierced on its way to us, or from us to that which we can only conjecture to be without. Every one of those impressions is the impression of the individual in his isolation, each mind keeping as a solitary prisoner its own dream of a world. (*R*, 235)

Speaking as he does here, Pater sounds much like a British empiricist, and one imagines that he is not far from Hume's phenomenalistic idealism, which marked the end of the scientific trend charac-

---

[6] 402[a]. I have not, however, used Jowett's translation.

terized by interest only in what can be weighed and measured. Pater accepted this scientific world of relative, finite realities without regret or reservation, and in his essay on Coleridge, we see him taking the poet to task for his refusal to accept the modern precept that "nothing is, or can be rightly known, except relatively and under conditions." The desire of Coleridge "to fix thought in a necessary formula, and the varieties of life in a classification by 'kinds,' or *genera*" (*Ap,* 66) seemed to Pater an idle dream indeed.

One is tempted to say that in siding with the empiricists Pater found himself snarled in the subjective prison of the mind's impressions and perceptions and that his philosophy of experience, as the product of a sort of Humian skepticism, became ultimately the old hedonistic philosophy of the *carpe diem.* The individual seemingly has no alternative but to throw metaphysics to the winds, to plunge himself into the flux, and to find there, in a single fleeting moment, that sense of reality denied him everywhere else. "While all melts under our feet," writes Pater,

we may well grasp at any exquisite passion, or any contribution to knowledge that seems by a lifted horizon to set the spirit free for a moment, or any stirring of the senses, strange dyes, strange colours, and curious odours, or work of the artist's hands, or the face of one's friend. Not to discriminate every moment some passionate attitude in those about us, and in the very brilliancy of their gifts some tragic dividing of forces on their ways, is, on this short day of frost and sun, to sleep before evening. With this sense of the splendour of our experience and of its awful brevity, gathering all we are into one desperate effort to see and touch, we shall hardly have time to make theories about the things we see and touch. (*R,* 237)

Our problem, as readers of Pater, lies in how we should assess this philosophy of experience. One is reminded of the modern undergraduate who saw the Conclusion as simply echoing the familiar witticism: "What is the best thing the rat can do when caught in a trap? Eat the bacon!"

But such an estimate of Pater's philosophic stance would be a grave mistake. "*Let us eat and drink, for to-morrow we die!—*is a proposal," says Pater, "the real import of which differs immensely, according to the natural taste, and the acquired judgment, of the guests who sit at the table" (*ME,* I, 145). Dante's Ciacco used it as a justification for mere physical gluttony. But for another, perhaps, food is spiritual, and for such a soul, "conforming to the highest moral ideal it can clearly define for itself" (*ME,* I, 145) may well be the practical application of the proposal.

5

Certainly in Pater's philosophy the world of sense had as its context some such divine referent, for it is necessary to recall that Pater's treatment of Heraclitus, both in *Marius the Epicurean* and in *Plato and Platonism*, attributes to the flux of phenomena the transcendent framework of divine reason as well as discrete mental and material content. In *Marius* Pater writes:

That continual change, to be discovered by the attentive understanding where common opinion found fixed objects, was but the indicator of a subtler but all-pervading motion—the sleepless, ever-sustained, inexhaustible energy of the divine reason itself, proceeding always by its own rhythmical logic, and lending to all mind and matter, in turn, what life they had. In this "perpetual flux" of things and of souls, there was, as Heraclitus conceived, a continuance, if not of their material or spiritual elements, yet of orderly intelligible relationships, like the harmony of musical notes, wrought out in and through the series of their mutations—ordinances of the divine reason, maintained throughout the changes of the phenomenal world; and this harmony in their mutation and opposition, was, after all, a principle of sanity, of reality, there. But it happened, that, of all this, the first, merely sceptical or negative step, that easiest step on the threshold, had alone remained in general memory; and the "doctrine of motion" seemed to those who had felt its seduction to make all fixed knowledge impossible. (*ME*, I, 130–31)

The stricture here applied to the followers of Heraclitus also has its application to the readers of Pater, who have somewhat too hastily concluded that Pater taught all knowledge to be relative because he could "make no sincere claim to have apprehended anything beyond the veil of immediate experience" (*ME*, I, 145). Pater, differing from Coleridge, certainly did not look for some static and absolute pattern above and beyond the world of relative, finite entities; rather, he held that within the shifting fabric of the sensuous veil itself—for those eyes and ears delicately attuned to the changes of the material world—there can be discerned the eternal outline of the Absolute.

Time and again Pater protests that the uncritical acceptance of a scientific empiricism plunges one into the yielding sands of skepticism. In *Plato* he asserts the same ideas he did in *Marius*, using the same metaphor of music to describe the divine life within the shimmering flux of phenomena. Pater writes:

Yet from certain fragments in which the *Logos* is already named we may understand that there had been another side to the doctrine of Heraclitus; an attempt on his part, after all, to reduce that world of chaotic mutation to *cosmos*, to the unity of a reasonable order, by the search for and the notation, if there be such, of an antiphonal rhythm, or logic, which, proceeding uniformly from movement to movement, as in some intricate musical theme, might link together in one those contending, infinitely diverse impulses. It was an act of recognition, even on the part of a philosophy of the inconsecutive, the incoherent, the insane, of that Wisdom which "reacheth from end to end, sweetly and strongly ordering all things." (*PP*, 17–18)

All change is contained within a framework, a harmony of the whole. Something akin to the "intelligible relationships" of an Absolute Reason unites all diverse psychic and material entities; the world of Eternal Ideas is not lost, only immersed within the flowing stream of phenomena. Paradoxically, then, both the Absolute idealist and the empiricist could subscribe to Heraclitus and his flux:

It is the burden of Hegel on the one hand, to whom nature, and art, and polity, aye, and religion too, each in its long historic series, are but so many conscious movements in the secular process of the eternal mind; and on the other hand of Darwin and Darwinism, for which "type" itself properly *is* not but is only always *becoming*. (*PP*, 19)

Whatever one does choose to say about the discontinuous and subjective entities in flux, one need not deny the existence of that eternal and objective order which unites them. This relation between the subjective and objective worlds was fundamental to Pater's philosophy and recurs in his thoughts in a variety of ways.

Of all the writers whom Pater undoubtedly read in the years that followed the appearance of the first edition of *The Renaissance*, Karl Ottfried Müller perhaps most strongly influenced his thoughts on the subject-object relationship, on becoming as opposed to being, on the individual self as opposed to the eternal type.[7] Müller's *History and Antiquities of the Doric Race* treated the psychology, politics, and art of the Greeks in terms of a systematic subject-object conflict, the opposed tendencies labeled "Ionian" and "Dorian" by him. Pater accepted the distinction, and in "The Marbles of Aegina," in the *Greek Studies*, he creates his own terms for the Ionian-Dorian opposition—"the centrifugal and centripetal tendencies, as we may perhaps not too fancifully call them" (*GS*, 252).[8] On the one side, says Pater,

[7] Pater acknowledged his debt to Müller in *PP*, pp. 199–200. Müller's work, *Die Dorier*, was published in 1824 and was translated into English by Henry Tufnell in 1830.

[8] Helen Young, in *The Writings of Walter Pater* (Bryn Mawr, 1933), p. 77, suggests that Pater borrowed his centripetal-centrifugal terms from William Wallace's *The Logic of Hegel* (London, 1874), p. lvii.

there is the centrifugal, the Ionian, the Asiatic tendency, flying from
the centre, working with little forethought straight before it, in the
development of every thought and fancy; throwing itself forth in endless play of undirected imagination; delighting in brightness and
colour, in beautiful material, in changeful form everywhere, in poetry,
in philosophy, even in architecture and its subordinate crafts. In the
social and political order it rejoices in the freest action of local and
personal influences; its restless versatility drives it towards the assertion
of the principles of separatism, of individualism,—the separation of
state from state, the maintenance of local religions, the development
of the individual in that which is most peculiar and individual in
him. Its claim is in its grace, its freedom and happiness, its lively
interest, the variety of its gifts to civilisation; its weakness is self-evi-
dent, and was what made the unity of Greece impossible. (*GS*, 252–53)[9]

One could compile a list of a dozen or more qualities, each of
which Pater somewhere employs to describe the centrifugal. It
is Ionian, Asiatic, colorful, undirected, restless, individual, varie-
gated, subjective, myriad-minded, and releasing, among other
things. For Pater, the centrifugal was best expressed in the philosophy of Heraclitus. It revels in the rich variety and flux of the
phenomenal world, emancipating the individual from the weary
weight of custom and external authority; but its trap lies in its
individuality, which eventually becomes solipsistic—"each mind
keeping as a solitary prisoner its own dream of a world."

Pater continues his discussion with a description of the centripetal, or Dorian, aspect of existence which served as a counterbalance to the centrifugal. Plato, in particular, saw the need to
invoke the centripetal as a corrective:

It is this centrifugal tendency which Plato is desirous to cure, by
maintaining, over against it, the Dorian influence of a severe simplifica-
tion everywhere, in society, in culture, in the very physical nature
of man. An enemy everywhere to *variegation*, to what is cunning
or "myriad-minded," he sets himself, in mythology, in music, in poetry,
in every kind of art, to enforce the ideal of a sort of Parmenidean
abstractness and calm. (*GS*, 253)

When Plato laid down the rules of the ideal republic, he forbade
"all those episodes of mythology which represent the gods as assuming various forms, and visiting the earth in disguise." In Plato's
rule, says Pater,

---

[9] Identical wording is used by Pater in *PP*, pp. 103–5. The idea is also
found in *PP*, pp. 24–25. Notice how Athens, the home of individuality, is
itself "shut off" with "but one narrow entrance."

we may perhaps detect that instinctive antagonism to the old Heraclitean philosophy of perpetual change, which forces him . . . on an
austere simplicity, the older Dorian or Egyptian type of a rigid, eternal
immobility. The disintegrating, centrifugal influence . . . had laid
hold on the life of the gods also, and, even in their calm sphere, one
could hardly identify a single divine person as himself, and not another. There must, then, be no doubling, no disguises, no stories of
transformation. (*GS*, 118–19)

Perhaps, writes Pater, Plato carried his battle against the disinte-
grative forces too far, but he was nevertheless essentially right:

This exaggerated ideal of Plato's is, however, only the exaggeration
of that salutary European tendency, which, finding human mind the
most absolutely real and precious thing in the world, enforces everywhere the impress of its sanity, its profound reflexions upon things
as they really are, its sense of proportion. It is the centripetal tendency,
which links individuals to each other, states to states, one period of
organic growth to another, under the reign of a composed, rational,
self-conscious order, in the universal light of the understanding.
(*GS*, 253)

While other races may also reflect such qualities, the Dorian race,
says Pater, has historically best manifested the centripetal tendency
"in its love of order, of that severe *composition* everywhere, of
which the Dorian style of architecture is, as it were, a material
symbol—in its constant aspiration after what is earnest and dig-
nified, as exemplified most evidently in the religion of its predilec-
tion, the religion of Apollo" (*GS*, 253). A list of the qualities of
the centripetal tendency would be, in effect, a list of opposites
to the centrifugal tendency: the centripetal is Dorian, European,
colorless, limiting, calm, unifying, simple, objective, universal, and
ordered.

The whole of Pater's world view is structured around this
tension between the Heraclitean centrifugal tendency and the
Parmenidean centripetal tendency. It is a relation which is described again in Pater's interesting Postscript to *Appreciations*, in
which the political ideas of the *Greek Studies* are translated into
aesthetic theory. The terms *romantic* and *classic*, says Pater, are
"but one variation of an old opposition, which may be traced from
the very beginning of the formation of European art and literature"
(*Ap*, 243–44). Romanticism, we are told, is characterized by
strength, energy, liberty, strangeness, and curiosity, and it seeks,
as an illustration of these qualities, the medieval world "because,
in the overcharged atmosphere of the Middle Age, there are un-
worked sources of romantic effect, of a strange beauty, to be won,

by strong imagination, out of things unlikely or remote" (*Ap*, 248). Romanticism, says Pater, represents the addition of these qualities to the underlying classical objective of beauty: "the desire of beauty being a fixed element in every artistic organisation, it is the addition of curiosity to this desire of beauty, that constitutes the romantic temper" (*Ap*, 246).

"There are," says Pater,

the born classicists who start with *form*, to whose mind the comeliness of the old, immemorial, well-recognised types in art and literature, have revealed themselves impressively; who will entertain no matter which will not go easily and flexibly into them. . . . On the other hand, there are the born romanticists, who start with an original, untried *matter*, still in fusion; who conceive this vividly, and hold by it as the essence of their work; who, by the very vividness and heat of their conception, purge away, sooner or later, all that is not organically appropriate to it, till the whole effect adjusts itself in clear, orderly, proportionate form; which form, after a very little time, becomes classical in its turn. (*Ap*, 257–58)

For Pater, *form* designates the fixed outline or type which belongs to the objective centripetal world, whereas *matter* is the fluid or individual ingredient belonging to the subjective centrifugal realm.[10] The Dorian world of the centripetal is truly the classic tendency, and the Ionian centrifugal is the romantic tendency; for romanticism derives its energy and strength from some inward source and is subjective in nature, whereas classicism, on the other hand, is not related to the revolutionary, individualistic world of romanticism, but belongs to the fixed world of the type and tends instead to be authoritative.

[10] The following is a clear definition of the meaning which Pater attaches to the word *form*: "So (i.) form means outline, shape, general rule, *e.g.* for putting together a sentence, or an argument; or it means the metre in poetry, or the type of poem, sonnet or what not. In all these it is something superficial, general, diagrammatic. We speak of empty form, mere form, formal politeness; it is opposed to the heart and soul of anything, to what is essential, material, and so forth. But (ii.) when you push home your insight into the order and connection of parts, not leaving out the way in which this affects the parts themselves; then you find that the form becomes (as a lawyer would say) 'very material;' not merely outlines and shapes, but all the sets of gradations and variations and connections that make anything what it is—the life, soul, and movement of the object." Quoted in Bernard Bosanquet, *Three Lectures on Aesthetic* (London, 1915), pp. 15–16. Pater is driving for the deeper meaning behind the idea of form when he relates it to the centripetal, for the centripetal is the visible vesture of the Absolute, and the sensuous form of (i) becomes the ideal form of (ii) if it expresses the Absolute. The pure form of the Absolute, form "as it is" devoid of the properties of sense, cannot be apprehended by mortals, Pater would say.

Pater takes great care to point out that the extremes of both the centrifugal romanticism and centripetal classicism are destructive of true art: "When one's curiosity is deficient . . . one is liable to value mere academical proprieties too highly, to be satisfied with worn-out or conventional types, with the insipid ornament of Racine, or the prettiness of that later Greek sculpture, which passed so long for true Hellenic work" (*Ap*, 246). Also, the opposite extreme, romanticism, is equally faulty: "When one's curiosity is in excess, when it overbalances the desire of beauty, then one is liable to value in works of art what is inartistic in them; to be satisfied with what is exaggerated in art" (*Ap*, 246). Thus, in romantic works of art "a certain distortion is sometimes noticeable, . . . something of a terrible grotesque, of the macabre" (*Ap*, 253).

Because romanticism is always transforming itself into its opposite, classicism, and because classicism constantly needs the rejuvenating touch of romanticism, these tendencies seem to alternate in periods. Although romanticism is "a spirit which shows itself at all times, in various degrees" (*Ap*, 257), it may also, says Pater, be considered

a product of special epochs. Outbreaks of this spirit, that is, come naturally with particular periods—times, when, in men's approaches towards art and poetry, curiosity may be noticed to take the lead, when men come to art and poetry, with a deep thirst for intellectual excitement, after a long *ennui*, or in reaction against the strain of outward, practical things. . . . It is especially in that period of intellectual disturbance, immediately preceding Dante, amid which the romance languages define themselves at last, that this temper is manifested. Here, in the literature of Provence, the very name of romanticism is stamped with its true signification: here we have indeed a romantic world, grotesque even, in the strength of its passions, almost insane in its curious expression of them, drawing all things into its sphere, making the birds, nay! lifeless things, its voices and messengers, yet so penetrated with the desire for beauty and sweetness, that it begets a wholly new species of poetry, in which the *Renaissance* may be said to begin. (*Ap*, 250–51)

Romanticism is often the instrument of a cultural reawakening, but only when it exists in conjunction with the classical "desire for beauty and sweetness." Toward the end of his Postscript, Pater quite clearly defines what he feels the highest art must be:

But explain the terms as we may, in application to particular epochs, there are these two elements always recognisable; united in perfect art—in Sophocles, in Dante, in the highest work of Goethe, though

not always absolutely balanced there; and these two elements may
be not inappropriately termed the classical and romantic tendencies.
(*Ap*, 260)

One can perhaps detect in this theory of art the influence
of Baudelaire and Poe who, like Pater, believed that beauty must
be mingled with strangeness. Be that as it may, Pater's formula
for artistic success is curiously allied with his theory of political
dynamics, for in both spheres final reality is the product of the
same perfect interaction of the classic and the romantic. It is a
balance which, if we probe closely, is not primarily that of sense
and spirit, if by *spirit* we mean the Logos, for God is without
finite location in time and space. At any rate, one should not suppose that even the most formal work of classical art could be purely
spiritual. However much classic form may mirror transcendent
divinity, the vehicle of that divine order, pattern, or type is always
the particular romantic entity rooted in time and space. The balance which Pater seeks to strike is that between the highly stylized
and the painfully grotesque, and the achievement of this balance
is the mutual accommodation of the centripetal and the centrifugal
tendencies within the work of art.

What Pater wrote in *Appreciations* and in the *Greek Studies*
about this balance sheds a great deal of light on the earlier essays
in *The Renaissance*, for he seems consciously to have conceived
his essays in terms of this distinction. Hellenic art, he writes in
The Renaissance, was for the most part interested in the objective,
in the type, and had "nothing in common with the grotesque"
(*R*, 216); the Greek sculptors sought

to abstract and express only what is structural and permanent, to
purge from the individual all that belongs only to him, all the accidents, the feelings and actions of the special moment, all that (because
in its own nature it endures but for a moment) is apt to look like
a frozen thing if one arrests it. In this way their works came to be
like some subtle extract or essence, or almost like pure thoughts or
ideas. (*R*, 66)

Romantic art, on the other hand, is "concerned with individual
expression, with individual character and feeling, the special history of the special soul" (*R*, 67). As in the *Greek Studies* and
Appreciations, so here in the essays of *The Renaissance*, Pater
is at pains to show us that the artistic revival of fifteenth-century
Italy was neither merely classic nor merely romantic; it consisted
in a balance between the centripetal and the centrifugal. For this
reason, the Renaissance, says Pater, is an "enchanted region" in
which "there are no fixed parties, no exclusions: all breathes of

that unity of culture in which 'whatsoever things are comely' are reconciled, for the elevation and adorning of our spirits" (*R*, 26–27). Time and again, Pater's emphasis in *The Renaissance* is upon the curious blending of antithetical elements. "For us," he writes, "the Renaissance is the name of a many-sided but yet united movement" (*R*, 2). And just as the Italian Renaissance is presented as the East in Italy, so the French Renaissance is seen as a "new Italy in France" (*R*, 171), while North blends with South in DuBellay's contemplation of his homeland as he writes in Rome. Whenever a moment of transition occurs in which romantic confronts classic or classic becomes romantic, there is an awakening.

For example, in the essay on Leonardo da Vinci, Pater describes Leonardo's success as an artist in the same terms used in the Postscript:

> Curiosity and the desire of beauty—these are the two elementary forces in Leonardo's genius; curiosity often in conflict with the desire of beauty, but generating, in union with it, a type of subtle and curious grace. . . . Sometimes this curiosity came in conflict with the desire of beauty; it tended to make him go too far below that outside of things in which art really begins and ends. This struggle between the reason and its ideas, and the senses, the desire of beauty, is the key to Leonardo's life at Milan. (*R*, 109, 112)

Precisely because there was a "struggle," Leonardo achieved a degree of success seldom realized by his predecessors. An examination of the art of Fra Angelico, for example, shows him too involved in the subjective, too romantic: "all that is outward or sensible in his work . . . is only the symbol or type of a really inexpressible world, to which he wishes to direct the thoughts; he would have shrunk from the notion that what the eye apprehended was all" (*R*, 205). Angelico's art is quite unlike classic art. With the "Venus of Melos," for example, "the mind begins and ends with the finite image, yet loses no part of the spiritual motive," for in Greek art

> the "lordship of the soul" is recognised; that lordship gives authority and divinity to human eyes and hands and feet; inanimate nature is thrown into the background. But just there Greek thought finds its happy limit; it has not yet become too inward; the mind has not yet learned to boast its independence of the flesh; the spirit has not yet absorbed everything with its emotions, nor reflected its own colour everywhere. It has indeed committed itself to a train of reflexion which must end in defiance of form, of all that is outward, in an exaggerated idealism. But that end is still distant: it has not yet plunged into the depths of religious mysticism. (*R*, 206)

Leonardo was, perhaps, not wholly free of Fra Angelico and the solipsism of his extreme subjectivity, for he had more "curiosity" than he really needed, but in his best art he strikes a balance between this romantic "curiosity" and the classic "desire of beauty."

Michelangelo is another artist whose work Pater treats in *The Renaissance* as the reconciliation of centripetal and centrifugal qualities. "The true type of the Michelangelesque," says Pater on the opening page of the essay, is "sweetness and strength" (*R*, 73). These were common opposites in Michelangelo's Italy, for, says Pater, "the Renaissance has not only the sweetness which it derives from the classical world, but also that curious strength of which there are great resources in the true middle age" (*R*, 15). That tradition, perpetuated in the medieval church, of the "mournful mysteries" of the "sad Chthonian divinities" (*R*, 203–4) of ancient Greece was the romantic element in Michelangelo's art. His romanticism sums up, says Pater, "the whole character of medieval art itself in that which distinguishes it most clearly from classical work, the presence of a convulsive energy in it, becoming in lower hands merely monstrous or forbidding, and felt even in its most graceful products, as a subdued quaintness or grotesque" (*R*, 73–74).

Even so, compared to the work of Fra Angelico, Michelangelo's art displays a very real return to the *Allgemeinheit* of the Greeks. But unlike later Greek sculpture, his art did not go too far in the direction of sterile and abstract pattern. While much late Greek art was simply content to stagnate in the world of exquisite but superficial and colorless form, the vanguard of Western civilization was swinging toward the centrifugal, romantic pole. Michelangelo, through his medieval heritage, restored anew to the Greek tradition the "lordship of the soul":

When Michelangelo came, therefore, with a genius spiritualised by the reverie of the middle age, penetrated by its spirit of inwardness and introspection, living not a mere outward life like the Greek, but a life full of intimate experiences, sorrows, consolations, a system which sacrificed so much of what was inward and unseen could not satisfy him. (*R*, 67)

But this precarious balance of romanticism and classicism which was the Renaissance did not last long, and the artists after Michelangelo could not duplicate his feat; it took another group of romanticists to revitalize the "insipid ornament" of another generation of classicists.

Perhaps one of the most famous of Pater's dicta is also one of his most succinct statements on this theme of artistic balance: "All art constantly aspires towards the condition of music," he writes in his essay on Giorgione. Pater, following certain Symbolist writers, held that music most perfectly fuses matter and form:

While in all other kinds of art it is possible to distinguish the matter from the form, and the understanding can always make this distinction, yet it is the constant effort of art to obliterate it. That the mere matter of a poem, for instance, its subject, namely, its given incidents or situation—that the mere matter of a picture, the actual circumstances of an event, the actual topography of a landscape—should be nothing without the form, the spirit, of the handling, that this form, this mode of handling, should become an end in itself, should penetrate every part of the matter: this is what all art constantly strives after, and achieves in different degrees. (*R*, 135)

In great art, then, the distinction between objective form and subjective matter no longer exists—as Hegel had said, the aesthetic object presents the universal incorporated in the particular. The "ideal examples of poetry and painting," says Pater, are

those in which the constituent elements of the composition are so welded together, that the material or subject no longer strikes the intellect only; nor the form, the eye or the ear only; but form and matter, in their union or identity, present one single effect to the "imaginative reason," that complex faculty for which every thought and feeling is twin-born with its sensible analogue or symbol. (*R*, 138)

Hence, for Pater, as well as for Hegel and the Symbolists, the creation of a work of art is inextricably bound up with the perfecting of a balance between the centripetal and the centrifugal tendencies. But what for the French or German thinkers is only a philosophy of aesthetics becomes with Pater the basis for a broader theory of cultural rebirth. Quite simply, Pater sees the Italian Renaissance as a bringing to the classical heritage of Greece a romanticism derived from the Middle Ages. It was, we might say, a rediscovery by the old Dorian tradition of what the Many contribute to the One. But while the Renaissance, the "enchanted" balance, lasted only momentarily, the reality of a great cultural flowering can be renewed repeatedly. The Age of Pericles, as well as the Age of Lorenzo, reflected the centripetal and centrifugal in perfect tension. Moreover, this rebirth belongs not merely to national awakenings: it occurs continuously on a more limited scale—in villages, in families, and in individuals—whenever the opposite ends of experience are momentarily fused.

We can immediately see from this that the so-called Hera-clitean philosophy of the Conclusion to *The Renaissance* was no mere *non sequitur* to the studies which preceded it. Pater's Conclusion is not a Humian attack upon the existence of material objects independent of perception, nor upon the belief in causality, nor upon the existence of the self; rather, it is directed against an idealism—or perhaps a better word would be *mysticism*—which ignored, to the peril of successful art, the multiplicity of the world. It is an attempt to lay down the conditions within which an artistic rebirth could occur, for fifteenth-century Italy or for nineteenth-century England, and it stresses the same lesson that needed to be stressed in the days of later Greek sculpture: the importance of the particular as the vehicle and only possible expression of the Absolute. "We are all *condamnés*," says Pater; "we have an interval, and then our place knows us no more. Some spend this interval in listlessness, some in high passions, the wisest, at least among 'the children of this world,' in art and song" (*R*, 238), for of such wisdom as can create or discover the fullest life, "the poetic passion, the desire of beauty, the love of art for its own sake, has most" (*R*, 239). That the Conclusion should culminate in a discussion of art is of prime significance, for here, in the aesthetic realm, we can find the ideal reality denied us by the Heraclitean, scientific world view which the Conclusion portrayed in its opening paragraphs. Art gives to the ideal its necessary concrete expression; for the aesthetic object, anchored in the world of sensuous perception, within the fabric of the veil of immediate experience, becomes the visible and empirical locus of the Absolute. The presence of "flux" need not rule out the existence of fixed form.

THE GODS OF ART

Consonant with his belief that abstract ideas must have concrete expression, Pater incarnates his centrifugal-centripetal romantic-classic dialectic in human personality. In clothing the bones of his abstract subject-object opposition in concrete and individual form, in personality, Pater moves out of philosophy altogether and into the realm of poetry and myth. R. T. Lenaghan has suggested that the terms *Dionysian* and *Apollonian* belong fully as much to Pater's thought as to Nietzsche's. Lenaghan says:

The descriptive utility of the Dionysian-Apollonian pattern derives from the concreteness of the imagery which is an essential part of the gods' make-up. The opposed "tendencies" could be made generally

significant by any number of antitheses: centrifugal and centripetal
come quickly to mind from *Plato and Platonism,* and Friedrich Staub
has gathered a good many interesting subsidiary antitheses into a
basic one between *Sinne* and *Geist.* The difficulty is that they are
all too abstract. When they are metaphoric—centripetal and centrifugal—they set abstract vehicles to abstract tenors; when they are not
metaphoric, they simply exchange abstractions of greater or lesser in-
clusiveness. They all lack the sensuous reference which is supplied
in the imagery of Dionysus and Apollo, and which Pater would require
for the full employment of the power of prose."[11]

This turn toward the drama of Dionysus and Apollo brings us
to a new level in our discussion of the subject-object role in Pater's
thought, and it deserves to be explored more intensively than has
hitherto been done.

As Pater tells us in the *Greek Studies,* Dionysus is "the vine-
growers' god, the *spiritual form* of fire and dew." The image of
Dionysus, says Pater, carries us back to a "world of vision unchecked by positive knowledge, in which the myth is begotten
among a primitive people, as they wondered over the life of the
thing their hands helped forward, till it became for them a kind
of spirit, and their culture of it a kind of worship" (*GS,* 28–29).
Dionysus is perhaps unique among the Greek gods, says Pater,
because he "came later than the other gods to the centres of Greek
life; and, as a consequence of this, he is presented to us in an
earlier stage of development than they; that element of natural
fact which is the original essence of all mythology being more
unmistakeably [*sic*] impressed upon us here than in other myths"
(*GS,* 29). For this reason, the later forms of Greek sculpture are
especially successful in portraying Dionysus, since in Greek art
the office of the imagination, when it treats of the gods, is "to
condense the impressions of natural things into human form; to
retain that early mystical sense of water, or wind, or light, in
the moulding of eye and brow; to arrest it, or rather, perhaps,
to set it free, there, as human expression" (*GS,* 32–33). Of course,
says Pater, "the human form is a limiting influence also; and in
proportion as art impressed human form, in sculpture or in the
drama, on the vaguer conceptions of the Greek mind, there was
danger of an escape from them of the free spirit of air, and light,

---

[11] "Pattern in Walter Pater's Fiction," *Studies in Philology,* LVIII (Janu-
ary, 1961), 88–89. My debt to Lenaghan and to Staub, whom Lenaghan mentions, is here acknowledged. However, the analysis in the following pages
of the functioning of Dionysus and Apollo in Pater's thought and fiction is
wholly new, for no commentator has either demonstrated or perceived the full
mythic pattern and its relation to Pater's theory of art.

and sky. Hence, all through the history of Greek art, there is a struggle, a *Streben*, as the Germans say, between the palpable and limited human form, and the floating essence it is to contain" (*GS*, 34). The artistic embodiment, then, of the old wine-god reflects a dynamic tension between "the teeming, still fluid world, of old beliefs, as we see it reflected in the somewhat formless *theogony* of Hesiod" and "the spirit of a severe and wholly self-conscious intelligence; bent on impressing everywhere, in the products of the imagination, the definite, perfectly conceivable human form, as the only worthy subject of art; less in sympathy with the mystical genealogies of Hesiod, than with the heroes of Homer, ending in the entirely humanised religion of Apollo" (*GS*, 34–35).

Pater's theory of art, as expressed in the "Dionysus" essay of 1876, has been likened to that which Friedrich Nietzsche outlined four years earlier in his *Geburt der Tragödie*. And there is a very real similarity between the two thinkers. Nietzsche speaks of "the Apollonian appearances, in which Dionysus objectifies himself," the Apollonian art form being "the objectification of a Dionysian state." Whereas the purpose of the Apollonian plastic art, according to Nietzsche, is to arouse within us "a delight in beautiful forms," Dionysus endows these forms with "a convincing metaphysical significance, which the unsupported word and image could never achieve."[12] Nietzsche conceives of Dionysus as subjective and centrifugal and of Apollo as objective and centripetal. Pater, likewise, identifies the subjective or Ionian tendency with Dionysus—words like *teeming, fluid,* and *formless* describe his world—while asserting that the "Dorian or European influence embodied itself in the religion of Apollo" (*GS*, 254). Moreover, both Nietzsche and Pater agree that Apollo, in opposition to Dionysus, is the god of order and rationality. Contrasting Apollo and his religion to their opposites, Pater says that such centrifugal deities as the summer-time goddess

Demeter, the spirit of life in grass,—and Dionysus, the "spiritual form" of life in the green sap,—remain, to the end of men's thoughts and fancies about them, almost wholly physical. But Apollo, the "spiritual form" of sunbeams, early becomes (the merely physical element in his constitution being almost wholly suppressed) exclusively ethical,—the "spiritual form" of inward or intellectual light, in all its manifestations. He represents all those specially European ideas, of a reasonable, personal freedom, as understood in Greece; of a reasonable polity; of the sanity of soul and body, through the cure of disease and of

---

[12] *The Works of Friedrich Nietzsche*, trans. Orson Falk (New York, 1931), pp. 216, 219, 272, 312.

the sense of sin; of the perfecting of both by reasonable exercise or
ascésis; his religion is a sort of embodied equity, its aim the realisation
of fair reason and just consideration of the truth of things everywhere.
(*GS,* 254)

One would be tempted to see a borrowing from Nietzsche
on Pater's part were it not for two considerations: first, Pater seems
to have thought in these terms from his very earliest essay in
1864, some eight years before the appearance of Nietzsche's work,
and second, there is an important difference between Nietzsche
and Pater in the rendering of the personality of Dionysus. Just
what, then, is the actual nature of the gods, and how are they
related to Pater's theory of art?

To begin, it is necessary to note that for Pater the personality
of Dionysus is somewhat more complex than it was for Nietzsche.
Although Pater's Dionysus is certainly the god of the narrow, subjective world and its fear of death, he has, says Pater, "his alternations of joy and sorrow" (*GS,* 40). Pater devotes a considerable
amount of space in his first essay in the *Greek Studies* to an examination of the double nature of the god:

The whole compass of the idea of Dionysus, a dual god of both summer
and winter, became ultimately . . . almost identical with that of
Demeter. The Phrygians believed that the god slept in winter and
awoke in summer, and celebrated his waking and sleeping; or that
he was bound and imprisoned in winter, and unbound in spring; . . .
and a beautiful ceremony in the temple at Delphi, which, as we know,
he shares with Apollo, described by Plutarch, represents his mystical
resurrection. . . . He is twofold then—a *Doppelgänger;* like
Persephone, he belongs to two worlds, and has much in common with
her, and a full share of those dark possibilities which, even apart
from the story of the rape, belong to her. He is a *Chthonian* god,
and, like all the children of the earth, has an element of sadness;
like Hades himself, he is hollow and devouring, an eater of man's
flesh—*sarcophagus.* (*GS,* 43–44)

For Nietzsche, Dionysus was merely a personification of a component in an abstract philosophical scheme. Pater's handling of the
god, on the other hand, is poetically far superior, for he introduces
him as a protagonist not merely in an ideological pattern but in
a truly mythic pattern. Dionysus' alternations between summer
and winter mark him as a vegetative god, a representative of the
seasonal cycle, and his relation to Apollo resembles that of
Persephone to Demeter. As Pater has described it at length in
the *Greek Studies,* Demeter is the *Magna Mater,* the goddess of
the eternal earth itself, and Persephone is the cyclic, vegetative
deity of summer and winter. Pater has taken this Demeter-

Persephone pattern and, with the figures of Apollo and Dionysus, transposed it to the context of cultural history. Apollo, as we shall see in more detail in Chapter V, represents humanity itself, Pater's equivalent for the *Magna Mater* of the old fertility myth. The Paterian Dionysus is the consort or priest of humanity; his sacrificial death, by renewing the creative powers of humanity, makes way for the cultural awakening, for the "renaissance" which is the Apollonian phase of civilization.

The mythic pattern of Dionysus and Apollo is definitely related to the theory of art expressed in the Conclusion to *The Renaissance*, where the summer and winter phases of Dionysus are treated in the first and second paragraphs, respectively. In the former Pater considers "physical life" (*R*, 233), and in the latter he takes up "the inward world" (*R*, 234). Because there is a kind of resistance to change in nature, the summer side of Dionysus, which corresponds to the bloom of sensuous things, exhibits only a "gradual fading" (*R*, 234). In the antique world of the Greeks and in the world of childhood, the soul can find release from its own subjectivity in the sensuousness of nature. For the young there is always a classic quality in the world of the summer Dionysus. But precisely because the world of the summer Dionysus is finite, the soul can expand beyond it, its inner visions becoming too great to find their counterpart merely in nature. Suddenly, what had been the objective world becomes subjective. There is no external outlet; the bloom of nature has become a trap; the dreaming soul is imprisoned; it descends to the delirium of the winter god. The "sleeping" or "imprisoned" Dionysus corresponds to the psychic realm, with its vastly heightened awareness of the shortness of life and the sense of death—the mind imprisoned in its own dreams, as the Conclusion describes this winter world. We recall how Pater had identified a certain "strange," "macabre," and "grotesque" quality in the excesses of romanticism; it was this darker side of the Chthonian god that such a romanticism was mirroring.[13]

In one of his early essays, "Aesthetic Poetry," Pater discusses the youth of civilization and how this Greek world of the summer Dionysus became the wintry world of the Middle Ages. Writing of monastic religion, Pater tells us that it was, "in many of its bearings, like a beautiful disease or disorder of the senses: and a religion which is a disorder of the senses must always be subject

---

[13] The prisoner isolated in his dream is, of course, a recurrent image in Pater's writings. See, for example, *ME*, I, 146, or *PP*, p. 108. The opening pages of the "Prosper Mérimée" essay in *MS* are perhaps the most extensive reflection of these images and ideas.

to illusions. Reverie, illusion, delirium: they are the three stages of a fatal descent both in the religion and the loves of the Middle Age" (*Ap*[1889], 217). And Pater continues, describing the way in which the trapped soul poisons all that it touches:

A passion of which the outlets are sealed, begets a tension of nerve, in which the sensible world comes to one with a reinforced brilliancy and relief—all redness is turned into blood, all water into tears. Hence a wild, convulsed sensuousness in the poetry of the Middle Age, in which the things of nature begin to play a strange delirious part. Of the things of nature the medieval mind had a deep sense; but its sense of them was not objective, no real escape to the world without us. The aspects and motions of nature only reinforced its prevailing mood, and were in conspiracy with one's own brain against one. A single sentiment invaded the world: everything was infused with a motive drawn from the soul. (*Ap* [1889], 218–19)

Obviously, the summer Dionysus is inadequate for the service of the expanding soul. He is finite, bound by the restrictions of time and space—the present moment, the particular place—for he embodies the discontinuity of the flux. The mature soul, which dreams of an immortality stretching from past to future, cannot be happy in this narrow world of the present, this simple life of sensations enjoyed from moment to moment.

But we recall that, for Pater, the flux of Dionysus is contained within an eternal framework, a harmony, which unites all diverse mental and material entities. The significance of art for the Conclusion lies precisely here. Art represents, in sensuous form, that larger order of the Absolute. Art is as concrete and real as the world of the summer Dionysus, but its form mirrors the eternal world of the ideal, and the soul cannot outgrow it. The mature mind, the expanded soul with larger vision, can relieve itself of the burden of its subjective dreams in this greater world of Apollonian art. All art is indeed dream, the dream of the romantic Dionysus objectified. The truly successful aesthetic object, then, has a form adequate to the matter which it clothes. We do not see, as Pater will show us in the Watteau portrait, the forms of sense struggling vainly to encompass the visions of the mature soul in the finite objectivity of the summer Dionysus.

The hero of the historical and imaginary portraits has a very natural relation to Pater's theory of art. He is the Dionysian priest of Apollo, and his function is the awakening of art in a barren world. Pater's characteristic interest in all of his writings, fictional and non-fictional alike, is that first dawning of the light which indicates a return from the winter Dionysus to the summertime.

In his 1868 review of the poetry of William Morris, afterwards entitled "Aesthetic Poetry," Pater had written of the beginnings of the arts in Italy:

No writer on the Renaissance has hitherto cared much for this exquisite early light of it. Afterwards the Renaissance takes its side, becomes exaggerated and facile. But the choice life of the human spirit is always under mixed lights, and in mixed situations; when it is not too sure of itself, is still expectant, girt up to leap forward to the promise. Such a situation there was in that earliest return from the overwrought spiritualities of the middle age to the earlier, more ancient life of the senses; and for us the most attractive form of classical story is the monk's conception of it, when he escapes from the sombre legend of his cloister to that true light. The fruits of this mood, which, divining more than it understands, infuses into the figures of the Christian legend some subtle reminiscence of older gods, or into the story of Cupid and Psyche that passionate stress of spirit which the world owes to Christianity, have still to be gathered up when the time comes.[14]

That "exquisite early light" of the Renaissance represented a return not merely to the simple life of the senses, but to summer in terms of art. Certainly Pater's heroes, by their great love of the natural world, bring a new appreciation of physical nature to the dead world of the winter Dionysus. But they do more than that. They help humanity grow beyond its childhood to the maturity of artistic creation. By their mediation the first Golden Age of the summer Dionysus is replaced by that truer and greater Golden Age, the Age of Apollo. The Paterian hero, the bringer of art to humanity, possesses the Apollonian purity of the eternal type while simultaneously displaying true Dionysian selfhood; that is, living incarnated in time and space and enduring the pangs of death.

One of the most revealing studies of the character of the hero is found in the paper "Diaphaneitè," an *Ur*-portrait, which Pater read to the Oxford literary society the Old Mortality in 1864. One cannot doubt that the "diaphanous" character-type here being defined is truly Apollonian. According to K. O. Müller, Apollo, or Phoebus, is a name from which the words *bright, clear, pure,* and *unstained* can be derived etymologically, and again and again Pater returns to the metaphor of light in describing his ideal Apollonian personality. The Apollonian individual has a transparency of nature which allows the light of the Absolute to shine through him:

The artist and he who has treated life in the spirit of art desires only to be shown to the world as he really is; as he comes nearer

[14] "Poems by William Morris," *Westminster Review*, XXXIV, n.s. (October, 1868), 307–8.

and nearer to perfection, the veil of an outer life not simply expressive
of the inward becomes thinner and thinner. . . . It is just this sort
of entire transparency of nature that lets through unconsciously all
that is really lifegiving in the established order of things; it detects
without difficulty all sorts of affinities between its own elements, and
the nobler elements in that order. (*MS,* 249, 251)

In Pater's fiction, as in ancient statuary, it is the form of the
god which, by its lack of nonessential characteristics, gives expression to the eternal world of the type. For this reason the artist-
heroes of Pater's imaginary portraits have a certain Apollonian
neutrality about them and display all the attributes of the gods
of Greek statuary, sharing with them that "colourless, unclassified
purity of life, with its blending and interpenetration of intellectual,
spiritual, and physical elements, still folded together, pregnant with
the possibilities of a whole world closed within it, [which] is the
highest expression of the indifference which lies beyond all that
is relative or partial" (*R,* 218). Like the gods of ancient Greece,
Pater's Apollonian heroes "refuse to be classified" (*R,* 27). This
neutrality, the most striking aspect of the Apollonian personality,
is not, however, a reflection of the "colourless uninteresting existence" of the man who has been neutralized "by suppression of
gifts"; rather, it is the colorless all-color of those individuals among
whose talents there is a "just equipoise." "In these," says Pater,
"no single gift, or virtue, or idea, has an unmusical predominance"
(*MS,* 252).

The modern age, Pater tells us, demands "life in the whole"
(*R,* 228), and the aesthetic personality answers that demand by
living "not only as intense but as complete a life as possible"
(*R,* 188). "Every one who aims at the life of culture is met by
many forms of it, arising out of the intense, laborious, one-sided
development of some special talent"; it is the aesthetic personality,
however, that desires to

see into the laws, the operation, the intellectual reward of every divided
form of culture. . . . It struggles with those forms till its secret is
won from each, and then lets each fall back into its place, in the
supreme, artistic view of life. With a kind of passionate coldness, such
natures rejoice to be away from and past their former selves, and
above all, they are jealous of that abandonment to one special gift
which really limits their capabilities. (*R,* 228–29)

Goethe is one of Pater's favorite examples of the balanced personality, for he "illustrates a union of the Romantic spirit, in its adventure, its variety, its profound subjectivity of soul, with Hellenism,

in its transparency, its rationality, its desire of beauty" (*R*, 226–27). By capturing the divine light in the perfect sphere of his own life, a hero such as Goethe becomes the instrument of cultural renewal.

We are not left merely to deduce that Pater's bringers of the Renaissance are related to the gods of myth. Very often Pater specifically identifies the individual who, for example, brings a Greek love of nature into the rigid medieval Christian world as an ancient god exiled by the coming of Christianity. Pater borrowed this idea of the gods in exile from Heinrich Heine and made it one of the major themes in *The Renaissance*, a fact which indicates that the god-like nature is associated in Pater's thought with the rebirth of the arts.[15] Heine's idea was fundamental to Pater's world view, and because Pater's writings always describe artistic creativity, it is the constant subject of his portraits. Germain d'Hangest recognizes the value of Heine's myth for Pater's thought when he notes that the legend gave a more concrete and dramatic form to the whole complex process of artistic rebirth, to all the vague Platonic ideas of the cycle and the innumerable reincarnations of the individual soul which Pater had associated with the idea of the Renaissance.[16] D'Hangest is right in pointing to the Pico essay as the first lengthy and easily identifiable presentation of Heine's theme, for near the beginning of his essay, Pater quotes Heine concerning

"how the gods of the older world, at the time of the definite triumph of Christianity, that is, in the third century, fell into painful embarrassments. . . . They had then to take flight ignominiously, and hide themselves among us here on earth, under all sorts of disguises. . . . Many of these unfortunate emigrants, now entirely deprived of shelter and ambrosia, must needs take to vulgar handicrafts, as a means of earning their bread. Under these circumstances, many whose sacred groves had been confiscated, let themselves out for hire as woodcutters in Germany, and were forced to drink beer instead of nectar. Apollo seems to have been content to take service under graziers, and as he had once kept the cows of Admetus, so he lived now as a shepherd in Lower Austria." (*R*, 31–32)

[15] Heine's "Gods in Exile" appeared in 1853. The essay is to be found in Volume XII of C. G. Leland's translation. Heine's treatment of the exiled gods is light-hearted and humorous, while Pater is far more serious in his handling of the myth. See J. S. Harrison, "Pater, Heine, and the Old Gods of Greece," *PMLA*, XXXIX (September, 1924), 655–86.

[16] *Walter Pater* (Paris, 1961), II, 66–67. Actually, d'Hangest does not suggest quite so much as my context indicates, for he, like Harrison, simply notes the fact and ignores its implications. One will, however, find d'Hangest's two-volume the-man-and-his-works study extremely useful, for it contains the best bibliographic compilation available.

Pater opened his essay on Pico with this quotation from Heine's "Gods in Exile" because Pico's reconciliation of the classic and romantic worlds could be understood in terms of it, as evidenced by Pater's analysis of his character:

It is because the life of Pico, thus lying down to rest in the Dominican habit, yet amid thoughts of the older gods, himself like one of those comely divinities, reconciled indeed to the new religion, but still with a tenderness for the earlier life, and desirous literally to "bind the ages each to each by natural piety"—it is because this life is so perfect a parallel to the attempt made in his writings to reconcile Christianity with the ideas of paganism, that Pico, in spite of the scholastic character of those writings, is really interesting. (*R*, 44)

The "mixed lights" and "mixed situations" of the dawning Renaissance, the monk escaped from his somber cloister into Hellenic day—this is the idea which Heine's theme so aptly dramatizes in Pater's essay on Pico.

Other figures in *The Renaissance* are also treated in terms of Heine's myth. Aucassin and Nicolette, like Pico, are bathed in the light of a supernatural beauty, and they, also, represent the fusion of two antithetical cultures. In particular, Pater connects the story of Aucassin and Nicolette with the rebirth or reappearance of Venus:

In their search after the pleasures of the senses and the imagination, in their care for beauty, in their worship of the body, people were impelled beyond the bounds of the Christian ideal; and their love became sometimes a strange idolatry, a strange rival religion. It was the return of that ancient Venus, not dead, but only hidden for a time in the caves of the Venusberg, of those old pagan gods still going to and fro on the earth, under all sorts of disguises. (*R*, 24)

There is also Leonardo da Vinci, a sort of magician, not dissimilar to his own Mona Lisa, who "has been dead many times, and learned the secrets of the grave" (*R*, 125), or to his Saint John the Baptist, in the Louvre, which bears a "strange likeness to the Bacchus which hangs near it, and which set Théophile Gautier thinking of Heine's notion of decayed gods, who, to maintain themselves, after the fall of paganism, took employment in the new religion" (*R*, 118). And, of course, there is Botticelli, whose beautiful figures, "in a certain sense like angels, but with a sense of displacement or loss about them—the wistfulness of exiles, conscious of a passion and energy greater than any known issue of them explains" (*R*, 55), remind us once again of the wandering gods. And, finally, there is Winckelmann, whose Apollonian nature was "like a relic of classical antiquity, laid open by accident to our alien, modern atmosphere; . . . he seems to realise that fancy of the reminiscence of a forgotten knowledge hidden for a time in the mind itself; as if the mind of one, lover and philosopher at once in some phase of pre-existence, . . . fallen into a new cycle, were beginning its intellectual career over again, yet with a certain power of anticipating its results" (R, 220, 194).[17]

Pater relates this theme, the reappearance of the god-like hero, to the old mythic pattern of Dionysus. Pico, Aucassin and Nicolette, Leonardo and his Mona Lisa and Saint John, Botticelli's comely figures, Winckelmann—all are in some sense, like Dionysus, gods of renewal. But just as Christianity surpassed Mithraicism, so the Paterian hero surpasses the primitive Dionysus. He is not merely a god of the renewal of spring: like Christ Himself, he becomes an instrument of fertility in the cosmic pattern, the regenerative agent on all levels of life—religious, aesthetic, intellectual—as well as physical. Something of the revolutionary, then, can be seen in the character of the hero, but his is a revolution without violence:

> They who prosecute revolution have to violate again and again the instinct of reverence. That is inevitable, since after all progress is a kind of violence. But in this nature revolutionism is softened, harmonised, subdued as by distance. It is the revolutionism of one who has slept a hundred years. . . . In this nature the idea appears softened, harmonised as by distance, with an engaging naturalness, without the noise of axe or hammer. (MS, 252, 254)

There is no violence because the harmonious revolutionary principle is actually that perpetual and sleepless mind of God, which rounds and sustains the sleepy, intermittent lives of men. With the reverence in which Solomon's temple was built, where "neither hammer nor ax nor any tool of iron" (I Kings 6:7) was heard, the hero gives expression to this divine light as he calls forth the dawning of a new day.

Just as the original myth of Dionysus saw the birth of the new year already implicit in the destruction of the summer Dionysus, so in Pater's thought it is specifically the sacrificial death of the hero which quickens humanity. "Poetry and poetical history,"

---

[17] Whole sentences have been taken from "Diaphaneitè" and applied to Winckelmann. This last is only one such example (MS, pp. 251, 250). See Francis X. Roellinger, "Intimations of Winckelmann in Pater's Diaphaneitè," English Language Notes, II (June, 1965), 277–82. Pater sees in Winckelmann, as in the Greek statues, "a moral sexlessness, a kind of impotence, an ineffectual wholeness of nature" (MS, p. 253; R, p. 221). The hero seems not unrelated in Pater's mind to the ancient figure of the androgyne, a mystical symbol of "wholeness."

says Pater in "Diaphaneitè," "have dreamed of a crisis, where it must needs be that some human victim be sent down into the grave." It is the Dionysian hero "whom in its profound emotion humanity might choose to send" (*MS,* 253). Certainly this sacrifice is not an unalleviated tragedy, for his death is his final awakening from mortality, and the blaze of cultural renewal that follows is an echo within the human community of the renewal which has taken place within the soul itself. The dying hero, as the highest expression and representative of humanity, becomes the means by which civilization is purified of its mortality and initiated into the dawning light of Apollo. It is not difficult to see why the image of the mother plays such a large part in the lives of all of Pater's heroes, for, as the *Magna Mater* of the modern god, she is none other than humanity itself, and the love between hero and humanity is, for Pater, the most perfect love possible. This also explains why all of Pater's heroes are celibate. As gods, they have ritually consecrated their virility to their Great Mother, and the violent death of the hero comes as the ultimate expression of his love, for it is a giving, after the manner of the sexual act itself, of the very blood and members of his body to fructify the *Magna Mater.* Appropriately, Pater often presents the death of his hero as the consummation of marriage; as, for example, with Marius, Watteau, Denys, Sebastian, Carl, and Hippolytus. And because this self-sacrificial "marriage" is consummated by blood, it becomes also a kind of eucharist, a sacred communion of which humanity partakes. The greatest example of this Dionysian love for the Great Mother within the eucharistic-marriage context is, of course, one which Pater purposely avoided—that of Christ and the *Mater Ecclesia.*

No doubt because so much of the Dionysian pattern pervades his fiction, Pater has often been accused of being morbid, of being a high priest of decadence, who views existence as incompatible with engagement in the world. In a sense, a somberness does pervade Pater's world view, for the romantic element is certainly present. But the Greeks, according to Pater, also had this side to their thought. In his essay on Demeter in the *Greek Studies,* Pater writes that

the legend of Demeter and Persephone, perhaps the most popular of all Greek legends, is sufficient to show that the "worship of sorrow" was not without its function in Greek religion; their legend is a legend made by and for sorrowful, wistful, anxious people; while the most important artistic monuments of that legend sufficiently prove that the Romantic spirit was really at work in the minds of Greek artists, extracting by a kind of subtle alchemy, a beauty, not without the elements of tranquillity, of dignity and order, out of a matter, at first sight painful and strange. (*GS*, 111)

The Greeks had, indeed, anticipated the sadder and more romantic shadows of the Middle Ages with legends of the fall of divinities even earlier than Demeter and Persephone. In "the supreme and colourless abstraction of those divine forms" so long since departed, we have "a premonition of the fleshless, consumptive refinements of the pale, medieval artists. . . . Those abstracted gods, 'ready to melt out their essence fine into the winds,' who can fold up their flesh as a garment, and still remain themselves, seem already to feel that bleak air, in which like Helen of Troy, the wander as the spectres of the middle age" (*R*, 224). But the gods will be reborn, for in their death we see the destruction of death. Pater had written in his essay on "The Bacchanals of Euripides" that in the hunting by the winter Dionysus of the innocent summer Dionysus, we must see the winter god of death as his own victim "if we are to catch, in its fulness, that deep undercurrent of horror which runs below, all through this masque of spring, and realise the spectacle of that wild chase, in which Dionysus is ultimately both the hunter and the spoil" (*GS*, 78–79). Speaking of the Greeks and their Golden Age of the summer Dionysus, Pater says: "Let us not regret that this unperplexed youth of humanity, satisfied with the vision of itself, passed, at the due moment, into a mournful maturity; for already the deep joy was in store for the spirit, of finding the ideal of that youth still red with life in the grave" (*R*, 209).

One hardly need point out—though at times the obvious is worth stating—that the myth of rebirth is basically optimistic and charged with the maximum of hope. Pater tells us in his essay on Demeter that the persons and incidents of myth in its highest form "are realised as abstract symbols, because intensely characteristic examples, of moral or spiritual conditions" (*GS*, 91), and he points out, by way of example, that in Hesiod

the goddess of summer and the goddess of death, Kore and Persephone, are identified with much significance; and that strange, dual being makes her first appearance, whose latent capabilities the poets afterwards developed; among the rest, a peculiar blending of those two contrasted aspects, full of purpose for the duly chastened intelligence; death, resurrection, rejuvenescence.—*Awake, and sing, ye that dwell in the dust!* (*GS*, 95)

Demeter as Kore is merely the summer Dionysus; as Persephone or the sorrowing mother, she is the winter Dionysus; but as Kore-

Persephone she embodies a life purged of its mortality by death—
"Demeter enthroned, chastened by sorrow, and somewhat advanced
in age, blessing the earth, in her joy at the return of Kore"
(*GS*, 136). "It is only when these two contrasted images," says
Pater, "have been brought into intimate relationship, only when
Kore and Persephone have been identified, that the deeper mythology of Demeter begins" (*GS*, 94–95). This third state, embodied
in the sculptured face of Demeter, conveys a message of hope to
the sensitive mind.[18] Death comes, it is true, but while the body
is a victim, the soul need never be. As Pater wrote of Pico, early
dead, "while his actual work has passed away, yet his own qualities
are still active, and himself remains, as one alive in the
grave . . . and with that sanguine, clear skin . . . as with the
light of morning upon it" (*R*, 49).

This, then, is the direction which the writings of Pater after
The Renaissance will take. He was, as his students so clearly saw,
no scholar "as the Universities understand the word," and, of
course, Edward Caird, T. H. Green, and F. H. Bradley gave the
"Universities" a rather clear idea of what a scholar should
be. Pater paid his way at the university with the coin of poetry,
not philosophy, for all his writing was infused with the sort of
imaginative drama not usually found in the more sober tomes of
the Oxford dons. His early apprenticeship at writing *The Renaissance* proved a fine prelude to the art of imaginary portraiture,
and by a natural and almost imperceptible progress Pater moves
from a fictionalized criticism to a critical fiction, from the historical
portrait to the imaginary portrait. The subject matter and technique remain essentially identical, for Pater's concern in the fiction
is the same as it was in *The Renaissance*—culture, its birth and
flowering—and all of his Dionysian heroes are represented as
bringers of artistic and cultural enlightenment to their ages. In
the writing of his essays for *The Renaissance*, in asking himself
what cultural rebirth means, Pater seems to have found the materials of fiction; and one may say that the title of his first slim
volume will serve as the metaphor of his future thought, for it
involves an attitude toward life fundamental to his art, and each
of his portraits will recount anew the myth of renaissance.

[18] There is, according to Pater, an actual tripartite evolution of the myth
toward the "ethical" (*GS*, p. 91) or highest artistic-religious plane. First, there
is the stage of folklore which reflects the world of the summer Dionysus;
then there is the poetic stage reflecting the sorrow of the winter Demeter
as recounted in the Homeric hymn; and finally there is the stage of statuary
in which the figure of Demeter, enthroned and chastened, unites the first
two phases.

II

PORTRAITURE AND THE EARLY PORTRAITS

In the August, 1878, issue of *Macmillan's Magazine* appeared Pater's first and perhaps his finest piece of prose fiction. Its title was printed as follows:

Imaginary Portraits
1. The Child in the House

We can discover from a letter (April 17, 1878) to George Grove, editor of the magazine, what Pater's intentions were when he gave his portrait this title. Pater tells Grove that "it is not, as you may perhaps fancy, the first part of a work of fiction, but is meant to be complete in itself; though the first of a series, as I hope, with some real kind of sequence in them. . . . I call the M.S. a portrait, and mean readers, as they might do on seeing a portrait, to begin speculating—what came of him?"[1] After his second fictional piece—"Imaginary Portraits / 2. An English Poet"—Pater abandoned in his future portraits whatever idea of "sequence" the series might originally have had. Nevertheless, "The Child in the House" stands at the beginning of a long line of prose fictions, sequential or not; and on one of those small scraps of paper which he habitually used to compose little notes to himself, Pater gives credit to his first piece for being the germinating work which shaped the form of his future imaginative writing.[2]

Yet if one examines Pater's art from a twentieth-century point of view and asks, as one frequently does, what literary devices are employed, one may well wonder if Pater's fiction is truly imaginative. Percy Lubbock, in his *Craft of Fiction*, discusses "scenic presentation" in Henry James and contrasts it to the "vi-

[1] Quoted in *IP*B, p. 2, from Lawrence Evans, *Some Letters of Walter Pater* (Harvard dissertation, 1961), No. 40 (MS: *Letter Books* of Macmillan & Co., Ltd.).

[2] Evans, *Letters of Pater*, p. xxiv.

sionary fiction" of Pater. Writing in particular of *Marius the Epi-curean*, which makes as good a test case as any, Lubbock says:

> In *Marius* probably, if it is to be called a novel, the art of drama
> is renounced as thoroughly as it has ever occurred to a novelist to
> dispense with it. I scarcely think that Marius ever speaks or is spoken
> to audibly in the whole course of the book; such at least is the impres-
> sion that it leaves. The scenes of the story reach the reader by refrac-
> tion, as it were, through the medium of Pater's harmonious murmur.
> But scenes they must be; not even Pater at his dreamiest can tell
> a story without incident particularized and caught in the act.[3]

One cannot quarrel with Lubbock's estimate. There is little that is true scene and less that is true dialogue. Pater simply cannot draw convincing characters. Few of his central figures are "three-dimensional," to use E. M. Forster's somewhat too simple test of artistic success. Pater's subsidiary figures are frankly two-dimensional. In the portrayal of women, Pater's limitations are particularly evident. Only Marie-Marguerite in the Watteau portrait is a central feminine character, and she is never named. Cecilia in *Marius* and Colombe in *Gaston* have, seemingly, both been flattened by the weight of ideology, whereas such *femmes fatales* as La Gioconda in the da Vinci portrait, Faustina in *Marius*, and Phaedra in "Hippolytus," although they have a certain depth which the others lack, are hardly normal women—hardly women at all, one might say.

In the area of interior scene and drama Pater also seems often to fall short. In a sense, he anticipates Henry James, Joseph Conrad, and such stream-of-consciousness writers as James Joyce and Virginia Woolf, for with him, as with these later writers, the mental process is the focus of treatment. Yet Pater differs from them, for he denies himself certain literary techniques which they use fully. His successors were able to achieve dramatic power by giving the reader a view into the inchoate world of ideas below the threshold of verbalization, but the mental processes of Pater's heroes are never the raw materials of unformed thoughts. A character such as Marius, for example, thinks in beautifully polished, euphuistically structured sentences which are even far above the level of ordinary discourse. His "sensations and ideas" reach us through a variety of literary genres seemingly far removed from first-hand experience: a Platonic fable in the form of a translation of Apuleius' tale of Cupid and Psyche; stanzas from the second-century Latin poem the *Pervigilium Veneris*; orations by Marcus

[3] Lubbock, *Craft of Fiction*, p. 195.

Aurelius and Cornelius Fronto; translations of two dialogues by Lucian, *The Hermotimus* and *The Halcyon;* selections from the *Epistle of the Churches of Lyons and Vienne;* a diary which we read over Marius' shoulder; and various historical quotations, epitaphs, hymns, and so forth.

When confronted with a work which defies classification as a true novel, the usual procedure of the literary critics has been to multiply names. *Marius* is called "ideological" or "critical" or "ruminative" fiction; the shorter portraits are called "character studies," "narrative" or "fictive" essays, and sometimes "*récits*" or "*fabulae.*" But this does not convince us that *Marius* or the other portraits are more imaginative than history of philosophy or art criticism. If we are to be convinced, we must first examine the relation of Pater's fiction to a number of distinctive literary forms.

Surely one of the major strains in Pater's fiction is the prose romance, a late development of classical mythology to which it bears certain strong affinities.[4] The supernatural hovers on the fringes of romance, and its events lie closer to the violent emotions of tragedy than to the everyday give-and-take of the novel. The stylized, idealized hero stands somewhere between the ordinary men of the novel and the supernatural gods of myth, and his archetypal nature tends to invest his actions with a certain quality of allegory. The impact of this genre upon Pater's portraits is obvious—the single god-like hero of unsurpassed purity, courage, and nobility, whose life reduplicates the tragic myth of Dionysus, derives directly from this tradition. The two-dimensional, allegorical nature of Pater's characters is also related to the romantic mode.

A second major component in Pater's fiction is the autobiography—the tradition of the confessions of Augustine or Pascal or Rousseau.[5] This tradition exhibits an interest in ideas rather than,

---

[4] In the following paragraphs I have found Northrop Frye's *Anatomy of Criticism* (Princeton, 1957) to be of help. I refer the reader to pp. 303–13.

With the exception of Apuleius's *Metamorphoses,* Pater's indebtedness to any particular romance, prose or verse, is not immediately obvious, but names of works with which we can assume Pater was intimately familiar easily come to mind. Prose exemplars of the romance form, in addition to Scott's, would include such works as Malory's *Morte Darthur,* Sidney's *Arcadia,* and Bunyan's *Pilgrim's Progress.* The half dozen or so romances written by William Morris during his last years are good Victorian examples though they appeared somewhat too late to have influenced Pater. Pater had, of course, written a review on Morris' poetry. About the time Morris began writing prose romances, Pater was publishing *Gaston* in installments; its final subtitle was "An Unfinished Romance."

[5] Its practitioners in the English language are numerous: Browne's *Religio Medici,* Bunyan's *Grace Abounding,* DeQuincy's *Confessions of an English*

as in the novel, personal relationships. The influence of this genre upon Pater is as important as it is obvious, and we do not have to go to the lengths of Thomas Wright, who interprets the portraits as a kind of wish-fulfillment, to note how closely at times Pater seems able to identify with his heroes or how remarkably similar are places and events in the portraits to those in Pater's life. Further, the genre certainly reinforced Pater's tendency to concentrate upon a single character, and, of course, its intellectual interest in religion, politics, and art was eagerly accepted by a writer who desired something to take the place of physical action. The use of diaries in *Marius* and in the portraits of Watteau, Sebastian, and Emerald is the result of the direct influence of the confessional tradition.

A third genre, very closely related in form to autobiography, is that of the familiar essay, which Montaigne fathered for the modern world.[6] The temporal structure of the imaginary portraits is directly conditioned by the subjectivity of the essay genre. Pater often begins one of his historically distant portraits in the present time, using as a springboard for his story his own observations and experiences. "Apollo" and "Hippolytus" both open with references to books and writers Pater had read, while "Duke Carl" closes with remarks on the German *Aufklärung* and a quotation about Goethe. In these portraits the author assumes the essayist's role of the man of letters. In all the other portraits Pater also presents, to a greater or lesser extent, his story as the product of his own experiences, often portraying himself as following a favorite pursuit of essayists, traveling. In "Gaudioso," for example, Pater begins with a discussion of a picture by Romanino, an obvious echo of his own travels through North Italy while collecting his "Art Notes." The only exception to this temporal crosscutting be-

---

Opium-Eater, Newman's *Apologia Pro Vita Sua*, to name but a few. Often, of course, the subject of the confession is not the author but some fictional character, a technique which produces such fictional autobiographies as Defoe's *Moll Flanders*.

   [6] The essay was the contribution of the Renaissance to prose, and the idea behind it differed radically from medieval writing. While the medieval author tried to keep personal qualities out of his writing, the Renaissance essayist desired to express his personality. Of Charles Lamb, who was greatly influenced by seventeenth-century writers such as Burton and Browne, Pater writes: "With him, as with Montaigne, the desire of self-portraiture is, below all more superficial tendencies, the real motive in writing at all—a desire closely connected with that intimacy, that modern subjectivity, which may be called the *Montaignesque* element in literature" (*Ap*, p. 117). The seventeenth-century essay becomes, then, a new, shortened form of autobiography and is, indeed, says Pater, the "characteristic literary type of our own time" (*PP*, p. 174).

tween past and present is the Watteau portrait, for it is presented entirely as a journal, and we have no direct sense of Pater's personality: it belongs wholly to the confessional tradition.

In the longer fiction, the influence of the essay structure is similarly noticeable. In *Marius* and *Gaston* Pater often violates the illusion of past time by alluding to the present, showing how the past resembles the present. For example, Pater tells us that Gaston "'almost anticipated our modern idea, or platitude, of the *Zeit-geist* (*GdL*, 70), and in *Marius* he mentions Giotto, Rousseau, Hamlet, Dante, Augustine, Montaigne, Renan, and Gregory the Great—all in one chapter!

One should perhaps mention two further forms which had a noteworthy, if not striking, impact on Pater's fiction. The fourth influence on the fiction is prose satire, which lies close to both the essay and the fictional autobiography.[7] Satire differs from the novel and resembles autobiography in that it deals not with people but with intellectual themes or mental attitudes, and the dramatic interest is, therefore, in the clash of ideas rather than of characters. Pater was undoubtedly aware of and influenced by this distinction even when he was not being consciously satiric. He does, however, specifically employ a trenchant irony in his description of Marcus Aurelius and the *Confarreation* doings, of Sebastian's love of Spinoza's philosophy, and of the Rosenmold court, as well as elsewhere. Finally, a fifth genre sometimes related to satire, as in Erasmus and Voltaire, and sometimes related to the essay, as in Landor, is the dialogue or symposium.[8] Pater is very obviously drawing on this genre when he reworks Lucian's *Hermotimus* and *Halcyon* in *Marius*. One may also see its influence on the orations by Aurelius, Fronto, and Bruno in *Marius* and *Gaston*. Many times Pater removes himself one step from the dialogue by reporting it in essay form, turning it back into a genre from which it had never been entirely separated.

While all these types are represented from antiquity onward, the seventeenth century is particularly rich in examples, and it is not surprising that Pater felt especially attached to the rhetorical

---

[7] Early practitioners of this form were Petronius, Apuleius, and, of course, Lucian, who provided the great stimulus for the seventeenth-century satiric essay. In the Renaissance, Erasmus and More were both contributors to this form, as was Burton with his *Anatomy*, while somewhat later Voltaire added his *Candide* and Swift his *Gulliver's Travels*.

[8] Plato, of course, was the father of this tradition, and from his time onward we hear edifying conversation—moral conversation for the medieval man in Boethius' *Consolations of Philosophy*, urbane conversation for the secular Renaissance man in Castiglione's *Courtier*, and satiric conversation for the man of the Enlightenment in Johnson's *Rasselas*.

prose writers of this period. His portraits are the direct heirs of the century that discovered the familiar essay, the form most basic to his fiction. If one applies a crude but perhaps telling test, he might note that only one of Pater's finished works, *Marius*, is longer than usual essay length and that it seems often to be only a collection of separate studies. Of course, the implication is not that *Marius* is less at home in the nineteenth century than the seventeenth. As the novel was expanded in scope and improved in technique, it carried with it a sort of penumbra of experiments in which definitely fictional elements were applied in works that could not qualify as novels by any accepted definition. There was a wide range of such "semi-fiction," such as Southey's *Colloquies*, Wilson's *Noctes Ambrosianae*, Carlyle's *Sartor Resartus*, Arnold's *Friendship's Garland*, and so on. While Pater's work is not closely related to any one of these, they nevertheless form a sort of context for his attempt to find a middle ground between pure fiction and exposition.

This "semi-fiction" of Pater, however, is in a way a unique genre. Pater's particular name for his form, "imaginary portraits," may have been suggested, so Thomas Wright tells us, "by his old friend McQueen's *Imaginary Countries*, though it is more probable that it was derived from the title of a favorite book of his, Landor's *Imaginary Conversations*."[9] Since Pater deliberately parodied Landor's title in Chapter XXIV of *Marius*, "A Conversation Not Imaginary," we can assume with reasonable certainty that the word *imaginary* was borrowed from Landor. As to the word *portrait*, this may have been Pater's own contribution. However, since Pater was certainly familiar with Sainte-Beuve's *Portraits littéraires* and *Portraits contemporains*, he may have taken the word from the Frenchman's carefully classified history of intellects and temperaments.

At any rate, the tendency to portraiture was already evident in the method which Pater used in *The Renaissance*, exploring the cultural awakening by means of individual lives rather than by systematic analysis of ideological components. To assert, as does Germain d'Hangest,[10] that Pater had a spontaneous tendency to incarnate abstract ideas in human form is not to deny that he was influenced by the historical method of, say, Jakob Burckhardt,

---

[9] Thomas Wright, *The Life of Walter Pater* (London, 1907), II, 91. Landor's conversation between "Joseph Scaliger and Montaigne" may have played its part in the portrayal of Montaigne in *Gaston*. In *Plato*, Landor is cited with approval as one of several "effective writers of dialogue" (*PP*, p. 176).

[10] *Walter Pater*, II, 43.

whose *Civilization of the Renaissance* concentrated on single bright moments in order to define the period. One may perhaps also consider Pater influenced by the historical methods of Michelet, Sainte-Beuve, the German romantic historians, and even Carlyle—all of whom explored their subjects through selected individual lives. But with Pater portraiture was probably not purely a matter of outside influence. His primary interest as a critic had always been the realization of the living personality behind the philosophic idea or the work of art.[11] "The best sort of criticism," Pater once wrote, is "imaginative criticism; that criticism which is itself a kind of construction, or creation, as it penetrates, through the given literary or artistic product, into the mental and inner constitution of the producer, shaping his work" (*EG*, 29). And again, in *Plato*, Pater reminds us:

> It might even be said that the trial-task of criticism, in regard to literature and art no less than to philosophy, begins exactly where the estimate of general conditions, of the conditions common to all the products of this or that particular age—of the "environment"—leaves off, and we touch what is unique in the individual genius which contrived after all, by force of will, to have its own masterful way with that environment. If in reading Plato, for instance, the philosophic student has to re-construct for himself, as far as possible, the general character of an *age*, he must also, so far as he may, reproduce the portrait of a *person*. (*PP*, 124–25)[12]

We can see, then, a very strong resemblance and continuity between the objective of Pater's literary, artistic, and philosophic criticism and the goal which he held out for his imaginary portraits: "Imaginary—and portraits: they present not an action, a story; but a character, [a] personality, revealed especially in outward detail."[13]

Hence, to say merely that Pater had a "spontaneous tendency" toward such portraiture is somewhat too vague. The idea of the por-

---

[11] Pater's "impressionism" bears a strong resemblance to an ever increasing number of Continental and American critics, such as Georges Poulet and J. H. Miller, who attempt, like Pater, to reconstruct the interior world of the writer. This tradition differs from that of I. A. Richards and the New Critics and explains why Pater as a critic has not been widely read in our time. On the subject of Pater's "impressionism" consult René Wellek, "Walter Pater's Literary Theory and Criticism," *Victorian Studies*, I (September, 1957), 29–46.

[12] Perhaps part of the charm which Plato exercised over Pater was the result of Plato's ability to fulfill this "trial-task" of good philosophizing. Pater writes that in the thought of Plato, "abstract ideas themselves became animated, living persons, almost corporeal, as if with hands and eyes" (*PP*, p. 170). See also *PP*, pp. 166–67.

[13] Quoted in d'Hangest, *Walter Pater*, II, 45.

trait is intimately related to the core of religious myth which pervades each of the historical and fictional studies, for the significance of the old legends, their ethical or religious quality, was in ancient Greece conveyed by portraiture, by the "personages" of sculpture. "The myths of the Greek religion," says Pater, became

parts of an ideal, visible embodiments of the susceptibilities and intuitions of the nobler kind of souls; and it is to this latest phase of mythological development that the highest Greek sculpture allies itself. Its function is to give visible aesthetic expression to the constituent parts of that ideal. As poetry dealt chiefly with the *incidents* of the story, so it is with the *personages* of the story—with Demeter and Kore themselves—that sculpture has to do. (*GS*, 137)

The function of the figures in ancient sculpture—"elevating and refining the religious conceptions of the Greeks" (*GS*, 138)—is identical with that of Pater's ideal heroes. Imaginary portraiture, like ancient statuary (Pater's heroes often seem allied more to the plastic arts than the graphic), seeks to proclaim a message of religious hope, and just as the figure of "Demeter enthroned, chastened by sorrow" embodied an immortality purged of the dark and grotesque elements of the world of mortals, so Pater's heroes seem to emanate an Apollonian light, to anticipate and call forth the dawning day of immortality.

In writing his portraits, Pater's purpose is not some "actual revival" of the childhood world of the summer Dionysus: "such vain antiquarianism is a waste of the poet's power" (*Ap*[1889], 223). If from his perspective of maturity he cannot recapture fully that childlike unconsciousness, he can at least recognize in the past its contribution to his spiritual maturity. "The composite experience of all the ages," says Pater,

is part of each one of us: to deduct from that experience, to obliterate any part of it, to come face to face with the people of a past age, as if the Middle Age, the Renaissance, the eighteenth century had not been, is as impossible as to become a little child, or enter again into the womb and be born. But though it is not possible to repress a single phase of that humanity, which, because we live and move and have our being in the life of humanity, makes us what we are, it is possible to isolate such a phase, to throw it into relief, to be divided against ourselves in zeal for it; as we may hark back to some choice space of our own individual life. We cannot truly conceive the age: we can conceive the element it has contributed to our culture: we can treat the subjects of the age bringing that into relief. Such an attitude . . . is what is possible for art. (*Ap*[1889], 223-24)

Pater's heroes are, so to speak, the eternal human face behind the outward events of the age; and imaginary portraiture is, then, an attempt to isolate a cultural phase by portraying the contribution which the hero, the representative of his age, makes as he breaks through the veil of mortality into the immortal world of light. Just as in his first portrait, "The Child in the House," Pater attempts to "hark back to some choice space" in his own childhood, so in all the portraits we go back to an earlier age—not by an impersonal repression of our experience, of who and what we are, but "imaginatively," by an appreciation of the implications of what the hero has contributed to his age and ours. The projection of this single figure against the background of humanity is the sort of artistic relief work which constitutes imaginary portraiture.

When one considers that Pater's first major work, *The Renaissance*, had been severely criticized, one is tempted to suspect that Pater used imaginary portraits as a more flexible and less vulnerable form for the presentation of his historical, philosophical, or critical ideas. Yet the genre of portraiture in Pater's hands rightly belongs to no discipline but imaginative literature. His portraits are in every case a triumph of fictional art, for the religious myths of renewal endow the lives and deaths of Pater's heroes with an undeniably dramatic pattern. The Paterian hero is not merely a passive reflection of his intellectual environment, as critics have alleged.[14] Rather, the task of the portrait is to delineate that mythic element in the hero by which he has his "own masterful way with that environment" and transcends his age. Being god and man at the same time, the hero mediates between time and eternity, bringing renewed life to those around him through his powers of synthesis. Each portrait ends with a single act charged with spiritual victory: Florian saves a pet bird, Marius dies in Christ-like fashion for another, Watteau produces a cross, Denys builds the organ, Sebastian rescues a child, Duke Carl marries a German peasant girl, Hippolytus preserves his sacred purity, Emerald dies a hero, Prior St. Jean learns to love the distant view. Often the Dionysian cycle of life and death overtly assists the denouement; sometimes it remains implicit, to be recognized only in the extraordinary creative capacity of the hero for harmonizing the discordant elements of his life. But whether explicit or implicit, this delineation of the mythic pattern in the life of the individual and the history of the human race makes Pater's portraiture truly literary and imaginative. "In his firm hold on the harmonies of the human face," wrote Pater in the *Greek Studies*, the designer of the head of Demeter "is on the one road to a command over the

---

[14] A typical example would be U. C. Knoepflmacher, *Religious Humanism*, p. 168, who asserts that Pater creates an "atmosphere" which then is seen to "mold the mind and will of his characters."

secrets of all imaginative pathos and mystery" (*GS*, 138–39). Much the same can be said of Pater in the fashioning of his portraits.

"THE CHILD IN THE HOUSE" (1878)

Until the publication of "The Child in the House," Pater had written of historical personages mythically in *The Renaissance,* and he had also written of mythical figures historically in the *Greek Studies*. He had never, however, simply created a figure and endowed him imaginatively with both historicity and myth. "The Child in the House" and the portrait that followed represent Pater's first step in this direction—a step away from the historical portrait and toward the imaginary. Of course, we should not minimize the importance of the factual material on which these two portraits are based. By virtue of the vividness of its descriptions and the nostalgic tone of its narration, "The Child in the House," for example, seems inescapably a retrospective essay of sorts.[15] In one sense, then, Florian is Pater, and "The Child in the House" comes very close to being the first chapter in Pater's autobiography. When Pater tells us that Florian's suddenly revived memory of his childhood home "was just the thing needed for the beginning of a certain design he then had in view, the noting, namely, of some things in the story of his spirit—in that process of brain-building by which we are, each one of us, what we are" (*MS*, 173)—we wonder if perhaps Pater's aim may not also have been to define those early impressions from which all his major sentiments sprang. Doubtless the series of sequential portraits which he contemplated at this time was designed to take the form of a thinly veiled autobiography, this present portrait being intended to describe the first steps in awakening selfhood and to define the relation between the growing soul and the external world.

Florian's "remembrance of things past" takes the form of a dream-vision:

[15] When Pater tells us here that "after many wanderings I have come to fancy that some parts of Surrey and Kent are, for Englishmen, true landscape, true home-counties" (*MS*, p. 179), we recall that this was the area where he, like Florian, had been reared, and we are not surprised to note that Florian's home, with its big garden, resembles the old house at Enfield in the neighborhood of Chase Side, where Pater spent his youth. Other elements of the story as well seem to come from Pater's own biography—the father who died early, for example, and the saintly aunt who believed young Walter destined for an ecclesiastical career both have their counterparts in Florian's life. And, interestingly, Florian and Pater are about the same age. We are told it was "almost thirty years" (*MS*, p. 173) since Florian left the house, when he was "about the age of twelve" (*MS*, p. 195). The portrait appeared in August of 1878, when Pater had just turned thirty-nine. If we take into consideration the "almost" and the "about," there is a rather close resemblance in age.

A dream of that place came to Florian, a dream which did for him
the office of the finer sort of memory, bringing its object to mind
with a great clearness, yet, as sometimes happens in dreams, raised
a little above itself, and above ordinary retrospect. The true aspect
of the place, especially of the house there in which he had lived
as a child, the fashion of its doors, its hearths, its windows, the very
scent upon the air of it, was with him in sleep for a season; only,
with tints more musically blent on wall and floor, and some finer
light and shadow running in and out, along its curves and angles. . . .
In that half-spiritualised house he could watch the better, over again,
the gradual expansion of the soul which had come to be there—of
which indeed, through the law which makes the material objects about
them so large an element in children's lives, it had actually become
a part; inward and outward being woven through and through each
other into one inextricable texture—half, tint and trace and accident
of homely colour and form, from the wood and the bricks; half, mere
soul-stuff, floated thither from who knows how far. In the house
and garden of his dream he saw a child moving, and could divide
the main streams at least of the winds that had played on him, and
study so the first stage in that mental journey. (*MS*, 172–74)

Childhood is the "tiring-room" where the soul clothes itself for
the life ahead as it blends the external world with its own divine
essence. The events of these years are charged with a specific potential strength for the mind of the adult, for from these experiences
come the initial awareness of the self and its close relation to the
world.

Florian's reverie is just the opposite of the narrow, wintry
Dionysian dream world where, as Pater describes it in "Aesthetic
Poetry," "the bodily senses sleep" (*Ap*[1889] 221). There the soul
cannot incorporate its dreams in any objective order; they are
confined with no outlet. But because Florian's soul has found its
freedom in the sensuousness of nature, his dream world resembles
the realm so aptly described by the later poetry of William Morris,
a realm which Pater says is

full of happy, childish wonder as in the earlier world. It is a world
in which the centaur and the ram with the fleece of gold are conceivable. The song sung always claims to be sung for the first time. There
are hints at a language common to birds and beasts and men. Everywhere there is an impression of surprise, as of people first waking
from the golden age, at fire, snow, wine, the touch of water as one
swims, the salt taste of the sea. (*Ap*[1889], 222)

Such a dream world of simple, first-hand experiences, according
to Pater, presents "a strange contrast to the sought-out simplicity
of Wordsworth," who cherished not experience itself, but its recol-
lection in tranquility—"the fruit of experience," as the Conclusion

to *The Renaissance* contemptuously calls it (*R*, 236). The young Florian loves "the body of nature for its own sake, not because a soul is divined through it" (*Ap* [1889], 222), and this direct acceptance of sensuous impressions is the quality which makes his childhood unique and gives to it the classic elements of the Golden Age.

Pater opens "The Child in the House" with an archetypal image probably as old as the imaginative mind of humanity itself. Florian meets "by the wayside a poor aged man, and, as he seemed weary with the road, helped him on with the burden which he carried, a certain distance" (*MS*, 172). We, as readers, should have no trouble in recognizing this road, for all men are traveling along it. Chaucer's Theseus was among the first to give voice to the ancient image in the English tongue: "This world nys but a thurghfare of wo, / And we been pilgrymes, passynge to and fro."[16] The old man's last journey, save that of death perhaps, reminds Florian of the first trip which he had made along this road in leaving the home and city "he had never since seen" (*MS*, 172).

Somehow, all the commentators on Pater have missed this central allegory in the portrait, perhaps because no one has connected it with the one work which might most appropriately be recalled here, and have, therefore, failed to see any significance in such images as the road, the house, the child, and the bird. The fusion of the pilgrimage-of-life allegory and the technique of the dream-vision derives from one of Pater's favorite writers, whose greatest work opens with these famous words:

As I walked through the wilderness of this world, I lighted on a certain place where was a Den, and I laid me down in that place to sleep; and, as I slept, I dreamed a dream. I dreamed, and behold, I saw a man clothed with rags, standing in a certain place, with his face from his own house, a book in his hand, and a great burden upon his back.[17]

The man with the burden, who begins his long pilgrimage from his original home through the Slough of Despond, the Valley of the Shadow of Death, Vanity Fair, and the House Beautiful on his way back to the Celestial City, has traveled through several centuries to appear once more as the augury of Florian's coming dream-vision, infusing its images with a depth far beyond that

[16] *Canterbury Tales*, "The Knight's Tale," Bk. IV, ll. 2847–48.

[17] John Bunyan, *The Pilgrim's Progress*. Bunyan supplies Pater with a number of names: "Celestial City" (*Marius*), "Apollyon" ("Apollo"), and "House Beautiful" (*Appreciations*), to name a few.

of mere autobiographical retrospection. The framework of the Everyman myth, with which Pater surrounds his hero, makes Florian the first of his archetypal figures to re-enact the universal experiences of mankind.

The allegorical or mythical nature of the portrait is most evident when one considers the idea of the house. A passage in *Marius* gives us the key to the symbol, and the verbal echoes between this passage and the one in which Pater describes the spiritualizing quality of Florian's dream are strong, for the perfect relationship envisioned between house and occupant in *Marius* is the same as that between the house and child of Florian's dream. Phrases such as "expansion of the soul," "light and shadow," "inward and outward," and "its windows, the very scent upon the air" recur here:

"The house in which she lives," says that mystical German writer quoted once before, "is for the orderly soul, which does not live on blindly before her, but is ever, out of her passing experiences, building and adorning the parts of a many-roomed abode for herself, only an expansion of the body; as the body, according to the philosophy of Swedenborg, is but a process, an expansion, of the soul. For such an orderly soul, as life proceeds, all sorts of delicate affinities establish themselves, between herself and the doors and passage-ways, the lights and shadows, of her outward dwelling-place, until she may seem incorporate with it—until at last, in the entire expressiveness of what is outward, there is for her, to speak properly, between outward and inward, no longer any distinction at all; and the light which creeps at a particular hour on a particular picture or space upon the wall, the scent of flowers in the air at a particular window, become to her, not so much apprehended objects, as themselves powers of apprehension and doorways to things beyond—the germ or rudiment of certain new faculties, by which she, dimly yet surely, apprehends a matter lying beyond her actually attained capacities of spirit and sense." So it must needs be in a world which is itself, we may think, together with that bodily "tent" or "tabernacle," only one of many vestures for the clothing of the pilgrim soul, to be left by her, surely, as if on the wayside, worn-out one by one, as it was from her, indeed, they borrowed what momentary value or significance they had. (*ME*, II, 92–93)[18]

[18] In his essay on Rossetti, Pater wrote: "The dwelling-place in which one finds oneself by chance or destiny, yet can partly fashion for oneself; never properly one's own at all, if it be changed too lightly; in which every object has its associations; . . . the house one must quit, yet taking perhaps, how much of its quietly active light and colour along with us!—grown now to be a kind of raiment to one's body, as the body, according to Swedenborg, is but the raiment of the soul—under that image, the whole of Rossetti's work might count as a *House of Life*, of which he is but the 'Interpreter' " (*Ap*, p. 214). The reference to leaving the house seems an echo of the conclusion to this portrait.

This passage presents in no uncertain terms the Platonic allegory basic to "The Child in the House": the body is to the soul as the house is to the inhabitant as the world is to humanity. And how are soul, inhabitant, and humanity related to body, house, and world? The answer is obvious: by pilgrimage.

Childhood, then, is that perfect state in which the "pilgrim soul" is momentarily in harmony with the sensuous world before it must move on to higher syntheses as it begins its pilgrimage toward the Celestial City. Yet never again, save in art, will the balance between sense and spirit be quite so perfect as in childhood. There is a touch of the prelapsarian in this youthful world, and the spacious garden which surrounds the house awakens in the reader echoes of another Garden. So vivid and so real are the experiences that pass through the soul of the child that they constitute the essence of the grown man. Recalling those experiences, Florian reflects:

How indelibly, as we afterwards discover, they affect us; with what capricious attractions and associations they figure themselves on the white paper, the smooth wax, of our ingenuous souls, as "with lead in the rock for ever," giving form and feature, and as it were assigned house-room in our memory, to early experiences of feeling and thought, which abide with us ever afterwards, thus, and not otherwise. (MS, 177)

The mature Florian is, so to speak, the "spiritual form" of his childhood home, for by the combining of these impressions in one harmonious whole, he himself is created. Were he able to pick sides in the real world of philosophical dispute, Florian would take issue with Hegel, for example, who asserted that the essence of selfhood lies in reason; he would probably prefer the philosophy of Plato, for Plato was too great an artist ever to say anything as positively as Hegel. Selfhood, Florian held, is not reason, but sensuous impressions linked aesthetically, not rationally. Florian accepted the One, but he also believed passionately in the reality of the Many. The "great poplar in the garden," "fallen fruit in autumn," "the glossy blackbirds," "the white angora," "Cecil, early dead," "the languid scent of ointments," and "the red hawthorn" indelibly inscribe upon the *tabula rasa* the nature of the future man.

In what is perhaps the most crucial philosophical passage in "The Child in the House," Pater almost seems to drop the guise of Florian completely, so intent is he upon explaining what he believes:

In later years he came upon philosophies which occupied him much in the estimate of the proportion of the sensuous and the ideal elements in human knowledge, the relative parts they bear in it; and, in his intellectual scheme, was led to assign very little to the abstract thought, and much to its sensible vehicle or occasion, . . . and he remembered gratefully how the Christian religion, hardly less than the religion of the ancient Greeks, translating so much of its spiritual verity into things that may be seen, condescends in part to sanction this infirmity, if so it be, of our human existence, wherein the world of sense is so much with us, and welcomed this thought as a kind of keeper and sentinel over his soul therein. But certainly, he came more and more to be unable to care for, or think of soul but as in an actual body, or of any world but that wherein are water and trees, and where men and women look, so or so, and press actual hands. (*MS*, 186–87)

If it is true that all of Western philosophy is merely a collection of footnotes to Plato, then surely Pater's footnote was, for his day at least, one of the more vigorous pleas against tipping the scales too far in favor of abstract universals. No artist, says Pater, can truly believe the things of this world merely shadows. Of the child's encounter with the red hawthorn, Pater writes: "for the first time, he seemed to experience a passionateness in his relation to fair outward objects, an inexplicable excitement in their presence, which disturbed him, and from which he half longed to be free" (*MS*, 186).[19] Pater has already described the meaning of the phenomenon, for us in the essay on Winckelmann, in which, speaking of "the artistic life, with its inevitable sensuousness," he tells us that "it has sometimes seemed hard to pursue that life without something of conscious disavowal of a spiritual world; and this imparts to genuine artistic interests a kind of intoxication" (*R*, 222). The child, drunk with the beauty of the hawthorn, is certainly not an incipient mystic. And if we begin to speculate on "what came of him," as Pater hoped his readers might, we would hardly be wrong in assuming that he became an artist.

Because Pater can only conceive of the soul as actually incarnated in a world of sense, he insists upon its inherent individuality. In *Plato and Platonism*, Pater condemns a determinism that blots out the individual self in favor of some impersonal secular process which accumulates

[19] This is one of the points where there is a tangential crossing with Proust and evidence that Proust had read Pater. The experience with the hawthorn in *MS*, p. 185, is strongly suggestive of a parallel experience in *Swann's Way*.

into its "colossal manhood" the experience of ages; making use of, and casting aside in its march, the souls of countless individuals, as Pythagoras supposed the individual soul to cast aside again and again its outworn body. So it may be. There was nothing of all that, however, in the mind of the great English poet at the beginning of this century whose famous Ode on *The Intimations of Immortality from Recollections of Childhood,* in which he made *metempsychösis* his own, must still express for some minds something more than merely poetic truth. For Pythagoreanism too, like all the graver utterances of primitive Greek philosophy, is an instinct of the human mind itself, and therefore also a constant tradition in its history, which *will* recur; fortifying this or that soul here or there in a part at least of that old sanguine assurance about itself, which possessed Socrates so immovably, his masters, his disciples. (*PP*, 73)

Pater concludes by quoting Henry Vaughan's "The Retreat" as exemplifying, as does Wordsworth's ode, the Pythagorean belief that the soul retains its inherent divinity even in a world in which the impressions of external things seem to be so important in our personalities. It is a belief that persists—and for this reason must have some basis in actual truth—despite the assurances of science that "we come into the world, each one of us, 'not in nakedness,' but by the natural course of organic development clothed far more completely than even Pythagoras supposed in a vesture of the past, nay, fatally shrouded, it might seem, in those laws or tricks of heredity which we mistake for our volitions; in the language which is more than one half of our thoughts; in the moral and mental habits, the customs, the literature, the very houses, which we did not make for ourselves" (*PP*, 72).

Pater, like Vaughan and Wordsworth, then, saw childhood as that state in which the spiritual self and the brute, irreducible facts of the external world are in perfect balance. He writes that for Florian, "the sense of harmony between his soul and its physical environment became, for a time at least, like perfectly played music" (*MS*, 180). Frequently in Pater's writings music becomes the great symbol of this fusion of the inward and outward worlds, and the whole of Florian's dream-vision of childhood is pervaded by the delicately attuned Pythagorean music of the spheres. Even Florian's musically alliterative name tells us that he effects in his person a harmony of sense and soul, for it reveals to us his Dionysian-Apollonian nature. The secret of the name Florian Deleal lies in the anagrammatic form, in which the endings have been neatly transposed from Floreal Delian. The child, we note, is "of French descent," (*MS*, 174) and his first name derives from the eighth month of the French Republican calendar, Floréal, which extends from mid-April to mid-May. The noun form of Florian's surname is *Delian*, meaning one who comes from the island of Delos, birthplace of Apollo and sacred for its sanctuary and festival to him.[20]

The Latin base of Florian's first name aligns him closely with that world of flowers which scatters such exquisite perfume through the whole of the portrait. We see him as a sort of male counterpart to Flora, goddess of spring, and similar in function to the vegetative god Dionysus. Florian is, then, intensely aware of the romantic as well as the classic quality of life: "he could trace two predominant processes of mental change in him—the growth of an almost diseased sensibility to the spectacle of suffering, and, parallel with this, the rapid growth of a certain capacity of fascination by bright colour and choice form" (*MS*, 181). So, as he says, "with this desire of physical beauty mingled itself early the fear of death—the fear of death intensified by the desire of beauty" (*MS*, 189–90). Florian is early aware of the cyclic pattern in the flux of phenomena, and "he yielded himself to these things, to be played upon by them like a musical instrument, and began to note with deepening watchfulness, but always with some puzzled, unutterable longing in his enjoyment, the phases of the seasons and of the growing or waning day, down even to the shadowy changes wrought on bare wall or ceiling" (*MS*, 188). This seems a verbal echo of the 1868 version of the Conclusion, in which Pater sees the winter Dionysus even in the bloom of the sensuous world—"the gradual darkening of the eye and fading of colour from the wall."[21]

In a way, Pater here seems to be echoing Poe, Baudelaire, and Keats in the belief that death and physical beauty are reciprocally related, and we recall that line in *Marius* about "the fatality which seems to haunt any signal beauty" (*ME*, I, 93). Certainly

[20] This explanation of Florian's name has not been given before. Pater occasionally uses such characterization by names elsewhere, too. For example, Sebastian van Storck's Christian name is an echo of St. Sebastian, who died a Dionysian death, transfixed by arrows and afterwards beaten. And just as the first Sebastian was a Roman officer, so the teacher of the Dutch Sebastian fancied "that his ultimate destination may be the military life" (*IP*, p. 83). Sebastian's surname may reflect the traditional Dutch belief that it is the presence of the stork that brings children; the relevance of this to the portrait as Pater tells it is clear enough. Emerald Uthwart is another good example of such characterization; his name will be explained in Chapter VI. Pater also seems to borrow names from his favorite romantic writers. For example the name "Marius" may very well come from Victor Hugo's *Les Miserables* (Pater mentions Hugo's hero in *Ap*, p. 248) and Gretchen, the girl Duke Carl marries, may well come from Goethe's *Faust*. (Goethe, of course, is a very important figure in the portrait.)

[21] *Westminster Review*, XXXIV, 310.

this combination of opposites is the basis of all art and defines the Apollonian temper for us. Speaking of the necessity under which the romantic spirit feels itself for associating beauty and strangeness, Pater writes in *Appreciations:* "Its desire is for a beauty born of unlikely elements, by a profound alchemy, by a difficult initiation, by the charm which wrings it even out of terrible things; and a trace of distortion, of the grotesque, may perhaps linger, as an additional element of expression, about its ultimate grace" (*Ap,* 247–48). In the childhood vision of the boy Florian, these two qualities of beauty and pain reach their fullest expression; it is a hearing of the musical harmony in the joy and sorrow of the world. Life and death, beauty and pain—"In music sometimes the two sorts of impressions came together, and he would weep, to the surprise of older people" (*MS,* 181).

This ideal harmony of beauty and strangeness finds its fullest expression not in art but in the hope of Christianity:

To Florian such impressions, these misgivings as to the ultimate tendency of the years, of the relationship between life and death, had been suggested spontaneously in the natural course of his mental growth by a strong innate sense for the soberer tones in things, further strengthened by actual circumstances; and religious sentiment, that system of biblical ideas in which he had been brought up, presented itself to him as a thing that might soften and dignify, and light up as with a "lively hope," a melancholy already deeply settled in him. (*MS,* 192–93)

For Florian, religion was "a constant substitution of the typical for the actual," a blending of two realms of experience, as in art, so that inner and outer are one ideal world:

His way of conceiving religion came then to be in effect what it ever afterwards remained—a sacred history indeed, but still more a sacred ideal, a transcendent version or representation, under intenser and more expressive light and shade, of human life and its familiar or exceptional incidents, birth, death, marriage, youth, age, tears, joy, rest, sleep, waking—a mirror, towards which men might turn away their eyes from vanity and dullness, and see themselves therein as angels, with their daily meat and drink, even, become a kind of sacred transaction—a complementary strain or burden, applied to our everyday existence, whereby the stray snatches of music in it re-set themselves, and fall into the scheme of some higher and more consistent harmony. (*MS,* 193–94)

Three qualities "the child took away with him, when . . . he left the old house": a "sensibility" to the sorrow in the world, a "desire of physical beauty," and, transmuting both the pain and the

beauty, "a strange biblical awe" (*MS*, 195). It is this ideal Apollonian world, neither merely soul nor merely sense, and expressed
here (as later in *Marius*) in terms of religion rather than art,
which Florian possessed as a child.

"The Child in the House" opens with a single vividly realized
image of the aged man with the burden, and it closes with an
equally vivid description of the empty house "like the face of one
dead" (*MS*, 196). Each stage on the road of life is marked by
a Dionysian dying—a dying to the old in order to be born into
the new. This cycle of life and death appears often in Pater's
portraits, perhaps most clearly in *Marius*, where stages of Marius'
mental growth are marked by the death of those who had symbolized a particular way of looking at reality which Marius is
about to transcend. Writing in *Appreciations* of Wordsworth's "Intimations" ode, Pater finds in the poem the same sort of nostalgia
for the "half-ideal" world of childhood that he himself expressed
in "The Child in the House." Wordsworth had pondered deeply,
says Pater,

on those strange reminiscences and forebodings, which seem to make
our lives stretch before and behind us, beyond where we can see or
touch anything, or trace the lines of connexion. Following the soul,
backwards and forwards, on these endless ways, his sense of man's
dim, potential powers became a pledge to him, indeed, of a future
life, but carried him back also to that mysterious notion of an earlier
state of existence—the fancy of the Platonists—the old heresy of
Origen. It was in this mood that he conceived those oft-reiterated
regrets for a half-ideal childhood, when the relics of Paradise still
clung about the soul—a childhood, as it seemed, full of the fruits
of old age, lost for all, in a degree, in the passing away of the youth
of the world, lost for each one, over again, in the passing away of
actual youth. (*Ap*, 54–55)

When writing "The Child in the House," Pater must have thought
of Vaughan's poem as well as Wordsworth's ode. Vaughan, like
Wordsworth, wistfully admitted the impossibility of any "retreat"
into the prelapsarian state:

> *O! how I long to travel back*
> *And tread again that ancient track!*
> *That I might once more reach that plain,*
> *Where first I left my glorious train.—*
> *But Ah! my soul with too much stay*
> *Is drunk; and staggers in the way.* (*PP*, 74)

The Dionysian "intoxication" with the things of this world
demands a forward progress, the closing off of the past behind

one. As happened to the simple antique life of the Greeks, so with the childhood of Florian: the problem of unity could no longer be solved by "any joyful union with the external world: the shadows had grown too long, the light too solemn, for that" (R, 228).

In the last scene of "The Child in the House," as Florian salvages from a dead past a single spark of life, the truth of the impossibility of retreat dawns on him for the first time. The family has forgotten a pet bird, and Florian returns to save it from starvation:

> As he passed in search of it from room to room, lying so pale, with
> a look of meekness in their denudation, and at last through that little,
> stripped white room, the aspect of the place touched him like the
> face of one dead; and a clinging back towards it came over him, so
> intense that he knew it would last long, and spoiling all his pleasure
> in the realisation of a thing so eagerly anticipated. And so, with the
> bird found, but himself in an agony of home-sickness, thus capriciously
> sprung up within him, he was driven quickly away, far into the rural
> distance, so fondly speculated on, of that favourite country-road.
> (MS, 196)

The expanding soul has grown beyond the bounds of the house, which suddenly has become a trap, and in its death-like atmosphere it becomes the first of the many images in Pater's fiction of that wintry Dionysian world of the Conclusion: "the individual in his isolation, each mind keeping as a solitary prisoner its own dream of a world" (R, 235). The old world of the summer Dionysus must be abandoned, for some new external order is needed to match the larger dreams of the soul. Never again can the Golden Age be found in merely the bloom of the red hawthorn; now it must be in the greater world of art, in the realm of Apollo himself, where Florian finds his ideal. Perhaps Florian's growing need to interpret life religiously was an indication that already he had outgrown the childish unconsciousness of the summer Dionysus.

Florian's act of pity is the perfect denouement, for the bird is a traditional image of the soul. Marius' mother had inscribed this same image deeply on her son's mind when he was a child at White-nights, the home so like Florian's own:

> A white bird, she told him once, looking at him gravely, a bird which
> he must carry in his bosom across a crowded public place—his own
> soul was like that! Would it reach the hands of his good genius on
> the opposite side, unruffled and unsoiled? And as his mother became
> to him the very type of maternity in things, its unfailing pity and
> protectiveness, and maternity itself the central type of all love;—so,
> that beautiful dwelling-place lent the reality of concrete outline to

a peculiar ideal of home, which throughout the rest of his life he seemed, amid many distractions of spirit, to be ever seeking to regain. (*ME*, I, 22)[22]

Life and death successively replace each other as the pilgrim soul journeys out to some distant world of love, where once again the concrete ideal of home can be found. Pater has given us in "The Child in the House" a chronicle of "the first stage in that mental journey" (MS, 174) which he, like all men, had made.

Pater has drawn his inspiration for this portrait seemingly from Bunyan's *Pilgrim's Progress*, as he works into the actual facts of his own life the elements of the Everyman myth. The allegorical framework of the dream-vision universalizes the particular experiences, turning the simple images of the child, the house, the bird, and the road into symbols of the experiences of all mankind. Perhaps there is a certain quiet irony in Pater's use of Bunyan's Christian as Florian's prototype. Christian stands always "with his face from his own house," whereas Florian stands with his face toward his old home, an ideal, as it was with Marius, that he seemed "to be ever seeking to regain." But perhaps there is no irony, for Christian, by going forward, and Florian, by going back, ultimately reach the same point. As Vaughan realized, God is without direction, both the Alpha and Omega of existence:

> *Some men a forward motion love,*
> *But I backward steps would move;*
> *And when this dust falls to the urn*
> *In that state I came return.* (PP, 74)

"AN ENGLISH POET" (1878)

Pater had written to George Grove, as we have already noted, that "The Child in the House" was not intended to be part of some larger fictional work, but was meant to be the first of its kind in a series of such portraits. The second installment in the series, not generally realized as such, was "An English Poet," the full heading of which resembled the preceding portrait, except that it was numbered as the second piece. We know that Pater devoted the autumn of 1878 to its composition, for he had written Grove in early September that he was working on the second installment, and Grove had replied by asking Pater to send it when finished

[22] In a section cut from the next to the last paragraph of Chapter XIX, "The Will as Vision," in the later editions of *Marius*, Pater had described the golden moments of epiphany as "birds of passage . . . soon out of sight or with broken wing; yet not really lost, after all, on their way to the enduring light, in which the fair hours of life would present themselves as living creatures forever before the perpetual observer."

to his assistant since he himself would be abroad. But by December Grove had returned, and Pater wrote to say that the delay had been caused by his having to take up again work of another sort which he thought he had finished. Pater never did send Grove his second installment, and the manuscript was not published until 1931, when Mrs. May Ottley, Hester Pater's legatee, discovered it and published it in the *Fortnightly Review*.

Although Pater had abandoned the idea of a sequence in his series sometime during the composition of the second portrait—indeed, his failure to complete the portrait may have been owing to his change in plans—Pater's letters cast light on his intentions and encourage us to read "An English Poet" in relation to "The Child in the House." If we suppose "The Child in the House" to describe the initial awareness by the soul of itself and its identity with the external world, then "An English Poet" deals with the second major stage in the development of the creative personality, namely, the awakening of the "imaginative reason," of artistic vision, in the expanding soul. If the first portrait represents the simple world of a Golden Age based on a harmony of soul and nature, the world of the summer Dionysus, then the second defines the more complex world of a Golden Age in which the dreams of the soul are embodied in the objectivity of art, the world of Apollo.

In this second portrait the center of interest moves one step farther down the autobiographical path in chronicling the stages of Pater's mental growth. We can trace in this portrait, though to a lesser extent than in the preceding one, the same incorporation of autobiographical facts; and although Pater attempts to place a certain distance between himself and his hero, the reader will probably still feel that the autobiographical basis of the narrative is betrayed by an almost too circumstantial account of the young poet's literary apprenticeship.[23] The objectives of the young poet

[23] While both Pater's evident confusion following the death of his mother and his youthful desire for a poetic vocation are undoubtedly reflected in this work, a greater distance between author and hero is undeniably present. In part, this distance is the result of a more fully differentiated narrative personality. Pater appears in his authorial intrusions under the guise of a traveller among "Swiss or English" (*IP*B, p. 36) mountains who is describing in best essayistic fashion his reactions to his readers. While there is no real necessity to deny a close link between subject and author, the fact that there are now two distinct personalities takes us one step further from the retrospective essay. Pater further distances himself from his hero by providing a more elaborate fictional setting—the Pays de Caux and the Cumberland Lake Country. This greater geographical coverage is matched by a considerably greater temporal span, for we begin with the young poet's parents and continue following his fortunes to his "earliest manhood" (*IP*B, p. 46), when he finally breaks loose for his *Wanderjahre*.

52

match almost exactly the goals laid down in Pater's own criticism, as, for example, in the famous essay "Style." One has the inescapable feeling that in this second portrait, as in the first, Pater is curiously scrutinizing the "process of brain-building," which resulted in his being the man he was.

"An English Poet" opens, as do so many of Pater's portraits, in the style of a travelogue, with a brief but very sensuous description of the Pays de Caux, which blends into the event of the young English girl's finding "in the furrow one autumn morning a golden Roman coin with a clear high profile on it which looked to her as might an image of immortal youth" (*IPB*, 35). Afterwards, the Curé, to whom she showed the coin, "told her how in the old Pagan times the darkened minds of men had been wont to think much more of the perishable beauty of the body than Christians are allowed to do" (*IPB*, 35). Then, at about the same time, the coin came alive for her in the form of "a slim figure with delicate hands and golden hair growing crisply half down his forehead, and just such a profile as that on the golden medal. He has too, what the medal has not, colour—white and pale red, and just a touch of amber where the salt air of the channel has taken him" (*IPB*, 35).

The slim woman-like figure "of immortal youth" was the summer Dionysus returned to haunt her mind with the unsuspected possibilities of a new plenitude of life. The Dionysian influence built in her, as it did in Florian, a sensitivity to the beauty of growing things and a corresponding awareness of pain and death in the natural cycle: "She sheltered the budding rose bush in its pot near the chimney corner and began to fancy that such things as flowers really felt neglect even, and pined over their own short lives, and a little heart seemed breaking in each leaf that glided golden from the trees" (*IPB*, 36). Dionysian ecstasy invaded her heart as well, for with the renewal of the year, heralded in its pagan way by the blossoming of the rose bush in the red light of the hearth on Christmas Day, "the fire in her heart was burning strong and wild and the light fancies were no longer at her will" (*IPB*, 36).[24] But the "bright figure" (*IPB*, 36) of the golden god did not return and the English girl died in childbirth, heartbroken, the following winter. As always, however, winter death gives birth to life, and the child is evidence of that renewal.

[24] As Pater tells us in "The Bacchanals of Euripides," the involuntary fancies of the poet's mother were the inspiration of Dionysus: "Himself a woman-like god,—it was on women and feminine souls that his power mainly fell" (*GS*, p. 57).

The boy was taken to be reared by relatives among "the stern Cumberland mountains," which seemed like "some place of exile or punishment" (*IPB*, 36, 38). Certainly the Pays de Caux had its wintry side in the Curé, who distrusted "perishable beauty" and in "the plain young Frenchman" (*IPB*, 36) whom the poet's mother married, just as the Cumberland mountains had a summer side, "its morsels of more delicate texture" (*IPB*, 40). But there is no real doubt as to the primary nature of either the Pays de Caux or the Cumberland mountains. The lad's home takes the "stillness and isolation" of the world of the "day-dreams" of the poet's mother (*IPB*, 35) and carries them to their extreme limit. His new home is "stern," "chill," "grotesque," "graceless," "northern," "hard," and "narrow" (*IPB*, 36, 37, 38, 40, 41, 47)—a perfect list of romantic, wintry qualities. When we recall the mention of the "adventure which ended in loss of life" (*IPB*, 36), we sense the lethal quality which haunts the boy's home. For him, the "sacred fire" (*IPB*, 37), the warm and happy centripetal world, lay elsewhere—"the tide of real existence, great affairs and great creations," flowed beyond "those impassable mountains reinforcing the barrier of his birth" (*IPB*, 40).

The sensitive lad suffered greatly in this wintry Dionysian prison. In the whole of his environment, there were only two things that

had coaxed out his capacity for liking—a red honeysuckle over the gateway of the grange, the one more stately habitation in the place, in remarkably free flower this year, and a range of metal screen-work, twisted with fantastic grace into wreaths of flames or flowers, noticed now for the first time, making fine shadows in the pale sunlight on the mellow whitewashed wall of the old church as he sat there on Sundays, himself except that thing, the one touch of delicacy in its rudeness, and which seemed to him to hold somehow of that honeysuckle in flower and belong with it to a warmer heaven. (*IPB*, 39)

The red honeysuckle, like the red hawthorn in "The Child in the House," seems to represent sensuous reality and the bloom of physical things, while the metal work is its artistic counterpart, so to speak, by which it has been elevated into an ideal Apollonian art world. The red vine and its artistic transfiguration are related to the southern world of the centripetal: "the honeysuckle was an exotic from France . . . and that ancient metal hand-work with its dainty traces of half-vanished gilding, an exotic that too from Augsburg where such metal flowers and flames are plenteous" (*IPB*, 39). The northern environment gave the lad vision, but it failed, except in the case of the excitingly strange red honeysuckle, to supply him the means of embodying it. What the boy needed was a "fitting stimulus for the senses, some concrete imagery which might fix the wandering vision, that visible garment of which he saw not so much as the hem, means of expression or translation through which that dim brooding infinite sense, imaginativeness, might take hold, and he be relieved of the stifling weight of it" (*IPB*, 40–41).

Through his reading in literature, he finds the sensuous world he so longed for: "out of the greyness and austerity of a school in which the senses pined while the fancy declined fondly towards a more exquisite mode of living, the boy required from words . . . all that was not actually there for ear and eye. . . . So written language came to be form and colour as well as sound to him, exotic perfume almost" (*IPB*, 44–45). Eagerly grasping at whatever has form or color, the lad embodied his inner vision in it:

For the strange boy himself there was a curious sense of relief in seeing thought or fancy, housed at last in the fragment of writing compressed, truly by many shapings, to some delightful inward pattern or ideal, which yet had weighed on him like a burden; for if your words regarding it are to be fragrant, he would say, you must have been for a time in slavish possession of the flower. (*IPB*, 46)

The lad escaped the oppressive weight of his wintry dream by embodying it objectively in the "hard, gemlike flame" of art. His poetry, we are told, had "a certain hardness like that of a gem . . . somehow not altogether unlike that of the metal honeysuckle" which wreathed itself in "metal flowers and flames" (*IPB*, 46, 39):

This, a peculiar character as of flowers in metal, was noticed by the curious as a distinction in his verse, such an elastic force in word and phrase, following a tender delicate thought or feeling as the metal followed the curvature of the flower, as seemed to indicate artistic triumph over a material partly resisting, which yet at last took outline from his thought with the firmness of antique forms of mastery. (*IPB*, 39)[25]

[25] If there is any writer who is the stylistic model for Pater's imaginary poet, it would probably be Wordsworth, whose art, like that of the young English poet, was a product of the Cumberland lake district. Pater's imaginary portrait is a kind of prose counterpart to Wordsworth's great poetic autobiography, *The Prelude*, in which the "Growth of a Poet's Mind" (as the subtitle has it) is the subject. According to Pater, Wordsworth achieved as well as any man the ideal of poetry, for the word and the idea were united "in the imaginative flame, becoming inseparably one with the other, by that fusion of matter and form, which is the characteristic of the highest poetical expression" (*Ap*, p. 58). It is hardly surprising that, having written such an "appre-

Much of what Pater says about the art of poetry in this portrait later becomes expanded in *Marius* and in his essay "Style." In the chapter on "Euphuism" in *Marius*, for example, Pater echoes the metaphor of the metal screen-work in his description of Flavian's poem. The *Pervigilium Veneris*, he says, is "a composition shaping itself, little by little, out of a thousand dim perceptions, into singularly definite form (definite and firm as fine-art in metal, thought Marius), . . . a firmness like that of some master of noble metal-work, manipulating tenacious bronze or gold" (*ME*, I, 104, 115). And we are reminded again of the poet and his attempt to find an objective outlet for his inner states of awareness in "Style," in which Pater writes, for example, that "into the mind sensitive to 'form,' a flood of random sounds, colours, incidents, is ever penetrating from the world without, to become, by sympathetic selection, a part of its very structure, and, in turn, the visible vesture and expression of that other world it sees so steadily within" (*Ap*, 31). But not only are such echoes of the stylistic principles of the "English Poet" found throughout Pater's writings; even Pater's own handling of syntax and diction follows those precepts defined in the portrait.

Since a great deal of the meaning in the portrait of the young poet lies in its poetic theory, a brief consideration of the physical structure and tone of Pater's own style may shed considerable light on the subject of the original idea of inner vision expressed in visible form. There is a marked lack of significant stylistic evolution in the works of Pater, and from the very earliest essays to the very latest, the hesitating, precious rhythms of his prose are apparent everywhere. As a result, most commentators on Pater's style seem entranced by its music. Percy Lubbock speaks of Pater's "harmonious murmur," and Graham Hough mentions "the languor of its rhythms."[26] It is as if Pater had very much the same sort of ear as had his hero Duke Carl, who liked in church music "those passages of a pleasantly monotonous and, as it might seem, unending melody—which certainly never came to what could rightly be called an ending here on earth" (*IP*, 132). This may also be

---

ciation" of Wordsworth some four years previously, Pater should have employed him as the model for the growth of his own imaginary poet's mind.

While we are searching for models, we should not overlook the underprivileged youth of J. J. Winckelmann. There is much in the last essay of *The Renaissance* which resembles this early portrait. And perhaps also the English poet in his poverty and "bitter self-reliance" (*IP*B, p. 47) anticipates the Roman poet Flavian in *Marius*.

[26] Lubbock, *Craft of Fiction*, p. 195; Graham Hough, *The Last Romantics* (London, 1949), p. 172.

a reasonably apt description of some of Pater's longer and more trying sentences. I think, however, that it would be a mistake to draw any sort of extended comparison between Pater's style and the quality of music. Music, for the most part, has a driving, linear movement. It goes places. But Pater's style, with its interminable qualifications and afterthoughts, with its parallelisms and antitheses, with its connotative richness and frequent ambiguity, is certainly anything but fluid. It is static, pictorial. It resembles the highly inflected structure of the classical languages in that it permits a more arbitrary order of words so that the sentence seems to present to the reader all of its parts simultaneously. Describing this pictorial kind of style, Northrop Frye tells us that all the elements of the sentence "are fitted into a pattern, and as one point after another is made, there emerges not a linear process of thought but a simultaneous comprehension. What is explained is turned around and viewed from all aspects, but it is completely there, so to speak, from the beginning."[27]

Moreover, Pater's is a style in which the sentence, not the paragraph, is the basic unit. Writing in paragraphs provides a sense of linear movement, but composition in sentences conveys a sense of stasis. Edmund Chandler, who made an extensive survey of the style of Pater's *Marius*, writes:

The aspect of the revision that strikes [one] as most curious is that Pater felt he could dismantle *Marius* into its component sentences, and then revise each as an entity in itself—an undertaking rather like cleaning a watch. For though the essay on "Style" gives little support for such a view, it is clear from the revision that for Pater the art of writing was synonymous with the composition of sentences. . . . The reader of Pater's prose soon becomes aware that a definite pause is essential after each sentence in order to adjust oneself to the rhythm of the next. Each sentence carries a complete impact and impression of its own, so that complementary sentences rarely occur. Such a manner is unusual, and we are so much more used to authors who think in terms of paragraphs and their total impression that Pater's method comes as somewhat of a shock.[28]

Interestingly, Pater was in the habit of composing sentences on small squares of paper which he would then rearrange into paragraphs.

The structure of Pater's style duplicates his *Weltanschauung*. It is a style which breaks up the flux of phenomena into isolated moments, for it is in these intervals only that reality is to be found,

[27] Frye, *Anatomy of Criticism*, p. 267.
[28] Edmund Chandler, *Pater on Style* (Copenhagen, 1958), p. 82.

Pater believed. It is a style which reflects those moments in which the stream has been arrested and the spirit incarnated in a form that lasts but briefly, but undeniably is achieved for an instant. Pater's style obviously differs from that of the later stream-of-consciousness writers, who present thought as a process: their style reflects the stream itself, and its structure gives the reader, as Frye puts it, "the process or movement of thought instead of the logical word-order of achieved thought."[29]

This tendency to atomize both paragraph and sentence is also reflected in the over-all structure of Pater's fiction. The portraits likewise are crystallizations of a precarious balance. On the one hand, there is the finite classic quality which provides the "general character"(R, 215) of the work, or what Pater in the essay "Style" calls "mind." On the other hand, there is the infinite romantic quality which gives to the work its "special situation" (R, 215), or what in the same essay is called "soul." The meaning of any portrait, however, lies not in its classic design or romantic atmosphere, but in a combination of the two. Just as the disparate elements of Pater's sentences call for simultaneous comprehension, so the portrait demands a total view. We see in this demand a reflection of Pater's contention that mind and soul, outer and inner, must be united in art: the theories expressed in the essay "Style" are no different from those basic to his concept of the Renaissance itself.

The tone of Pater's style is a second method by which he conveys meaning. In his cadences there is a gentle sadness akin to the wistfulness in the faces of Botticelli's exiles or to the longing in Florian's enjoyment. It is the prose of quiet suffering, and its tones reach one as in a dream, as from across a distance. The nostalgia seems to testify to those shadowy memories of ideal patterns echoing in the soul here on earth[30] and arises from the sense that the Golden Age which those patterns had inspired in youth, or in the youth of the human race, are now gone. Only by death will those pure forms again be seen. The poignancy and sentiment with which Pater invests the past come, however, not from the feeling that one's own past or the historical past is outwardly more perfect than the present. Childhood may be a high point, as was the age of ancient Greece, but there is no literal Golden Age for Pater. In *Marius* Pater referred to belief in such an age as "the

[29] Frye, *Anatomy of Criticism*, p. 266.
[30] Pater's influence on his most famous student, G. M. Hopkins, is evident here, for Hopkins, in his journals and other writings, also speaks of philosophical ideas which recur, of universal principles, and of an inner energy which gives pattern to all the diverse objects within the evanescent flux.

enchanted-distance fallacy" (*ME*, I, 101). For Pater there are moments, "golden" moments of ecstasy, periods of renaissance in nations and in individual lives, which shed light on that "whole long chaplet of sorrowful mysteries" (*ME*, II, 175) which constitutes the major part of existence for most men. Childhood or youth is, certainly, the most perfect of such periods, but it passes, as do all future moments. Pater's deep awareness of this sorrow of the world, of the suffering of grown people and children and animals, and of the shortness of such "golden" moments, sets for each portrait its tone of nostalgia, its mist of sentiment. In Pater's writings, as in the poetry of Tennyson, for example, the moment of ecstasy always lies in the past. It is ineffable when it is present, and it is gone when it is understood. There are left for the present only the suffering caused by its loss and the patient hope that soon again the self-divided world will be harmonized anew.

Undeniably, then, Pater's own writing fulfills those principles of good style which he first set forth in "An English Poet," and the structure and tone of his own works are in perfect accord with his critical theories. But the ultimate goal toward which Pater and his young English poet both strive is not merely that of a successful fusion of form and matter. Art should have a moral end as well. Pater was to write some years after his second portrait, in his essay "Style," that, given a successful fusion of mind and soul in a work,

then, if it be devoted further to the increase of men's happiness, to the redemption of the oppressed, or the enlargement of our sympathies with each other, or to such presentment of new or old truth about ourselves and our relation to the world as may ennoble and fortify us in our sojourn here, or immediately, as with Dante, to the glory of God, it will be also great art. (*Ap*, 38)

Pater was at pains in his portrait of the English poet to point to this quality of moral elevation in the boy's art. There could be seen in the character of the young poet, says Pater, a certain mood "which with the desire of literary form, the ideal of literary life—became a motive high enough to purge out of an ambitious youth all that was common or unclean, and prompted an ideal so high that once to have conceived it, '*il suffit que la pensée vous en soit venue pour que ma vie en demeure consolée et charmée*'" (*IPB*, 43).[31]

---

[31] This passage recalls what George Moore had to say about Pater: "He made me understand that the object of art is to aid us in forgetting all that is violent and cruel, and to orient us toward certain normal aspects of life." Quoted in d'Hangest, *Walter Pater*, II, 35. See also *Ap*, pp. 62–63.

This is the true outcome of Pater's "aestheticism," and "An English Poet" could well serve as the imaginative embodiment of his own artistic creed which, at about this time, was being so grossly misinterpreted. Art, Pater here seems to say, purifies the soul. It was pointed out in the discussion of the idea of portraiture that the sublimity of Greek sculpture lay in its power to purge the mind of the melancholy, impure, and gloomy shadows of the winter Dionysus. The noble figure of Demeter, says Pater, was impressed "with all the purity and proportion, the purged and dainty intelligence of the human countenance" (GS, 138). Certainly Pater's conception of the ideality of art is hardly surprising when one considers that he shared with Hegel the belief that art is the expression of Truth, that it is the particular embodiment of the Absolute Idea. But Pater's emphasis differs from Hegel's. The moments of ultimate truth are moments of hard-core experience, true and valid in themselves, of which the woof is sense and the warp is reason. Indeed, just as Hegel stressed the universal as primary, so Pater stressed the particular; he exaggerated the importance of the subjective element in art to give this neglected side of the aesthetic object its proper due. Pater's enthusiastic disciples sadly forgot that their master's definition of true beauty included the classic as well as the romantic qualities. This unfortunate lapse in such followers as Wilde, Beardsley, Dowson, Johnson, and Moore produced a philosophy of art which displayed a narrow interest in artistic subjectivity. They slipped into a belief that the work of the artist, isolated from society, has no relation to morality, and they tended to rely upon personal emotion, demanding only novelty of sensation or a passion of the grossest kind of intensity as an artistic criterion. Pater naturally was horrified that such a construction should be put upon the philosophy of art advanced in *The Renaissance*. In opposition to the "decadents," he believed that Dionysian romanticism is only one ingredient in aesthetic beauty; he also insisted, as even George Moore tells us, that the function of art was to orient one toward the normal and natural rather than toward the artificial, rare, and abnormal. Certainly, when speaking of art for the sake of the full life, Pater did not mean art for the sake of sheer intensity.

The particular moment at which "The Child in the House" and "An English Poet" appeared in Pater's career is of crucial significance, for it seems that they were meant to be his *apologia* for the philosophy of art that he had expressed in the Conclusion to *The Renaissance*. The series of sequential portraits that Pater had originally planned may have been devised to serve the purpose that *Marius* eventually fulfilled. In them Pater originally had hoped to answer those who misunderstood what he meant to say in *The Renaissance*, and it is interesting to note how closely at first even *Marius* approximated a sequence of portraits, for Pater had originally intended to publish it serially and had actually submitted his first two chapters before changing his mind.[32]

Because of their unique position in the history of Pater's attempt to explain himself—why he was as he was and why he believed what he did—"The Child in the House" and "An English Poet" quite naturally differ from the portraits which follow in several very interesting ways. The most obvious difference between these and the later ones is their openly autobiographical, essay-like quality. One need not conclude, however, that the autobiographical quality of the portraits was unintentional, a mistake that embarrassed the author.[33] The portraits depend for their unity on the reader's perceiving that each reflects a particular period in the life of a single contemporary artistic mind, and the reader would have to be very obtuse indeed not to realize that it is the artistic mind of Pater himself which they express.[34] Secondly, the later portraits do not share the same contemporary setting, for it is no longer needed as a unifying device. Pater is free to choose whatever time setting he desires, from a century before his time in "Emerald" to the mythical past in "Hippolytus." Finally, in "The Child in the House," at least, a third differentiating quality is the absence of the physical death of the young hero. In all the other portraits there is one decisive moment of choice and action which leads the hero to an early, often violent, death. This lack of the Dionysian denouement is probably an indication, again, that the projected sequence of portraits was originally meant to trace successive stages of development and not whole lives, though there is a symbolic, if not a physical, death in "The Child in the House."

"An English Poet," on the other hand, ends in the middle of a sentence, and we can only guess about its probable conclusion. Pater does, however, supply us with a few clues. The young poet, steadily weakening from tuberculosis, returns in the end, as do so many of Pater's heroes, to the area of his birth: "the coming even *so* far southwards from the narrow Cumberland valley he felt like a removal in the abstract from North to South" (*IPB*, 47). It appears that he, like most of Pater's heroes, is destined for an

---

[32] Evans, *Letters of Pater*, No. 61 (MS: Macmillan & Co., Ltd.), to Alexander Macmillan, September 9, 1884.

[33] D'Hangest, *Walter Pater*, I, 366, n. 5.

[34] Arthur Symons, *A Study of Walter Pater* (London, 1932), pp. 105-6.

early end. Like DuBellay, writing of his northern home while in the south at Rome, this young poet, too, lived long enough to mingle north in south:

And a time came when the sense of certain gracious things not exotic, neglected in that early mountain abode . . . came to him freshly as if then first seen, and with great reaching out of appetite towards them out of a feverish southern land, all the softer elements of that life at the lake side detached themselves from his memory and hung like a mirage over an imagined place he would fain have been in. (*IPB*, 40)

One might almost regard this death an anticipation of Flavian's death in *Marius the Epicurean* except that the delirious sensuousness of Flavian's poetry remains tortured to the end. Here the poet turns from the "exotic" aspects of the "feverish" land toward the simple, primary experiences of his childhood home itself, discovering the classic even in the very stronghold of the romantic. He is himself that summer Dionysus which his mother loved and for whom she gave her life; he is the life springing from death, and though he must himself die, his death will give birth to a new world. There is a curious resemblance between the young poet and Rousseau of the Conclusion. Like the English poet, "an undefinable taint of death had clung always about him," says Pater, "and now in early manhood he believed himself smitten by mortal disease." Rousseau's decision to dedicate himself to art was, according to Pater, "the awakening in him of the literary sense" (*R*, 238). So, too, with the young poet: the discovery of the centripetal world, his dedication to Apollo, and his creation of poetry represent an "awakening" not only in himself, but ultimately in the whole sphere of human affairs. Certainly the idea of a Dionysian death as the climax of the portrait must have been contemplated by Pater; but perhaps, as he told Sharp concerning "The Child in the House," it would have required too much reworking to fit it into the usual pattern of the imaginary portrait.[35]

In *Marius*, Pater returns to a more historical subject matter which resembles, in a sense, the material he had dealt with in *The Renaissance*. But between Pater's handling of Marius and, for example, his handling of Pico della Mirandola, there is a difference. The advance in understanding achieved in these two early imaginary portraits is carried over into the novel. The historical life of Pico had rough edges and did not fit easily into a precon-

[35] Evans, *Letters of Pater*, No. 72 (MS: Warden of All Souls College, Oxford), to John Sharp, May 23, 1887.

ceived fictional pattern of denouement. Few historical lives do. (It was only an accident, for example, that Winckelmann should have been so dramatically strangled.) Pater needed more freedom, both with respect to external events and also inner motives. In *Marius*, when speaking of the old masters of the Cyrenaic philosophy, Pater says that some among them realized "a vision, almost 'beatific,' of ideal personalities in life and art" (*ME*, II, 22). In the fiction which follows, Pater attempts to portray such "ideal personalities," who unite within themselves antithetical elements. And because he is free to create as he wills, he achieves a portrayal of this ideal state of synthesis more fully in his imaginary portraits than he does in his strictly critical or semi-autobiographical writings.

III

⚘ MARIUS THE EPICUREAN (1885)

It has been suggested that the need to excise the offending Conclusion from the second edition of *The Renaissance* (1877) may have prompted Pater to compose "A Child in the House" and "An English Poet." Since *Marius the Epicurean* takes over from the early portraits their original function as a defense, we can date the inception of *Marius* at about the time when Pater abandoned work on "An English Poet"—in the fall of 1878—and we can assume that from this time on Pater devoted most of his energies to the creation of his novel.[1] Perhaps as he sat down to write his "apology," Pater felt himself a little like Socrates of old, who was caught between the radical Sophists and "the good old men of Athens" (*PP*, 89), for Pater also was accused by the conservative forces of undermining with a new morality those old values which he in fact respected. His words in the footnote to the restored Conclusion, those about not wishing to "mislead" the young men, seem a conscious echo of the charge brought against Socrates. Perhaps this is why in *Plato* he was so drawn to Socrates' attempt to steer a middle course between the pursuit of "experience" and the observance of traditional morality. At any rate, Pater structures his novel in terms of this dialectic and dramatizes it with archetypal myth.

Only among recent writers—Osbourn, Hafley, Sudrann,

---

[1] For a résumé of possible sources for *Marius*, see Louise M. Rosenblatt's "The Genesis of *Marius the Epicurean*," *Comparative Literature*, XIV (Summer, 1962), 242–60. Rosenblatt should perhaps have also noted that *Marius* seems to belong to a sort of sub-genre of the nineteenth century not unrelated to the Oxford Movement and "tractarianism": the novel of the primitive church written by an ecclesiastically minded author—among them, Kingsley's *Hypatia* (1853), Wiseman's *Fabiola* (1854), and Newman's *Callista* (1856). Of course, *Marius* came some thirty years later, but there can be no doubt that, for example, Newman's rather public religious struggle was an important intellectual stimulus for the novel. Verbal echoes from the writings of Newman are easily found; phrases such as "undeniable possibilities," "sense of economy," "gain and loss," and many others create a Newmanesque atmosphere.

Inman—has *Marius* found critics willing to champion its structural coherence.[2] Henry James, for example, grumbled to a friend that the novel fell apart in the middle—"that the first volume of *Marius* was given over to paganism, and a large part of the second to an equal admiration of Christianity, and that it was not possible to admire opposites equally."[3] And, of course, T. S. Eliot's famous critique is the most brutal of all. Having cast doubts on Pater's mental ability, Eliot then proceeds to call *Marius* "incoherent; its method is a number of fresh starts; its contents is a hodge-podge of the learning of the classical don, the impressions of the sensitive holiday visitor to Italy, and a prolonged flirtation with the liturgy."[4] Surely objections such as those of James and Eliot can be met simply by pointing to the autobiographical element in the novel; that is, its unity of mental development and its reflection of the nineteenth-century *Zeitgeist*. Yet the ultimate unity of the novel does not lie in any such ideological structure—in its religious autobiography (Osbourn) or in the process of "learning to hope" (Hafley) or in the interaction of the metaphors of the rose, the heavenly city, and the face of death (Sudrann) or in "the consistency of Marius's fundamental character" (Inman). All such unities tend more to reflect a static and theoretical structure than a dramatic one. The drama, the real action of the novel, is a duplication of the allegorical and mythical pattern of the quest of Psyche for Cupid, a pattern reflected in Marius' quest for the God of Love. Just as Cupid and Psyche are ultimately united on Olympus, so the Christian community as a reflection of the Celestial City foreshadows the eventual unification of the soul with Christ. If Lubbock is right in saying that in *Marius* Pater dispensed with drama as thoroughly as it ever occurred to any novelist to dispense with it, we shall have to qualify his statement by noting that Marius' quest for Love and his discovery of the Christian community carries with it all the drama of a mythic re-enactment.

BOOK I

The young Marius, like Pater's English poet, is a dreamer. his mind nesting upon the still waters of the soul, creating a world

---

[2] R. V. Osbourn, *"Marius the Epicurean," Essays in Criticism*, I (October, 1951), 387–403; James Hafley, "Walter Pater's 'Marius' and the Technique of Modern Fiction," *Modern Fiction Studies*, III (Summer, 1957), 99–109; Jean Sudrann, "Victorian Compromise and Modern Revolution," *ELH*, XXVI (September, 1959), 425–44; Billie Inman, "The Organic Structure of *Marius the Epicurean*," *Philological Quarterly*, XLI, II (April, 1962), 475–91.

[3] Osbourn, *Essays in Criticism*, pp. 398–99.

[4] *Selected Essays*, p. 391.

in which everything is pervaded by a ubiquitous spirituality. "A dream in winter time, when the nights are longest"—this is the motto for *Marius,* taken from the seventeenth paragraph of Lucian's *Dream.* The first book of the novel, then, begins with the dreams of the winter Dionysus at Marius' childhood home of White-nights, a home which recalls in some of its aspects the world of the English poet who, like Marius, was burdened with a weary weight of visions. Marius' removal from White-nights to the ancient city of Pisa at the death of his mother corresponds roughly to the English poet's trip southward. Pisa is the world of the summer Dionysus, and this section of the first book stands in sharp contrast to the opening pages devoted to White-nights. In each of these two contrasting sections in Book I, Pater has carefully placed a vision of the ideal Apollonian world in the form of the Temple of Aesculapius and the story of Cupid and Psyche. However, this Apollonian ideal which harmonizes the winter and summer, the spiritual and the material, has as yet no actual embodiment, no tangible incarnation. The purpose of the succeeding books is to portray the progress of Marius' search for the concrete representation of the Apollonian ideal. One may say that Book I provides Marius with the two basic alternatives of matter and spirit. These alternatives will be explored in the following books in terms of the philosophies of Epicureanism and Stoicism, neither of which Marius will find satisfactory because neither transcends the narrow confines of Dionysus' solipsism.

Until the death of Marius' close friend Flavian, an event which ends the first book and the period of Marius' youth, the two worlds of White-nights and Pisa, of winter and summer, existed side by side in Marius' life in a kind of uneasy Roman equivalent to Florian Deleal's early environment. Certainly the heritage of White-nights remained a pervasive influence throughout Marius' life, even when he most eagerly plunged himself into the material world. The name White-nights itself should mean, says Pater, "nights not of quite blank forgetfulness, but passed in continuous dreaming, only half veiled by sleep" (*ME,* I, 14). In *Appreciations,* Pater had written of Rossetti that the "dream-land . . . is to him, in no mere fancy or figure of speech, a real country, a veritable expansion of, or addition to, our waking life" (*Ap,* 214). Though actual enough, the world of reverie is a sort of unreal world as well, for dreams, so Pater says in *Marius* as he quotes "a quaint German mystic," are like things which are white—" 'the doubles, or seconds, of real things, and themselves but half-real, half-material' " (*ME,* I, 13). This unreality of sleep and dreams is, for

Pater, a symbol for our veil of mortality. In this life we are asleep, and only when we awaken from sleep do we break through the immediate experience of the senses to God. Our dreams are, so to speak, those memories of that earlier state of existence celebrated by Wordsworth and Vaughan. This white unreality of our mortal dreams is a characteristic of Dionysus himself, whose "dazzling whiteness" (GS, 40) in winter contrasts with his summer tan. The white Dionysus, "son or brother" (GS, 45) of Persephone, has much in common with the goddess of death, whose domain is like that of the dreaming world of White-nights: she holds in her hand "the poppy, emblem of sleep and death by its narcotic juices, of life and resurrection by its innumerable seeds, of the dreams, therefore, that may intervene between falling asleep and waking" (GS, 148–49).

In this twilight world of mortality, Marius, the boy-priest, early endowed with "a spontaneous force of religious veneration" (ME, I, 5), acts out the rituals of the religion of his heritage, taking a leading role in the festival of the private *Ambarvalia*, with its processional of the images of Demeter, Dionysus, and the mysterious Dea Dia. But, of course, the gloomy shadows of the violent Dionysian death lie at the center of the festival. Marius had "a certain pity at the bottom of his heart, and almost on his lips, for the sacrificial victims and their looks of terror, rising almost to disgust at the central act of the sacrifice itself, a piece of everyday butcher's work" (ME, I, 9). The slaughter of the animals raises the specter of death generally. Is death in this supposedly religious context a breaking through the veil of mortality into the light of immortality? Will those dreams or half-recollections of the world beyond be proved real? The assurance of that reality is what Marius senses his religion lacks, and the real significance of his trip to the Aesculapian shrine lies in the fact that there he discovers that the visible counterpart, the proof, of the reality of his dreams can be found in this life.

The terror of the winter Dionysus is far removed from the shrine of Aesculapius, "that mild and philanthropic son of Apollo" (ME, I, 28). In the crystal sunlight and clarity of its air, a kind of immortal youthfulness seems to pervade everything, and the doctrine of the Apollonian mean, here taught, creates that pure and transparent nature of which Pater had written in his essay "Diaphaneitè"—the soul " 'made perfect by the love of visible beauty' " (ME, I, 32). During a nighttime talk with one of the priests, Marius notes that the priest's expression of "perfect temperance had in it a fascinating power—the merely negative element of purity, the mere freedom from taint or flaw, in exercise as a positive influence" (*ME*, I, 33–34). Here also at the Temple of Aesculapius Marius' original "ideal of home" (*ME*, I, 22), of the close-knit religious community experienced in the family worship of Numa, becomes expanded to something very like the New Jerusalem revealed to John on Patmos. Marius is told by the young priest in the night talk that "a diligent promotion of the capacity of the eye" (*ME*, I, 32) may issue in "the possibility of some vision, as of a new city coming down 'like a bride out of heaven,' a vision still indeed, it might seem, a long way off, but to be granted perhaps one day to the eyes thus trained" (*ME*, I, 32). It is an ideal, typically centripetal, of the unity of all men in an eternal order which transcends the narrow world of the single soul. Already at the temple there is an attempt to anticipate that vision when, on his last morning there, Marius looks through a hidden opening:

What he saw was like the vision of a new world, by the opening of some unsuspected window in a familiar dwelling-place. . . . It might have seemed the very presentment of a land of hope, its hollows brimful of a shadow of blue flowers; and lo! on the one level space of the horizon, in a long dark line, were towers and a dome: and that was Pisa.—Or Rome, was it? (*ME*, I, 40)

Marius discovers that the dwelling place of this world, so familiar and seemingly unenchanted, may afford a vision to the questing soul, but its indeterminacy—Pisa or Rome?—is indicative of the distance he must still cover before that vision is clearly perceived. Marius goes to Pisa, but it is not the new city. Afterwards, he goes to Rome; that, too, is not it. As yet, the young lad does not suspect how far he must go, but the beginning of his journey is already at hand.

The death of Marius' mother closes the first part of Book I and coincides with his removal as a "tall schoolboy" (*ME*, I, 44) to the old town of Pisa, where he seems to find "unlimited self-expansion in a world of various sunshine" (*ME*, I, 44), the sunshine of the summer Dionysus. Pater, in his Conclusion to *The Renaissance*, offers advice which can be considered applicable to young men in Pisa, and Marius, in effect, accepts this advice as he attempts to delve into the reality at the heart of the instant: "As in that gray monastic tranquility of the villa, inward voices from the reality of unseen things had come to him abundantly; so here . . . it was the reality, the tyrannous reality, of things visible that was borne in upon him" (*ME*, I, 47). Unlike his childhood world, this life was not oriented to the past, but to the present, and its ideal of modernity perhaps clashed a little with the heritage of White-nights:

> While the pursuit of an ideal like this demanded entire liberty of
> heart and brain, that old, staid, conservative religion of his childhood
> certainly had its being in a world of somewhat narrow restrictions.
> But then, the one was absolutely real, with nothing less than the
> reality of seeing and hearing—the other, how vague, shadowy, prob-
> lematical! Could its so limited probabilities be worth taking into ac-
> count in any practical question as to the rejecting or receiving of
> what was indeed so real, and, on the face of it, so desirable?
> (*ME*, I, 48–49)

Just as Pisa is the autobiographical equivalent of Canterbury, so young Pater's goal in life resembled that of Marius, for "the fame he conceived for himself at this time was . . . that of a poet" (*ME*, I, 47).

As a schoolboy, Marius looked for the incarnation of his dreams in the form of his friend Flavian. To Marius, Flavian—older, wiser, handsomer—was a kind of Apollo. Almost literally, Flavian, whose name probably derives from *flavus*, "golden-yel-low," seems the golden god: "He was like a carved figure in motion, thought Marius, but with that indescribable gleam upon it which the words of Homer actually suggested, as perceptible on the visible forms of the gods" (*ME*, I, 50). But Flavian, for all his attractive-ness, is not Apollo; he is only the summer Dionysus, who soon displays his sinister, wintry side. Marius' hero, together with his *magnum opus*, the *Pervigilium Veneris*, are in some undefined and obscure way involved in an excess of love quite the opposite of the Apollonian mean:

> How often, afterwards, did evil things present themselves in malign
> association with the memory of that beautiful head, and with a kind
> of borrowed sanction and charm in its natural grace! To Marius, at
> a later time, he counted for as it were an epitome of the whole pagan
> world, the depth of its corruption, and its perfection of form.
> (*ME*, I, 53)

Flavian seems almost a kind of precursor of the characters in Wilde's *Dorian Grey*, and Pater seems to be implying that the moral problem at the heart of the aestheticism of the *fin-de-siècle* rebels was also to be found in the rather sinister Epicureanism of Flavian. One could say of Flavian, as Pater so characteristically remarked apropos of Lord Henry Wotton, that "he has too much of a not very really refined world in and about him" (*UE*, 128). Flavian, like Wilde's characters, has a "doppelgänger" (*UE*, 131):

his two sides remain forever unreconciled, beautiful, yet sinister. Because of his experience at the Temple of Aesculapius, Marius' ideal of beauty, rooted in the golden mean, "made him revolt with unfaltering instinct from the bare thought of an excess in sleep, or diet, or even in matters of taste, still more from any excess of a coarser kind" (*ME*, I, 34) and came to be an important factor in counteracting "the less desirable or hazardous tendencies of some phases of thought, through which he was to pass" (*ME*, I, 41).

Marius' discovery of the tale of Cupid and Psyche in Apuleius' *Metamorphoses* strongly influenced his desire for an Apollonian beauty without taint or flaw. Pater makes it perfectly clear that this story from the Golden Book of Apuleius is closely interwoven with the history of Marius' mental development, and its appearance in the novel forms no mere digression, as Benson maintained.[5] Undoubtedly, the translation has a certain amount of independent interest—to teachers of Latin, at any rate—but its real value lies in its relation to the main theme of the novel. Although two recent articles by Brzenk and Turner[6] have discussed Pater's translation of this story, the most helpful consideration of the legend is that of James Hafley, who writes:

That awful moment at which Cupid awakes as the oil from Psyche's lamp falls upon his shoulder, at which her comforting sense of a shadowy ideal is transformed by her own curiosity to that of an invaluable but vanished reality, is in Marius's life the moment at which his apparently secure idealism becomes vanquished by experience and leaves him with only a longing for the "real ideal" he has glimpsed before its flight.[7]

Hafley then states that Marius' eventual "discovery of Cornelius and his meaning is Cupid's triumphant return." This is perhaps too simple, as we shall see, but Hafley's realization that the plight of Psyche parallels Marius' quest to harmonize subject and object in the ideal world of the concrete universal is of considerable importance.

Perhaps the best clue to the correct interpretation of the story of Cupid and Psyche is furnished by Pater when he tells us that "you might take it, if you chose, for an allegory" (*ME*, I, 61). As an allegory, the tale of Cupid and Psyche supplies the key to the novel, for it pinpoints the quest of Marius for the God of

---

[5] Benson, *Pater*, p. 92.

[6] Eugene Brzenk, "Pater and Apuleius," *Comparative Literature*, X (Winter, 1958), 55–60; Paul Turner, "Pater and Apuleius," *Victorian Studies*, III (March, 1960), 290–96.

[7] Hafley, *Modern Fiction Studies*, pp. 105–6.

Love. Pater knew that the story was, like the legend of the Phoenix, one of the few myths accepted by the early Christians. During his trip to Rome in 1882, he could hardly escape noting the allegorical use to which the early Christians put this legend.[8] But he probably was acquainted with the Christian allegorizing of Cupid and Psyche long before he saw it depicted on the sarcophagi and catacomb frescoes of Rome. From Martianus Capella in the fifth century to Boccaccio in the fifteenth, the allegorical interpretations grew increasingly more explicit, more familiar.[9] The story of Cupid and Psyche is the allegory of the mortal soul freed from the grip of death through the power of its "love of Love" (ME, I, 75). Christ became Cupid, and the marriage of Psyche to Cupid brings to mind the well-known image of Christ as the bridegroom of "the living soul" (ME, I, 65) or of the community of Christian souls, the Church (ME, II, 97, 111).[10] Pater is at pains to strengthen this allegorical quality of the old legend by the elimination of numerous extraneous personifications and the suppression of all the coarse and earthy humor of the original version. The focus is further sharpened by an elevation of the syntax and diction so that the language of the translation seems more appropriate to the King James Version of the Bible than to the *Metamorphoses* of Apuleius.

Not only does the Cupid-Psyche legend describe allegorically Marius' movement toward Christianity, but also the legend has its mythical Dionysian overtones, which support and amplify its Christian meaning. In the *Greek Studies*, Pater writes:

Semele, an old Greek word, as it seems, for the surface of the earth, the daughter of Cadmus, beloved by Zeus, desires to see her lover

[8] Elizabeth Haight, in *Apuleius and his Influence* (New York, 1927), pp. 169–70, tells of the sarcophagi in Christian cemeteries and decorative paintings and mosaics in churches and catacombs in which the legend of Cupid and Psyche appears.

[9] While Boccaccio's interpretation of the myth is its full-blown Renaissance form, it could, if simplified, have supplied Pater with something like the meaning which the legend must have had for the early Christians. The interested reader can find the Cupid-Psyche legend in the *Genealogia Deorum*, pp. 255–61 of Vol. CC of the *Scrittori D'Italia* series edited by V. Romano (Bari, 1951). A convenient English summary of the allegorical "kernal" can be found in D. C. Allen's *Image and Meaning* (Baltimore, 1960), pp. 28–29.

[10] E. O. James in *The Cult of the Mother Goddess* (London, 1959), pp. 192ff and p. 281, nn. 6, 7, has collected a number of traditional references to Christ as the bridegroom of the Church Universal and of the individual soul within the church. One feels that perhaps the influence of the syncretic mythographers upon Pater can here be seen. "The gods of Greek mythology," he says—and he might also have added the figures of Christian religion to this—"overlap each other; they are confused or connected with each other, lightly or deeply, as the case may be, and sometimes have their doubles" (*GS*, p. 100).

in the glory with which he is seen by the immortal Hera. He appears
to her in lightning. But the mortal may not behold him and live.
Semele gives premature birth to the child Dionysus; whom to preserve
it from the jealousy of Hera, Zeus hides in a part of his thigh, the
child returning into the loins of its father, whence in due time it
is born again. (*GS*, 24)

Semele's story, then, is a kind of allegory, says Pater; it turns
on the idea of

the love of the immortal for the mortal, the presumption of the
daughter of man who desires to see the divine form as it is; on the
fact that not without loss of sight, or life itself, can man look upon
it. The travail of nature has been transformed into the pangs of the
human mother; and the poet dwells much on the pathetic incident
of death in childbirth, making Dionysus, as Callimachus calls him,
a seven months' child, cast out among its enemies, motherless.
(*GS*, 24–25)

Semele incarnates "the mystical body of the earth" (*GS*, 25), and,
united with Zeus, she represents Demeter as the goddess of fertility
and life. But at the withdrawal of the immortal Zeus, part of her,
like Persephone, dies; and part of her, in the form of her son
Dionysus, remains alive and questing like the sterile and sorrowing
Demeter, whose face is veiled, whose godhead is in eclipse, as she
wanders over the earth in search of Persephone. The questing
Demeter and the dead Persephone—these two aspects of Semele
are the embodiment of her mortality; they constitute that state
which is best described as life-in-death—the condition of the soul
which has lost the light of the divine form, which is cast out into
the world of sense, homeless and a wanderer in a cold and hostile
environment.

Semele's state of life-in-death corresponds precisely to that
of Psyche and Marius, both of whom are searching for the fulfillment of those vague recollections of an immortal world beyond.
The guarantee of the reality of that world is to be found in the
sensuous realm, for the discovery of the visible counterpart of God
is an anticipation of that final awakening. Often in Pater's fiction
the sensuous vestment of the Absolute is represented in art. Here
in the novel it is that "city" beyond Pisa, beyond Rome, already
anticipated by the vision in the Aesculapian shrine. The relationship between the individual and this visible expression of the Logos
is a very close one, for the soul, in its discovery of the divine form,
is the representative of the larger community, even as the community is visible proof to the souls outside of the victory which

the souls inside have won. Pater often presents the role of the soul as that of priest-attendant and masculine counterpart to this larger society. Because his novel is explicitly a Christian allegory, it is possible to see Marius' name as the masculine form of *Mary*, the sorrowing and questing Demeter of the Middle Ages. Mary as the virgin Church, Marius as the virgin soul—both alike are searching for the supreme Lover.

For Marius, then, the legend of Cupid and Psyche becomes a parable of his own human situation, of his incarceration in the narrow prison of mortality, of his need to find some larger world which would answer to those dreams of a city of immortal Love. Psyche's story, as it formed itself in his memory, "with an expression changed in some ways from the original," served, says Pater, "to combine many lines of meditation, already familiar to Marius, into the ideal of a perfect imaginative love, centered upon a type of beauty entirely flawless and clean—an ideal which never wholly faded from his thoughts" (*ME*, I, 92). It is quite appropriate that Flavian should be Marius' companion in the "truant reading" (*ME*, I, 54) of Apuleius, for Flavian served as the foil for the kind of love which Marius saw in the Cupid-Psyche legend. Because Flavian's was a love not oriented toward the immortal world of Cupid or Zeus, but was a purely sensuous love turned wintry, he dies struck down by the plague, as Lucius Verus later will die, perhaps also as the penalty of some "amorous appointment" (*ME*, II, 31). The delirium of Flavian's plague-fever is the perfect issue of his Dionysian love, for, having no external or spiritual order as his goal, he suffers the fate of a mind imprisoned in its own subjectivity (his egotism and self-sufficiency are significant), making the fatal descent from dream to illusion to delirium and death. Unlike the eventual death of Marius, which is the climax of a steady ascent toward light and life, Flavian's life ends in the horror of the soul's extinction—"A Pagan End" (Chap. VII), both physical and spiritual.

Flavian's pagan end, however, is only symptomatic of the universal delirium sweeping through the ancient world of the second century. Pater turns the plague in *Marius* into an almost medieval personification of the subjective spirit: "It was by dishonour done to Apollo himself, said popular rumour—to Apollo, the old titular divinity of pestilence, that the poisonous thing had come abroad" (*ME*, I, 111). Indeed, "the unsuspected foe" (*ME*, I, 111), "the enemy" (*ME*, I, 116), "the destroyer" (*ME*, I, 116) seems very much like the well-known dragon or snake which has vexed so many allegorical kingdoms—a sort of Chthonian image of human mortality, with its grotesque and macabre romanticism. This snake of evil quite predictably haunts even the paradisaical garden of Marius' childhood. There was, says Pater, "a certain vague fear of evil, constitutional in him. . . . His religion, that old Italian religion, in contrast with the really light-hearted religion of Greece, had its deep undercurrent of gloom, its sad, haunting imageries, not exclusively confined to the walls of Etruscan tombs" (*ME*, I, 22–23). Indeed, the snake becomes even physically present as the image "of some unexplored evil, ever dogging his footsteps" when one day, as he walked along a "narrow road"—the narrowness suggesting the prison-like restriction of subjectivity—Marius had

> seen the snakes breeding, and ever afterwards avoided that place and its ugly associations, for there was something in the incident which made food distasteful and his sleep uneasy for many days afterwards. . . . There was humanity, dusty and sordid and as if far gone in corruption, in the sluggish coil, as it awoke suddenly into one metallic spring of pure enmity against him. (*ME*, I, 23–24)

After the death of Flavian, Marius begins his agonizing pilgrimage toward new light. He resembles the young Florian Deleal, whose soul finds itself caught like the bird, setting out on his journey in an agony of homesickness. The real seems on every hand tainted with corruption; the ideal seems unreal. With Flavian at Pisa, Marius has eaten of "The Tree of Knowledge," as the chapter heading expresses it. His eyes have been opened, and he has been cast out into the storm and stress of a hostile world. He has become, seemingly, "a materialist" (*ME*, I, 125). Like Psyche of the allegorical tradition, he has been plunged into sensuous nature, a fallen creature in a fallen creation. The world is out of joint, sick unto death, its plague-wracked frame evidence of its decay. And as Marius begins his quest and moves toward Rome, the heart of the empire, the evidences of the plague become increasingly prominent.

BOOK II

In the second book Marius explores the centrifugal world of Epicureanism and the centripetal world of its opposite, Stoicism. He also meets Cornelius, who heralds the higher Christian synthesis which Marius will eventually reach. Just as Flavian in the last book was the "spiritual form" of hedonism, so Cornelius in this book is the epitome of Christianity (*ME*, I, 233–34). The young Marius, setting out on the quest of life, has two paths open to him which correspond to these two figures: to awaken from sleep to

life or to slip back through sleep to death. Although the whole
of the novel is about his choice of the former, in his rejection
of Flavian, Marius refuses to abandon the material world. Somehow it must be reconciled with the spiritual. So here, at the beginning of Book II, Marius begins to build his philosophy by going
back beyond Epicurus and Lucretius to the master of both,
Heraclitus of Ionia, whose philosophy of the perpetual flux found
its practical application in the precepts of Aristippus of Cyrene.
In Pater's description of Marius' reaction to the thought of Heraclitus and Aristippus, we hear echoes of the Conclusion to
The Renaissance:

Conceded that what is secure in our existence is but the sharp apex
of the present moment between two hypothetical eternities, and all
that is real in our experience but a series of fleeting impressions:—so
Marius continued the sceptical argument he had condensed, as the
matter to hold by, from his various philosophical reading:—given,
that we are never to get beyond the walls of the closely shut cell
of one's own personality; that the ideas we are somehow impelled
to form of an outer world, and of other minds akin to our own, are,
it may be, but a day-dream, and the thought of any world beyond,
a day-dream perhaps idler still: then, he, at least, in whom those
fleeting impressions—faces, voices, material sunshine—were very real
and imperious, might well set himself to the consideration, how such
actual moments as they passed might be made to yield their utmost,
by the most dexterous training of capacity. (*ME*, I, 146)[11]

This beginning of Marius' journey through the philosophies
of the ancient world is paralleled by the beginning of his travels
to Rome, and the reader cannot help feeling that the latter bears
a certain metaphoric relation to the former: "The motion of the
journey was bringing his thoughts to systematic form. . . . His
philosophic scheme was but the reflection of the *data* of sense,
and chiefly of sight, a reduction to the abstract, of the brilliant
road he travelled on, through the sunshine" (*ME*, I, 164–65). In
Plato, Pater had used the metaphor of the journey to describe

[11] Elsewhere Pater calls the "sharp apex" the "little point of the present
moment . . . between a past which has just ceased to be and future which
may never come" (*ME*, I, 139). Pater is careful to show, however, that this
intense consciousness of the present moment does not issue in hedonism: "Not
pleasure, but fulness of life, and 'insight' as conducting to that fulness—energy,
variety, and choice experience, including noble pain and sorrow even, loves
such as those in the exquisite old story of Apuleius, sincere and strenuous
forms of the moral life, such as Seneca and Epictetus—whatever form of
human life, in short, might be heroic, impassioned, ideal: from these the 'new
Cyrenaicism' of Marius took its criterion of values" (*ME*, I, 151–52).

the dialectic method of Socrates, so like this dialectic between the One and the Many in Marius' thought:

It was like a journey . . . to a mountain's top. . . . From this or that point, some insignificant peak presented itself as the mountain's veritable crest: inexperience would have sworn to the truth of a wholly illusive perspective, as the next turn in the journey assured one. It is only upon the final step, with free view at last on every side, uniting together and justifying all those various, successive, partial apprehensions of the difficult way—only on the summit, comes the intuitive comprehension of what the true form of the mountain really is. (*PP*, 180)

So Marius, on the seventh day of his journey to Rome, is climbing a winding mountain road. Just when his thoughts have reached their most refined stage, suddenly a heavy mass of falling rock plunges down the steep slope so close behind him that, like Achilles, "he felt the touch upon his heel" (*ME*, I, 166). This startling revelation of the proximity of death quite shakes Marius' fragile little scheme of Epicureanism, which would scarcely have been able to explain the meaningfulness of being crushed to extinction under several tons of stone: "A sudden suspicion of hatred against him, of the nearness of 'enemies,' seemed all at once to alter the visible form of things. . . . His elaborate philosophy had not put beneath his feet the terror of mere bodily evil; much less of 'inexorable fate, and the noise of greedy Acheron'" (*ME*, I, 166).

Precisely when Marius comes to realize that the Epicurean system cannot accommodate the fact of pain and death, he meets Cornelius of the Twelfth Legion. There at an inn at the top of the mountain—Marius goes "down the steep street" (*ME*, I, 167) the next day—his spirits are partially restored by the Spartan purity of the surroundings and the "reviving edge or freshness" (*ME*, I, 166) of the wine, so like the "unsweetened" (*PP*, 222) wine of the Lacedaemonians. "It was just then," says Pater, "that he heard the voice of one, newly arrived at the inn, making his way to the upper floor—a youthful voice, with a reassuring clearness of note, which completed his cure" (*ME*, I, 167). Marius naturally does not understand at this time that it is Christianity which provides the answer to evil and death, but he nevertheless strikes up an acquaintance with Cornelius, puzzling over his irrepressible blitheness and noting that he seems to belong to a group even more exclusive than the imperial guard. The following day the two enter a goldsmith's shop, and Marius marvels at the way in which pure matter has been given so clever a form. It is another detail which, like the asceticism of the inn and the military bearing of Cornelius, attests to the Apollonian principle of order that informs all creation and is the goal toward which Marius' quest is bent.

On the way toward Rome, the pair stops at the home of Cornelius' friend, who is absent, and in a scene charged with symbolism, Cornelius' Christian character is defined:

The great room of the villa, to which they were admitted, had lain long untouched; and the dust rose, as they entered, into the slanting bars of sunlight, that fell through the half-closed shutters. It was here, to while away the time, that Cornelius bethought himself of displaying to his new friend the various articles and ornaments of his knightly array—the breastplate, the sandals and cuirass, lacing them on, one by one, with the assistance of Marius, and finally the great golden bracelet on the right arm, conferred on him by his general for an act of valour. And as he gleamed there, amid that odd interchange of light and shade, with the staff of a silken standard firm in his hand, Marius felt as if he were face to face, for the first time, with some new knighthood or chivalry, just then coming into the world. (*ME*, I, 170)

Cornelius standing there is, says Edward Thomas, "a study from a picture, not from life," and it reminds him of a passage in Pater's "Giorgione" essay in *The Renaissance*, "of Giorgione's 'warrior saint, Liberale,' and the study for it 'with the delicately gleaming silver-grey armour' in our National Gallery, which Pater admired."[12] We, however, are perhaps even more strongly reminded by the plague-emptied villa of Pater's favorite metaphor of the world as a house. The world, like the house, has grown dusty and is emptied by plague. But at its center stands Cornelius. As Marius eventually comes to realize, "new hope had sprung up in the world of which he, Cornelius, was a depositary, which he was to bear onward in it" (*ME*, II, 209).

As Cornelius dons his armor piece by piece, he becomes the living incarnation of Paul's warrior against "the wiles of the devil":

Put on the whole armour of God . . . that ye may be able to withstand in the evil day, and having done all, to stand. Stand therefore, having your loins girt about with truth, and having on the breastplate of

[12] *Walter Pater* (New York, 1913), p. 15. The scene reminds me of Nicholas Wiseman's portrayal of St. Sebastian, who was both soldier and Christian. Wiseman describes a room illuminated only "by an opening in the roof; and Sebastian, anxious to be seen by all, stood in the ray which now darted through it, strong and brilliant where it beat, but leaving the rest of the apartment almost dark. It broke against the gold and jewels of his rich tribune's armour, and, as he moved, scattered itself in sparks of brilliant hues into the darkest recesses of that gloom; while it beamed with serene steadiness upon his uncovered head." *Fabiola* (New York, n. d.), pp. 50–51.

righteousness; and your feet shod with the preparation of the gospel of peace; above all, taking the shield of faith, wherewith ye shall be able to quench all the fiery darts of the wicked. And take the helmet of salvation, and the sword of the Spirit, which is the word of God. (Eph. 6:11–17)

"Every object of his knightly array," Marius later reflected, "had seemed to be but sign or symbol of some other thing far beyond it" (*ME*, I, 233). Cornelius' name, of course, derives from another early Christian warrior—the centurion Cornelius who, we are told in Acts 10, was baptized with all his house by Peter. Cornelius stands there, then, before Marius as a representative of a "new knighthood" that battles, in Paul's words, "not against flesh and blood, but against principalities, against powers, against the rulers of the darkness of this world, against spiritual wickedness in high places" (Eph. 6:12). Cornelius is the answer to Marius' old, vague fear of some shadowy adversary in the dark. He will restore light to the darkened heart of the Roman Empire. Significantly, as Marius approached Rome, "the highest light upon the mausoleum of Hadrian was quite gone out, and it was dark, before they reached the *Flaminian* Gate" (*ME*, I, 170).

Marius arrives in Rome, " 'The Most Religious City in the World,' " only to find that its welter of competing religions is mere gross superstition and that Aurelius patronized them all like a shrewd politician. Aurelius, however, has his own "religion," too, and it is to Stoicism that Marius is now exposed. Shortly after his arrival, Marius listens to a discourse by Aurelius, the ideas and images of which Pater derived directly from the *Meditations* themselves, but selected to drive home Aurelius' awareness of the shortness of life, the closeness of death, and the vanity of existence. Despair and renunciation are, seemingly, more evident in Aurelius' discourse as presented here than they actually are in the *Meditations,* for Pater has not included the more positive passages concerned with moral conduct. But Stoicism, despite all the extra awareness with which Pater endows it, fails as completely as did Epicureanism in finding significance in suffering and death. The Emperor's lecture offers only the cold mortality of the winter god: "the discourse ended almost in darkness, the evening having set in somewhat suddenly, with a heavy fall of snow" (*ME*, I, 211). And later, after the events in the amphitheater, Marius concludes that the bare fact that the wise Emperor could complacently sit through the "Manly Amusement" of the public spectale of suffering animals certainly seemed "to mark Aurelius as his inferior now and for ever on the question of righteousness. . . .

Surely evil was a real thing, and the wise man wanting in the sense of it, where, not to have been, by instinctive election, on the right side, was to have failed in life" (*ME*, I, 241–43). Even Aurelius' citadel of indifference does not offer him true protection, for when his child becomes sick and dies, his "pretence breaks down, and he is broken-hearted" (*ME*, I, 221; II, 56).[13]

On the note of an Epicureanism and a Stoicism that have failed to meet the test of pain and death, Book II ends. Neither the pure sensuousness of the summer Dionysus nor the pure spirituality of the winter god have offered Marius an escape from the subjective trap of his own narrow life. Pater, however, by the introduction of Cornelius, who stands both structurally and figuratively between the worlds of sense and spirit, vaguely sketches the ultimate Apollonian synthesis. But before Marius can recognize the success of Christianity, his mind must be broadened so that he is willing to concede the possibility of a reality which does not lie wholly in the present moment. For the time being, he is "Marius the Epicurean" of the here-and-now, the single concrete moment beyond which nothing exists.

BOOK III

The third book, shortest of the four, has a relatively simple function: to fashion for Marius the object of his quest, the Celestial City, and to provide him a more receptive frame of mind in which to apprehend it. To that end, the first chapter, "Stoicism at Court," introduces us to Cornelius Fronto, Aurelius' old teacher of rhetoric, who presents to Marius and others the idea that "the world is as it were a commonwealth, a city" (*ME*, II, 10). This idea of the community of all men gives rise to the idea "of that new, unseen, Rome on high" (*ME*, II, 11). " 'We are,' " Marius hears " 'citizens also in that supreme city on high, of which all other cities beside are but as single habitations' " (*ME*, II, 10). For Marius, Fronto is simply suggesting the old theme of the vision in the Temple of Aesculapius. Just as Marius could not then quite envision the city, so now he leaves the lecture hall wondering how that city is actually to be found—"Where were those elect souls? . . . Where was that comely order?" (*ME*, II, 12)—and he sees Cornelius riding by "with that new song he had heard once before floating from his lips" (*ME*, II, 13).

---

[13] This same technique was used by Johnson in *Rasselas* and by Fielding in *Joseph Andrews* to explode Stoic pretentions. Apparently Pater is not unmindful of literary antecedents in the romance-dialogue tradition.

In the following chapter, "Second Thoughts," Marius realizes that his earlier Epicureanism had been too narrow and inflexible, that he must make room in his scheme of things for possibilities, for the unfulfilled ideals being a reality which as yet cannot be wholly experienced. A little more "walking by faith," says Pater of the old Cyrenaics,

> a little more of such not unreasonable "assent," and they might have profited by a hundred services to their culture, from Greek religion and Greek morality, as they actually were. The spectacle of their fierce, exclusive, tenacious hold on their own narrow apprehension, makes one think of a picture with no relief, no soft shadows nor breadth of space, or of a drama without proportionate repose. (*ME*, II, 24)[14]

The proper goal of Cyrenaicism, then, should be to enlarge experience by making a concession to the reality of what is only partially manifested in any given moment or place. To ally oneself with some system larger than one's own circle of experience is surely one way to enrich the mind, to expand beyond the narrow moment of the present into a past and a future. As Pater says in an important passage, "The mere sense that one belongs to a system—an imperial system or organisation—has, in itself, the expanding power of a great experience; as some have felt who have been admitted from narrower sects into the communion of the catholic church; or as the old Roman citizen felt" (ME, II, 26). In an earlier edition of the novel Pater had written that if the Cyrenaic disciple adopts this more flexible approach, he finds himself "as a single element in an imposing system, a wonderful harmony of principles, exerting a strange power to sustain—to carry him and his effort still onward to perfection, when, through one's inherent human weakness, his own peculiar source of energy fails him, or his own peculiar apprehension becomes obscured for a while."[15] To someone rereading the novel, these words seem uniquely apropos of the

---

[14] In a paragraph cut in later editions from the chapter entitled "Second Thoughts," Pater had written of the Cyrenaics that "contrasted with the liberality of one like Socrates, their theory of practice, even at its best, has the narrowness—the fanatic narrowness—if, also, the intense force, of a 'heresy.'" But, says Pater, heresy is not so much positive error as "disproportion of truth," and so Cyrenaicism, "old or new"—Pater is thinking of Victorian England as well as second-century Italy—could be "at the least a very salutary corrective, in a generation which has certainly not overvalued the aesthetic side of its duties, or even of its pleasures. . . . It is in this way that Cyrenaicism, with its worship of beauty—of the body—of physical beauty—might perform its legitimate moral function, as a 'counsel of perfection,' for a few."

[15] This likewise was cut from the chapter "Second Thoughts."

dying Marius, admitted finally into the communion of the Church Universal and to the hope which it entertained.

Having described Marius' attainment of a more flexible philosophy, Pater now reintroduces him into the presence of Aurelius. This time Aurelius has something to say concerning the "Beata Urbs" (Chap. XVII). Indeed, it was from Aurelius that Fronto had borrowed much of his terminology describing the *"City on high"* (*ME*, II, 37), and the chapter gives us a more positive, less pessimistic, résumé of the Emperor's thoughts. Although Fronto does not give his city any "visible locality and abiding-place" (*ME*, II, 11), since it is for him no more than "an intellectual abstraction" (*ME*, II, 12), Aurelius sees that the heavenly city must be "incorporate somehow with the actual city whose goodly stones were lying beneath his gaze" (*ME*, II, 37). Yet, ironically, "with the descent of but one flight of steps into the market-place below" (*ME*, II, 40), the vision for Marius is destroyed. Aurelius' idea of the "one city" is typically centripetal in its conception of the existence of all men united in brotherhood, or at least in a single community. Although it carries forward the vision of the Aesculapian shrine, it is, of course, the Stoic idea of the One, of the single principle of the Logos which pervades the universe, that lies behind Aurelius' hope for the "Celestial City, Uranopolis, Callipolis, *Urbs Beata*—in which, a consciousness of the divine will being everywhere realised, there would be, among other felicitous differences from this lower visible world, no more quite hopeless death, of men, or children, or of their affections" (*ME*, II, 39). But Aurelius' helplessness in the face of evil—indeed, his tolerance of it—shows Marius that in Stoic thought there was "no real accommodation of the world as it is, to the divine pattern of the *Logos*, the eternal reason, over against it" (*ME*, II, 51).

Marius' response to Aurelius' visionary hopes is further conditioned by his first passing, in order to reach the Emperor, through a "subterranean gallery" (*ME*, II, 33) still haunted by memories of the assassination of the Emperor Caligula, which took place there. The thoughts of the Stoic Emperor about the brotherhood of men must have seemed woefully out of contact with reality to one who, only moments before, had been reflecting that Roman history resembled that sinister passageway: "had not almost every step in it some gloomy memory of unnatural violence?" (*ME*, II, 35) And Aurelius' philosophy must have seemed especially detached since he appeared content to tolerate such evil passively. Marius could not help noting that Aurelius' philosophy, with its "forced and yet facile optimism, refusing to see evil anywhere, might lack, after all, the secret of genuine cheerfulness" (*ME*, II, 52), and it undoubtedly contrasted oddly with the joy of Cornelius, whose cheerfulness was, unlike Aurelius', "certainly united with the bold recognition of evil as a fact in the world" (*ME*, II, 53). Inevitably, then, the *Urbs Beata* remains for Aurelius, even "in his clearest vision of it, a confused place" (*ME*, II, 40). It is a vision without content, for it is a vision without that power of love for specific individuals which can actually weld mankind into some pattern of heavenly order:

> Plato, indeed, had been able to articulate, to see, at least in thought, his ideal city. But just because Aurelius had passed beyond Plato, in the scope of the gracious charities he pre-supposed there, he had been unable really to track his way about it. Ah! after all, according to Plato himself, all vision was but reminiscence, and this, his heart's desire, no place his soul could ever have visited in any region of the old world's achievements. He had but divined, by a kind of generosity of spirit, the void place, which another experience than his must fill. (*ME*, II, 40)

This vision without individual content is ironically echoed by the physical circumstances of the interview. In order to raise funds for the war, Aurelius sold the imperial furniture, only himself remaining in the hollow rooms—"in his empty house, the man of mind, who had always made so much of the pleasures of philosophic contemplation, felt freer in thought than ever" (*ME*, II, 36). But the freedom is illusory, and even the tower room denied its possiblity, for the chamber was nearly "window-less," only "a quite medieval window here and there" (*ME*, I, 216) let in the light.

Plato, says Pater, had thought that Apollo's Golden Age would come when those in whom God mixed gold became the rulers (*PP*, 248). But in *Marius* Plato's ideal is tested against the "golden" (*ME*, I, 229) mediocrity of Aurelius—Pater is not above a pun on *aureus*—and both Roman Emperor and Greek philosopher fail, for neither perceives that if the golden world of Apollo is really to appear, it must have its local habitation and name, utilizing the individual as the vehicle for its expression. "By his peculiar gift of verbal articulation," says Pater of Plato,

> he divined the mere hollow spaces which a knowledge, then merely potential, and an experience still to come, would one day occupy. . . . His aptitude for things visible, with the gift of words, empowers him to express, as if for the eyes, what except to the eye of the mind is strictly invisible, what an acquired asceticism induces him to rank above, and sometimes, in terms of harshest dualism, oppose to, the sensible world. (*PP*, 143)

If Plato was at fault in his reasoning, it was precisely because he did not attempt to localize his ideal in the visible world. Like Aurelius, at times Plato, too, seemed little more than "a mind trying to feed itself on its own emptiness" (*PP*, 143). Certainly Aurelius was truly a moral person, not an egotist after the manner of Flavian, yet he, too, failed to escape from his Dionysian subjectivity into some larger objective order external to himself. That order was for him only a "void." Flavian's was a world of content without form; Aurelius' was one of form without content. Aurelius ignored, for the sake of some disembodied universal, the objective focal point of the One in the here-and-now; he loved humanity in terms of the type, but the type, without individuals, will always flatten to mere abstraction.

In the final chapter of the third book—introduced, significantly, by a quotation from Psalm 56 (Vulgate): "My heart is ready, O God, a ready heart is mine"—Marius has a mystic vision. He experiences one of those rare moments of heightened awareness akin to the epiphany of Joyce. Marius has his experience at an inn garden in one "peculiar and privileged hour" (*ME*, II, 68) as he ponders whether the "Will" itself might not be "an organ of knowledge, of vision" (*ME*, II, 65). At this moment he has an intense consciousness of the God in whom man lives and moves and has his being. Had there not been "besides Flavian, besides Cornelius even, and amid the solitude which in spite of ardent friendship he had perhaps loved best of all things—some other companion, an unfailing companion, ever at his side throughout?" (*ME*, II, 67) Marius feels an inexplicable but overwhelming sense of gratitude to someone not tangibly present. His sense of the divine assistant is closely related to the realization of the "celestial New Rome," and he continues to speculate:

Might not this entire material world . . . be . . . but . . . a creation of that one indefectible mind, wherein he too became conscious, for an hour, a day, for so many years? . . . The purely material world, that close, impassable prison-wall, seemed just then the unreal thing, to be actually dissolving away all around him: and he felt a quiet hope, a quiet joy dawning faintly, in the dawning of this doctrine upon him as a really credible opinion. It was like the break of day over some vast prospect with the "new city," as it were some celestial New Rome, in the midst of it. (*ME*, II, 69–70)

Pater writes of Marius that "himself—his sensations and ideas— never fell again precisely into focus as on that day, yet he was the richer by its experience" (*ME*, II, 71).

The heart of Marius' intellectual achievement is the perception of an order external to himself, that overarching spirituality to which Aurelius had dedicated himself. But Marius is now about to go beyond Aurelius: "Must not all that remained of life be but a search for the equivalent of that Ideal, among so-called actual things—a gathering together of every trace or token of it, which his actual experience might present?" (*ME*, II, 72) Marius' vision has passed beyond the veil of immediate experience; now he must find that ideal actually incarnated in the fabric of the visible world. His sense of a divine assistant is so real that he is certain its objective counterpart must be visible to the mortal eye, and, like Psyche, he goes in search of the real ideal. This surely is something that Aurelius, who ignored the physical world, had never done. But unless one accepts the fact that, like Psyche, all mortals are part of the visible world, one can never even take the first step, which is to apprehend clearly the spires and towers of that ideal city. Pater's wistful query of Plato would have been fully as applicable to Aurelius: "Ah, good master! was the eye so contemptible an organ of knowledge after all?" (*PP*, 97).

BOOK IV

As events move toward their dramatic climax, the pace of the novel becomes more rapid. The fourth book begins with a sharp juxtaposition of two chapters, the first chapter presenting the pagan house where Marius meets the idol of his youth, Apuleius, and the second describing the Christian home where Marius first sees Saint Cecilia, the well-known martyr of the second century. The opening scene of the first chapter is set some years after Marius' experience in the garden of the inn; he is attending a supper party given by a friend, a wealthy and aristocratic dilettante. The purpose of the party is to honor Apuleius, author of the Golden Book in which Marius had found the legend of Cupid and Psyche. The young Commodus is also there, already displaying those traits of character which will mark his reign. His crudity, however, seems less a contrast than a complement to the jaded aestheticism of the gathering, to the elegant conversation, soft entertainment, heavy wine, and light women. As Commodus and the other young men dance the *Death of Paris*, "their long swords weaving a silvery network in the air" (*ME*, II, 79), they act out the story of the passionate and fatal love of the young Trojan for the fair Helen.

The recitation of a supposed work of Lucian's, *The Halcyon*, which follows the dance, presents another kind of love, in marked contrast to the selfish and suicidal love of Paris and his deserted wife, Oenone. *The Halcyon*, which Pater inserted almost verbatim into the novel, becomes here an allegory, like the story of Cupid and Psyche, of a love stronger than death. It tells how the daughter of Aeolus, god of the winds, loved Ceyx, the son of the morning star. At his death, the wife of Ceyx "lamented his sweet usage" (*ME*, II, 81), to quote the same euphemism Pater had applied to Cupid's love for Psyche, and since she could not find Ceyx after a lengthy search of the land, Heaven, noting the strength of her love, turned her into a bird so that she could pursue her quest over the sea. The allegorical equation is not difficult to establish: the bird is Pater's usual image for the soul, while Ceyx's virtual identification with the morning star ties him closely to the traditional symbol for Christ. Some versions of the Halcyon legend tell of an eventual reunification of the two lovers, but Pater, on Lucian's authority, remains content only to leave the door open as to the outcome.

After the party, as Marius stands in the outer darkness, watching a great fire in the distance, Apuleius expounds to him his neo-Platonic theory of intermediary beings which link the human world to the divine. This is an abbreviated version of his oration *On the God of Socrates*. While listening to Apuleius, Marius recalls again *The Halcyon*, in which Socrates pleads with Chairephon for suspension of judgment in the face of the limitation of human knowledge, and Marius is further reminded of Plato's great image of the cave, with which the Seventh Book of *The Republic* opens. Apuleius' singular utterances "were sufficient to throw back on this strange evening, in all its detail—the dance, the readings, the distant fire—a kind of allegoric expression: gave it the character of one of those famous Platonic figures or apologues which had then been in fact under discussion" (*ME*, II, 89). Has Apuleius actually left the shadows and seen that of which he speaks? Is his vision absurd only to the dwellers in the cave? The epigraph to the chapter—"Your old men shall dream dreams" (Joel 2:28)— recalls that world of the winter Dionysus, in which dreams such as those of Plato and Aurelius, and now Apuleius, lack their objective counterpart. Apuleius, standing there with Marius, is metaphorically as well as literally a speaker "in the darkness" (*ME*, II, 89). He has committed the error of believing too readily his own wishes. Marius, on the other hand, realizes that he is in danger of not allowing enough for possibility; yet, as much as he would like to, he cannot accept Apuleius' guesses at the truth; he demands greater evidence: "he must still hold by what his eyes really saw" (*ME*, II, 90). Ironically, this neo-Platonism of Apuleius is almost identical with the childhood religion of Marius, in which "the whole of life seemed full of sacred presences, . . . conscious powers external to ourselves, pleased or displeased by the right or wrong conduct of every circumstance of daily life" (*ME*, I, 17, 5), and Marius' inability to recapture his early belief is extremely poignant: "For him certainly, and for his solace, the little godship for whom the rude countryman, an unconscious Platonist, trimmed his twinkling lamp, would never slip from the bark of these immemorial olive-trees.—No! not even in the wildest moonlight" (*ME*, II, 90). But Marius could concede that Apuleius' speculations "bore witness, at least, to a variety of human disposition and a consequent variety of mental view . . . regarding the world all alike had actually before them as their original premiss or starting-point; a world, wider, perhaps, in its possibilities than all possible fancies concerning it" (*ME*, II, 91).

If in this chapter we see how dead Marius' childhood religion was for him, in the next chapter we see how much more meaningful religion may become when the acknowledged "possibilities" are matched by evidence more concrete than that marshaled by Apuleius. In direct contrast to the soft decadence of the literary party at the villa at Tusculum is the church in Cecilia's house, reflecting the purity and the realization of the ideal which Marius so vainly sought in the crumbling world of the Roman Empire. One afternoon Marius and Cornelius visit a villa situated where the Latin and Appian Ways intersect. This house marks the crossroads in Marius' spiritual pilgrimage. It corresponds to the demand that he leave the shadows of the darkened cave and behold the light of the sun: "Was he willing to look upon that, the seeing of which might define—yes! define the critical turning-point in his days?" (*ME*, II, 95) The vague guesses of Apuleius are about to be exchanged for an actual vision of the ideal City.

The church in Cecilia's house does not, Marius sees, reject the culture and religious insights of the pagan world; rather, it remolds them according to a higher pattern. This is a key idea in Pater's thought, and it is closely related to his demand that one utilize the contents of actual experience rather than theorize *in vacuo*, as Apuleius had done. The primitive church of the second century represents a rebirth of those visible elements which veil the Logos; it enjoyed, says Pater, "an earlier, and unimpeachable *Renaissance* . . . as if in anticipation of the sixteenth century. . . . It was the old way of true *Renaissance*—being indeed the way of nature with her roses, the divine way with the body of man, perhaps with his soul—conceiving the new organism by no sudden and abrupt creation, but rather by the action of a new principle upon elements, all of which had in truth already lived and died many times" (*ME*, II, 125, 95–96). Marius senses in Christianity the continuity of his beautiful religion of childhood, and he is no stranger to the scene before him. He is well prepared to understand its significance:

His old native susceptibility to the spirit, the special sympathies, of places,—above all, to any hieratic or religious significance they might have,—was at its liveliest, as Marius, still encompassed by that peculiar singing, and still amid the evidences of a grave discretion all around him, passed into the house. That intelligent seriousness about life, the absence of which had ever seemed to remove those who lacked it into some strange species wholly alien from himself, accumulating all the lessons of his experience since those first days at White-nights, was as it were translated here, as if in designed congruity with his favourite precepts of the power of physical vision, into an actual picture. (*ME*, II, 96–97)

The early church as an "actual picture" is in a sense a metaphor of its acceptance of the visible world, and it is of prime significance that its central act of worship, the Mass, is presented with "all the vividness of a picture for the eye" (*ME*, II, 134).

As in the religion of Numa there was a closeness of the living to the dead, so here Marius perceives in the catacombs "the centre of the peculiar religious expressiveness, of the sanctity, of the entire scene" (*ME*, II, 98). And just as the religion of White-nights celebrated the seasonal cycle, so here birth, death, and rebirth seem to constitute the very essence of a somewhat more refined, less primitive, religious hope. Even the graves in the catacombs are "like cradles or garden-beds" (*ME*, II, 131–32), and the deaths of those who had died as martyrs are celebrated as *natalitiae*. In the context of this "bold paradox" (*ME*, II, 102) which treated death as birth, Marius meets the virgin saint, Cecilia:

Her temperate beauty brought reminiscences of the serious and virile character of the best female statuary of Greece. Quite foreign, however, to any Greek statuary was the expression of pathetic care, with which she carried a little child at rest in her arms. Another, a year or two older, walked beside, the fingers of one hand within her girdle. (*ME*, II, 105)

Cecilia, in her "virginial beauty" (*ME*, II, 106), calls to mind not only those Renaissance paintings of the Madonna with Her children, but the figure of Demeter, the Great Mother, herself.

Cecilia, the Madonna, Demeter, "our virgin mother, the

Church" (*ME*, II, 193–94) are all sorrowing for the soul which has lost its immortality in its separation from the Logos and, like Persephone, has died by its descent into the sensuous world. Because God cannot dwell in His Church, His visible vesture and expression, except through those individual souls which succeed in finding Him, the search of the individual soul for the Logos is likewise the search of the whole Christian community. Like the death of Christ, the Dionysian deaths of the martyrs—Sanctus, " 'his corpse, a single wound, having wholly lost the form of man' " (*ME*, II, 193)—celebrate the marriage union by which the Church itself is constantly renewed, for the individual soul, by its sacrificial love, finds God and infuses the whole community with its life. Thus, in the church in Cecilia's house Marius senses his closeness to God when he beholds the people and their rites. The face of Cecilia is stamped on his memory, and he feels as though "that visionary scene was the close, the fitting close, of the afternoon's strange experiences. . . . That old longing for escape had been satisfied by this vision of the church in Cecilia's house, as never before" (*ME*, II, 105–6). Marius calls it a "new vision," undoubtedly thinking of the visions of the temple of Aesculapius and of the inn-garden, both of which have now been superseded. Here is the new city, the ideal community made visible. Interestingly, the chapter epigraph is retained with the unobtrusive addition of "and your young men shall see visions" (Joel 2:28; Acts 2:17).

The Christmas Mass which Marius shortly thereafter unexpectedly witnesses sums up "an entire world of complex associations" (*ME*, II, 128) for him. He hears the story of Christ told to the assembly in a manner which displayed as in a picture

> the mournful figure of him towards whom this whole act of worship still consistently turned—a figure which seemed to have absorbed, like some rich tincture in his garment, all that was deep-felt and impassioned in the experiences of the past. . . . It was the image of a young man giving up voluntarily, one by one, for the greatest of ends, the greatest gifts; actually parting with himself, above all, with the serenity, the divine serenity, of his own soul; yet from the midst of his desolation crying out upon the greatness of his success, as if foreseeing this very worship. (*ME*, II, 134, 138–39)

Marius does not feel himself the uncomfortable witness to this "sacrifice" that he had at the agricultural festival of the *Ambarvalia* or the Roman celebration of the *Lectisternium*. Within the Christian context, death is not brutal and senseless, but meaningful and charged with hope, for the Christmas Mass is a celebration of death on the anniversary of birth, and it stresses the relatedness of the two events. Indeed, the death and resurrection of Christ correspond to the seasonal Dionysian renewal of the year: on this day it seemed to Marius "as though the spring had set in with a sudden leap in the heart of things, the whole scene around him lay like some untarnished picture beneath a sky of delicate blue" (*ME*, II, 129). As he left the church, Marius felt "that he must hereafter experience often a longing memory, a kind of thirst, for all this, over again. And it seemed moreover to define what he must require of the powers, whatsoever they might be, that had brought him into the world at all, to make him not unhappy in it" (*ME*, II, 140).

To summarize, then, in this fourth book the evolution of Marius' "sensations and ideas" is following a very orderly progression by chapters. First comes a chapter in which Apuleius expounds his unfounded dreams. Then three chapters are used to present the actual vision of the church and the Mass.

In the two chapters which follow the Mass, Pater considers the nature of Revelation as the narrow theological question of transubstantiation becomes, naturally enough, the broader one of "evidence" for the reality of the *Deus Absconditus*. Does God really manifest Himself to the soul; will Cupid return to Psyche? The "Conversation Not Imaginary" which follows the chapter on the Mass is a chilling contrast to its warmth. It is a reasonably faithful translation of Lucian's *Hermotimus*, and its general import, much like David Hume's phenomenalism of a later age, is that metaphysical speculation is hopeless, that skepticism is the only reasonable philosophy, and that man is helpless because he has been given no divine Revelation. There is a quality about Lucian's mentality which indeed is "not imaginary": he lacks the " 'imaginative reason' " (*R*, 138) or "imaginative love" (*ME*, I, 92) to see spiritual form within the material veil. The mountaintop and the happy city of which he speaks are, for him, purely illusory.

Marius can agree with the destructive criticism which Lucian levels against the various sects, but he is not led into Lucian's skepticism. Marius comes to see that only some form of Revelation will serve, and he recalls to mind

an image, almost ghastly in the traces of its great sorrows—bearing along for ever, on bleeding feet, the instrument of its punishment—which was all Marius could recall distinctly of a certain Christian legend he had heard. The legend told of an encounter at this very spot, of two wayfarers on the Appian Way, as also upon some very dimly discerned mental journey, altogether different from himself and

his late companions—an encounter between Love, literally fainting
by the road, and Love "travelling in the greatness of his strength,"
Love itself, suddenly appearing to sustain that other. (*ME*, II, 171)

The Redeemer victorious through suffering (an image from Isa.
63:1) as He appeared to the fleeing Peter, giving him strength
to return to Rome and his martyrdom, is no doubt the legend Marius here recalls. Marius realizes that the hope of some such divine
intervention as this is needed if man is to look death in the face
with equanimity. Standing on the Appian Way, the road of tombs,
Lucian tells Hermotimus that they "have come round in a circle
to the spot whence we started, and to our first incertitude"
(*ME*, II, 168). Lucian asks his friend not to be angry because "I
would not suffer you to pass your life in a dream, pleasant perhaps,
but still only a dream—because I wake you up" (*ME*, II, 169).
But Lucian's awakening at the completion of the intellectual circle
does not bring the realization of the dreams. There is no immortality on the road which Lucian travels, and the contrast with
the catacombs is obvious. The plaintive cry inscribed on the tomb-
stones for those in the land of the living to remember the dead
is no more than that " 'subjective immortality' " (*ME*, I, 20) which
Marius' mother offered to her deceased husband. There must be
some superhuman order larger than the merely subjective world
which passes away, some concrete embodiment which is as permanent as is the divinity of which it is the expression. Marius recalls
a few stray snatches of that day's conversation: " 'Do they never
come down again,' he heard once more the well-modulated voice:
'Do they never come down again from the heights, to help those
whom they left here below?'—'And we too desire, not a fair one,
but the fairest of all. Unless we find him, we shall think we have
failed' " (*ME*, II, 171).

The following chapter makes the next logical step. It rejects
as insufficient—either for the second century or, for that matter,
the nineteenth—the traditional idea of a god who literally returns.
The chapter, introduced by a somber quotation from the *Aeneid:*
" 'Sunt lacrimae rerum et mentem mortalia tangunt' " (Bk. I, 462),
takes the form of a diary in which Marius notes the sufferings
of dumb animals, of children, of men and women in a world which
"seemed to present itself as a hospital of sick persons"
(*ME*, II, 174). In the privacy of his diary, Marius struggles with
the idea of the god who returns to help his people and wonders
what would really be gained by a literal return, as was envisioned,
for example, in the religion of Numa:

"That a Numa, and his age of gold, would return, has been the hope or the dream of some, in every period. Yet if he did come back, or any equivalent of his presence, he could but weaken, and by no means smite through, that root of evil, certainly of sorrow, of outraged human sense, in things, which one must carefully distinguish from all preventible accidents. Death, and the little perpetual daily dyings, which have something of its sting, he must necessarily leave untouched." (*ME*, II, 179–80)

Reasoning from the traditional definition "God is Love," Pater gives us a new insight into God revealed. What is needed to offset the ever present sorrow of this life is perhaps not so much the physical return of a god as love among men, a love which would itself become God:

"There have been occasions, certainly, when I have felt that if others cared for me as I cared for them, it would be, not so much a consolation, as an equivalent, for what one has lost or suffered: a realised profit on the summing up of one's accounts: a touching of that absolute ground amid all the changes of phenomena, such as our philosophers have of late confessed themselves quite unable to discover. In the mere clinging of human creatures to each other, nay! in one's own solitary self-pity, amid the effects even of what might appear irredeemable loss, I seem to touch the eternal." (*ME*, II, 183–84)

It is paradoxical that through love victory can be wrung from inevitable suffering. Marius observes something of the sort in Cecilia's attitude toward the dead child, and the quiet confidence in which the Christian burial is conducted serves as a foil to the hollow measures which the distraught Aurelius decrees at the death of Annius Verus.

Marius again clearly perceives the power of Christian love when, as he once more attends Mass the following spring, he listens to the *Epistle of the Churches of Lyons and Vienne*. This letter, drawn by Pater from the writings of Eusebius, testifies as vividly as any document can to a vision or a revelation which directly answers the inexorable sorrow of the world. Martyrdom seems unmistakably "the overpowering act of testimony that Heaven had come down among men" (*ME*, II, 214). It is a kind of Mass itself, in which Love is made visible in the willingness of the Christians to sacrifice their lives for their common religion. This is the Revelation for which Marius had been waiting, and the self-sacrificial death of the early martyrs becomes to him an ideal—the laying down of one's life, in Christ-like fashion, for another, for something greater than one's self. In the midst of the sorrow of death there is joy, for in the death of the body, death itself dies.

Marius has now reached a crucial stage in his spiritual development, for he has discovered an escape from his isolated dreams through a sympathetic identification with humanity. This love, he discovers, places him for the first time in possession of a larger world and a living future. At this point Marius journeys back to his childhood home of White-nights in order to visit the family burial place. Wandering through its dusty interior, he identifies closely with those buried around him, sees himself almost as one or another of the dead: "It seemed as if this boy of his own age had taken filial place beside her [his mother] there, in his stead" (*ME*, II, 206). Here, too, he suddenly realizes that his father had died at the age he has now reached—"And with that came a blinding rush of kindness, as if two alienated friends had come to understand each other at last" (*ME*, II, 207). These generations of ancestors stored away in the sterile vault represent Marius' own past—a dead past. He is shocked by the odd air of neglect, in strong contrast to the Christian graves he had seen: "With a vain yearning, as he stood there, still to be able to do something for them, he reflected that such doing must be, after all, in the nature of things, mainly for himself. His own epitaph might be that old one— "Εσχατος τοῦ ἰδίου γένους—*He was the last of his race!*" (*ME*, II, 207)

Marius stands, so to speak, between the generations of the past and those of the future. The world of the summer Dionysus has, as in the story of Florian, been closed off forever behind him by the somber shadows of death. In the dark world of the winter Dionysus, Marius must chose between, on the one hand, Cornelius, the Christians, the catacombs; and on the other, Lucian, Flavian, and the tombs on the Appian Way. The circle of his life is complete; he has returned to his starting point. Is this merely the inconclusive circle of Lucian's logic, or has he indeed found behind the material veil of mortality the divine form? Aware of the Christian belief in the resurrection of the body, Marius, as a symbol of hope for the future which the past may possess, buries the remains of his ancestors in the Christian manner. In the very jaws of death he snatches his victory. Later, when he lies mortally ill, Marius momentarily thinks his death an irony because it is not a spectacular martyrdom. In his depression he at first does not see that he has already made his peace with the Church here at White-nights, for it was here that he reached his turning point in aligning the generations of the past, the pagan world, with the hope of Christianity.

The epigraph for the concluding chapter—"Anima Naturaliter Christiana"—is taken from Tertullian's *Apologia*[16] and describes the state which Marius' soul has reached. As Marius returns to Rome, covering the same route he had taken as a young man, he is accompanied this time by Cornelius who, as the "unseen companion" now manifested, is a representative of Christianity and all humanity. In the person of Cornelius is concentrated all of Marius' hope for the future: "Identifying himself with Cornelius in so dear a friendship, through him, Marius seemed to touch, to ally himself to, actually to become a possessor of the coming world; even as happy parents reach out, and take possession of it, in and through the survival of their children" (*ME*, II, 209–10). On this journey, however, Marius arrives not at the old Rome, but at what is essentially the ideal community for which he had sought so long. Stopping to spend the night at a little town where Marius "remembered that he had been . . . on his first journey to Rome" (*ME*, II, 210), the two companions worship the next morning at the shrine of several local martyrs. They are caught in an earthquake and are arrested as the cause of it by the superstitious inhabitants. Marius, who is partly in love with Cecilia, substitutes himself for his friend and bribes the guards to release Cornelius, for he "believed that Cornelius was to be the husband of Cecilia; and that, perhaps strangely, had but added to the desire to get him away safely" (*ME*, II, 212).

On the way to Rome Marius becomes sick and is left by the soldiers to die at a Christian farmhouse. The peace, the pleasant fragrance of new-mown hay, and the sunlight made it seem as though "he was lying safe in his old home" (*ME*, II, 216). Gradually, out of his depression, it becomes clear to him that he has discovered the "new city" in the Christian community, part of which is now ministering to him. The ideal is made a reality: "Revelation, vision, the discovery of a vision, the *seeing* of a perfect humanity, in a perfect world— . . . how goodly had the vision

---

[16] The quotation is from Chap. 17. 6. Tertullian's words seem almost the perfect description of Pater's belief that the soul still remembers the God from whom it came and can indeed find His visible form in the world of sense: "He is invisible, although He may be seen; intangible, although He may be measured by human senses. . . . Do you wish us to prove His existence from His numerous, mighty works by which we are supported, sustained, delighted, and even startled? I repeat, do you wish us to prove Him from the testimony of the soul itself? . . . O testimony of the soul, which is by natural instinct Christian! . . . It knows the abode of the living God; from Him and from there it has come." *Apologetical Works*, trans. Rudolph Arbesmann, E. J. Daly, and E. A. Quain, Vol. X of *The Fathers of the Church*, ed. R. J. Deferrari *et al.* (New York, 1950), pp. 52–53.

been!—one long unfolding of beauty and energy in things, upon the closing of which he might gratefully utter his "*Vixi!*" (*ME*, II, 218).

There is, however, one step more which must be taken before the fruits of victory are wholly gained. As he slips toward death, Marius turns for the fulfillment of his ideal to the vision of the divine form, Love itself, behind or beyond the material veil:

At this moment, his unclouded receptivity of soul, grown so steadily through all those years, from experience to experience, was at its height; the house was ready for the possible guest; the tablet of the mind white and smooth, for whatsoever divine fingers might choose to write there. And was not this precisely the condition, the attitude of mind, to which something higher than he, yet akin to him, would be likely to reveal itself; to which that influence he had felt now and again like a friendly hand upon his shoulder, amid the actual obscurities of the world, would be likely to make a further explanation? . . . In the bare sense of having loved he seemed to find, even amid this foundering of the ship, that on which his soul might "assuredly rest and depend." (*ME*, II, 220, 223)

Like Psyche, Marius has found the visible vesture and expression of the divine face in the Christian community and in Cornelius, but he has not yet looked upon "the divine form as it is" (*GS*, 24).

James Hafley, as I have remarked, saw in the appearance of Cornelius Cupid's return to Psyche. This, I believe, is an oversimplification because Cornelius is not the end of Marius' quest in the sense that Cupid was Psyche's. Cornelius, like the Christian community of which he is a member, merely testifies to the presence of the divine behind the flux of life. At his death, Marius is still the questing soul, Psyche, who descends into the realm of the dead to beg a boon from Persephone, goddess of death. This was Psyche's last labor before Love comes down and makes her his. The moment of Revelation is at hand, and Pater emphasizes the open-endedness of the vision:

Throughout that elaborate and lifelong education of his receptive powers, he had ever kept in view the purpose of preparing himself towards possible further revelation some day—towards some ampler vision, which should take up into itself and explain this world's delightful shows. . . . Surely, the aim of a true philosophy must lie, not in futile efforts towards the complete accommodation of man to the circumstances in which he chances to find himself, but in the maintenance of a kind of candid discontent, in the face of the very highest achievement; the unclouded and receptive soul quitting the world finally, with the same fresh wonder with which it had entered

the world still unimpaired, and going on its blind way at last with
the consciousness of some profound enigma in things, as but a pledge
of something further to come. . . . For a moment he experienced a
singular curiosity, almost an ardent desire to enter upon a future,
the possibilities of which seemed so large. (*ME*, II, 219–21)

As he descends into the Valley of the Shadow, Marius, like Psyche,
hopes again to see the ideal, and just as Psyche took along the
bread which guaranteed her safety, so Marius, as he embarks upon
his last quest, has the bread placed gently between his lips: "In
the moments of his extreme helplessness their mystic bread had
been placed, had descended like a snow-flake from the sky, between
his lips" (*ME*, II, 224).

Psyche, however, did not escape from Hades unaided, we recall. Her "old error" (*ME*, I, 90) of desiring to look into "the
beauty of the divine countenance" (*ME*, I, 88) reasserted itself,
and she swooned into a sleep which would have been eternal had
not Cupid pricked her with his arrow and awakened her from
"the slumber of death" (*ME*, I, 89). Marius' death, too, comes like
sleep, but it is his dream that Love will be triumphant over death.
And we are given every reason to expect that it will be. Beginning
with the ideal of maternal love in the first book, Marius' conception
of love has gradually expanded, growing by accretion as more
and more experiences are added, until it culminates in this supreme
Christ-like act of laying down his life for "the least of these my
brethren" (Matt. 25:40). By his love, in which those relations
that bind men together are most clearly seen, Marius finds the
objective embodiment of divinity for which he had sought so long.
By his death, in which he transcends the mortal veil, he reaches
God. For Marius, as for Psyche, the sting of death is in reality
the prick of Cupid's arrow, an awakening from that life-in-death
which is the state of all mortals; it is a discovery that those dreams
of the immortal world are real, that Cupid has returned. We recall
what Fronto had told Aurelius' children: "in his dream the soldier
was victorious, the general was borne in triumph, the wanderer
returned home. Yes!—and sometimes those dreams come true!"
(*ME*, I, 228) For Marius the truth of his dream had already been
glimpsed in the Christian community itself.

We recall that a marriage ends the quest of Psyche for Cupid.
Here, too, at the end of the novel, a marriage takes place, though
not the expected one between Cornelius and Cecilia. The year is
177 A.D., and Aurelius has issued his first edict against the Christians. History says that Saint Cecilia died as a martyr that year
in the persecutions at Rome, and martyrdom, we are told by the

grave Eusebius, was considered by the early Christians to be a marriage with Christ. This was the image used to describe the martyrdom of the Christians at Lyons and Vienne: led out to the slaughter, " 'their bonds seemed but a goodly array, or like the golden bracelets of a bride' " (*ME*, II, 191); and, at the end of the *Epistle*, we are told that Blandina " 'as a mother that had given life to her children, and sent them like conquerors to the great King, hastened to them, with joy at the end, as to a marriage-feast' " (*ME*, II, 195). The God of Love, then, does save Marius' soul, for in the grey, austere evening the Christians took up his remains "and buried them secretly, with their accustomed prayers; but with joy also, holding his death, according to their generous view in this matter, to have been of the nature of a martyrdom; and martyrdom, as the church had always said, a kind of sacrament with plenary grace" (*ME*, II, 224).

"Anima Naturaliter Christiana" is perhaps a bit like the last chapter of Johnson's story of a search, *Rasselas*, a "Conclusion in which Nothing is Concluded." Yet the ending of Pater's novel is in no way vague or befuddled. The story itself stops short at the bounds of human experience, but a momentum has been generated which carries the reader into the future. It is this force of expectation which defines Marius' religious belief. What has been glimpsed through the darkened mirror of mortality is a love stronger than death, for, remarks Pater apropos of Rossetti's heroes, there is "a sense of power in love, defying distance, and those barriers which are so much more than physical distance, of unutterable desire penetrating into the world of sleep, however 'lead-bound' " (*Ap*, 214).

Throughout this last book of the novel, Pater has consistently used the dawn as an image of Christian hope (*ME*, II, 102, 114, 129, 132). The dark night of the soul, shrouded in the shadows of the wintry god of death, is over; the twilight of early morning is at hand; the veil of sleep and mortality is about to yield to the sunlight of Apollo. Marius, with the other Christians, now knows with certainty of the great light outside the cave of human experience, and he dies in expectation of that final union with the God of Light and Love.

IV

✑ THE COLLECTED IMAGINARY PORTRAITS

In 1883, while he was still dutifully laboring to bring *Marius* to a conclusion, Pater already had, as he told Violet Paget, "visions of many smaller pieces of work the composition of which would be actually pleasanter to me."[1] It is hardly surprising, then, that a sudden spate of portraits followed the publication of *Marius*. "A Prince of Court Painters" was published in 1885, the same year as the novel. Two other stories, "Sebastian van Storck" and "Denys l'Auxerrois," followed in 1886. The next year "Duke Carl of Rosenmold" appeared. That same year these four were collected from *Macmillan's Magazine*, where they had first been published, and were printed in the volume entitled *Imaginary Portraits*. "Which is the best of your books?" someone once asked Pater. "*Imaginary Portraits*," he replied, "for it is the most natural."[2] We should not be surprised that Pater's talent found these portraits "pleasanter" and more "natural," for it is precisely in such fine cameo work that he excels. Pater seems to be giving us here, in the single figure projected against the background of humanity, his equivalent to those delicate Greek coins stamped with the profile of Demeter—"an epitome of art on a larger scale" (*GS*, 138), as he remarks.

"A PRINCE OF COURT PAINTERS" (1885)

According to Thomas Wright, "A Prince of Court Painters" owed its inception to a visit Pater and a friend made to the Dulwich Gallery.[3] It is the imaginary portrait of Jean Antoine Watteau (or Antony Watteau, as he is called here), presented, as the subtitle

[1] Quoted in Benson, *Pater*, p. 90.
[2] Quoted in Wright, *Life of Pater*, II, 95.
[3] *Ibid.*, p. 92.

has it, by means of "Extracts From an Old French Journal."[4] Pater had already used the journal technique for a chapter in *Marius*, and he was to use it again for parts of "Sebastian van Storck" and "Emerald Uthwart." By giving many French turns to its syntax and diction, Pater has succeeded in making this purely imaginary journal seem quite authentic. The ostensible writer of it is actually the young sister of the historical Jean-Baptiste Pater, a protégé of Watteau. (Jean-Baptiste's surname, however, never is mentioned in the story; one finds it hard not to smile at such authorial reticence.) Jean-Baptiste had three younger brothers, some of whom appear as girls in this story, and a sister five years older than he, Marie-Marguerite Pater, born in 1690, who evidently keeps the journal.[5]

Although "A Prince of Court Painters" is the only imaginary portrait based completely upon historical incidents and personalities, Pater's primary concern is not with biography but with the portrayal of an imagined world. The relationship Pater constructs between Watteau and Marie-Marguerite, who loves him, takes this story out of the class of purely historical portraits and places it in the domain of invention. The fictional pattern to which all the facts are made to correspond is Pater's unique vision of the Dionysian priest in service to Apollo and the arts. The restless, gay,

---

[4] The journal technique supplies us with a first-person narrator and gives us not only another character in the drama but a more immediate and vivid presentation of the action as well. Its significance, however, goes beyond this. The precarious "now," so typical of Watteau's art, is reflected in the nature of the journal form itself, in its series of successive present moments. The date above each entry plunges the reader into the fractured world of temporal things, into the perpetual flux which is so much a part of Watteau's life and art, and in the very form which Marie-Marguerite's account takes we see a reflection of Watteau himself, vibrating, Dionysus-like, between subject and object and only momentarily synthesizing the two worlds in his fragile art. Pater's chosen structure is well suited to its purpose, and the device certainly does not rob the portrait of its color and drama, as has sometimes been alleged.

[5] These details concerning the life of J.-B. Pater are given in Florence Ingersoll-Smouse, *Pater* (Paris, 1928), p. 2. Just what significance the surname has for the writer of the story is not hard to guess. When Pater was once asked whether he was actually a descendant of Jean-Baptiste, he reportedly replied: "I think so; I believe so; I always say so" (*IPB*, p. 11). One wonders, indeed, if Pater would not have liked to have thought, believed, and said that he was related to an even more famous artist in his story, for one recalls Florian Deleal's house with that "element of French descent in its inmates— descent from Watteau, the old court-painter, one of whose gallant pieces still hung in one of the rooms" (*MS*, p. 174). But beyond allowing us to see that Pater was ready at the drop of a name to identify himself with his heroes and heroines, such genealogical details remain mere curiosities. It is the interaction of the various personalities that should be the true focus of our attention.

and myriad-minded life of the courtly city of Paris reflects, in all its freedom, the world of the summer Dionysus, whereas the calm, austere, and "sleepy" (*IP*, 8) atmosphere of the northern provincial capital of Valenciennes represents his winter world. The young artist, caught between the two, searches for some transcendent, Apollonian reality.

The heavy and restrictive nature of Watteau's early environment, the dream-prison of the winter Dionysus, finds its expression in images of stone. Watteau is the son of a stone mason who had built and lives in an all-stone house which, "big and gray and cold" (*IP*, 6), creates in the young lad a desire for the graceful and the elegant. Marie-Marguerite writes that "the rudeness of his home has turned his feeling for even the simpler graces of life into a physical want, like hunger or thirst, which might come to greed; and methinks he perhaps over-values these things" (*IP*, 7). Instinctively, young Watteau turns to what little gaiety he can find in the atmosphere of Valenciennes, painting the happy crowd at the September fair, the figures in his graceful pictures seeming to reflect "a sort of comedy which shall be but tragedy seen from the other side" (*IP*, 6). Watteau finds a partial refuge from the stifling weight of home and Valenciennes environment in the family of Antoine Pater, the sculptor: "he has become like one of our family" (*IP*, 8), writes Marie-Marguerite in her journal. Indeed, Pater improves upon the known historical facts so far as to have the admiring Marie-Marguerite record several years later that "young Watteau has returned home . . . and (it is agreed!) stays with us, instead of in the stone-mason's house" (*IP*, 11).

Watteau is essentially serious of mind, a true heir of Flemish solidity and Spanish austerity (Spain had ruled the lowlands for many years), but he turns, dissatisfied, from this native world to that of the Paris court. For him this Parisian world seems to embody the ideal for which he longs and which he devotes his whole life to capturing. In reality, Paris is too shallow to be that ideal, but because he has gained from his early environment great depth of vision, he is able to invest the trivial graces of Paris with a nobility far beyond their actual worth:

He will never overcome his early training; and these light things
will possess for him always a kind of representative or borrowed worth,
as characterising that impossible or forbidden world which the mason's
boy saw through the closed gateways of the enchanted garden. Those
trifling and petty graces, the *insignia* to him of that nobler world of
aspiration and idea, even now that he is aware as I conceive, of their

true littleness, bring back to him, by the power of association, all
the old magical exhilaration of his dream—his dream of a better world
than the real one. (*IP*, 34–35)

Marie-Marguerite's passage seems to recall the image of the momentarily opened gateway through which Florian saw the red hawthorn, and it also reminds us, more generally, of the young English
poet's longing for the warm southern world beyond his cold northern environment.

This striving after the ideal is the reason that Marie-Marguerite finds in Watteau's art "a sort of *moral* purity; yet, in the
forms and *colours* of things" (*IP*, 23), though she well knows that
"those fine ladies in Watteau's 'conversations,' who look so exqui-
sitely pure" (*IP*, 37) are certainly not guiltless. *Manon Lescaut*,
the popular novel of the Abbé Prévost, had taught her that. Yet
it is this appearance of purity, despite the actual fact of the matter,
which for her invests the work of Watteau with interest:

> The world he sets before us so engagingly has its care for purity,
> its cleanly preferences, in what one is to *see*—in the outsides of
> things—and there is something, a sign, a memento, at the least, of
> what makes life really valuable, even in that. There, is my simple
> notion, wholly womanly perhaps, but which I may hold by, of the
> purpose of the arts. (*IP*, 33)

In a certain measure, at any rate, Watteau has achieved a visual
representation of his ideal in form and color, and like the art of
the young English poet, his pictures purify and ennoble the soul.

But if Watteau succeeds in transforming the social graces of
the Parisian ladies into true art, still this world of the summer
Dionysus is not large enough to contain the whole of his vision;
thus, he is never at peace: "Those coquetries, those vain and perishable graces, can be rendered so perfectly, only through an intimate
understanding of them," writes Marie-Marguerite; but, she adds,
for Watteau "to understand must be to despise them" (*IP*, 27).
This is the secret of Watteau's anguish, his inability to incarnate
the vision of Valenciennes in the concrete world of Parisian life.
Paris, in all its tumult, has become for Watteau what Pisa became
for Flavian—a world unable to offer a truly objective escape for
the dreams of the soul. In the hot, feverish love of Manon Lescaut
and her world, Marie-Marguerite detects the "premature touch
of winter"; she identifies the ungoverned passion of the lovers
with the coldness of the October sun—"that glacial point in the
motionless sky, like some mortal spot whence death begins to creep
over the body!" (*IP*, 38). The same applies to Watteau's art: "The

storm is always brooding through the massy splendour of the trees, above those sun-dried glades or lawns" (*IP*, 32). It is the same sort of instability which haunted the bright world of Pisa in *Marius:* "the boy's superficial delight in the broad light and shadow of all that was mingled with the sense of power, of unknown distance, of the danger of storm and possible death" (*ME*, I, 45). There can be no Golden Age of the rococo: "People talk of a new era now dawning upon the world," writes Marie-Marguerite, but she adds that it is perhaps an era "of infinite littleness also" (*IP*, 33). Only Jean-Baptiste, whose child-soul has never expanded beyond the tiny world of the summer Dionysus, fails to find it restrictive. "As for me," says Marie-Marguerite, "I suffocate this summer afternoon in this pretty *Watteau* chamber of ours, where Jean-Baptiste is at work so contentedly" (*IP*, 30).

Watteau's failure to find a world large enough to contain his ideal creates in him a dissatisfaction with his art. Again and again Marie-Marguerite finds in his pictures the resulting incompleteness:

It is pleasanter to him to sketch and plan than to paint and finish; and he is often out of humour with himself because he cannot project into a picture the life and spirit of his first thought with the *crayon*. He would fain begin where that famous master Gerard Dow left off, and snatch, as it were with a single stroke, what in him was the result of infinite patience. . . . To my thinking there is a kind of greed or grasping in that humour; as if things were not to last very long, and one must snatch opportunity. (*IP*, 35–36)

And so, in 1714, when Antony begins his picture of her, she must write that "my own portrait remains unfinished at his sudden departure" (*IP*, 24). And after another visit, in 1717, her "own poor likeness, begun so long ago still remains unfinished on the easel, at his departure from Valenciennes. . . . He has commanded Jean-Baptiste to finish it; and so it must be" (*IP*, 35–36).[6] Not only are Watteau's pictures often incomplete, but what is finished is ephemeral. The painting "Four Seasons" replaces "that sombre style . . . which the Spaniards left behind them here" (*IP*, 20) with a "fairy arrangement" (*IP*, 22) which

[6] We can see this picture in Ingersoll-Smouse's book, Fig. 552: *Portrait de la Soeur de Pater*, p. 195. Marie-Marguerite is certainly not beautiful. On the same page we find a self-portrait of Jean-Baptiste himself. Perhaps the *donnée* for this story was not the visit to the Dulwich Gallery but an earlier visit which Pater had made to the municipal museum of Valenciennes. There he had seen this portrait of Marie-Marguerite that Watteau had begun (so Pater claims) and Jean-Baptiste had finished. Pater turns this picture into a symbol of the relation in which these three stand to each other.

lasts, like delicate music, only momentarily. When Marie-Marguerite first sees Watteau's picture, she thinks it "a pity to incorporate
so much of his work, of himself, with objects of use, which must
perish by use, or disappear, like our own old furniture, with mere
changes of fashion" (*IP*, 23). A few years later she writes of his
art in general and the "Four Seasons" and her portrait in particular:

Alas! it is already apparent that the result also loses something of
longevity, of durability—the colours fading or changing, from the
first, somewhat rapidly, as Jean-Baptiste notes. 'Tis true, a mere trifle
alters or produces the expression. But then, on the other hand, in
pictures the whole effect of which lies in a kind of harmony, the
treachery of a single colour must needs involve the failure of the
whole to outlast the fleeting grace of those social conjunctions it is
meant to perpetuate. This is what has happened, in part, to that portrait on the easel. (*IP*, 36)

The world of the summer Dionysus simply cannot endow Watteau's art with that Apollonian permanence above and beyond the
distintegration which erodes even the most beautiful objects of sensuous nature.

Marie-Marguerite, like Watteau, is a sensitive soul who feels
trapped in her environment. The day after young Watteau returns
from his first visit home to seek again the "freedom" of Parisian
life, Marie-Marguerite writes in her journal:

I am just returned from early Mass. I lingered long after the office
was ended, watching, pondering how in the world one could help
a small bird which had flown into the church but could find no way
out again. I suspect it will remain there, fluttering round and round
distractedly, far up under the arched roof, till it dies exhausted. I
seem to have heard of a writer who likened man's life to a bird passing
just once only, on some winter night, from window to window, across
a cheerfully-lighted hall. The bird, taken captive by the ill-luck of
a moment, re-tracing its issueless circle till it expires within the close
vaulting of that great stone church:—human life may be like that
bird too! (*IP*, 14–15)

The writer of whom she "seems to have heard" is, of course, the
Venerable Bede, in whose *Ecclesiastical History* that famous passage occurs which she recalls.[7] But the problem facing the worthy

[7] *Historia Ecclesiastica*, ed. Alfred Holder (Tubingen, 1882), Bk. II, Chap.
XIII, p. 90. A translation might run: "Another of the king's chief men, ap-
proving of the wise words and exhortations, added thereafter: 'The present
life of man upon earth, O king, seems to me, in comparison with that time

thane and his king some thirteen centuries ago was what came before and after life, not life itself. For Marie-Marguerite, however, sheer existence presents the problem. Some years later, in 1714, she writes: "With myself, how to get through time becomes the question,—unavoidably; though it strikes me as a thing unspeakably sad in a life so short as ours" (*IP*, 25). Somehow, in the restrictive, death-like world of the subjective, that shortness is all too long, and her plight is like that of a bird trapped in the stone church, an image which recalls not only the stone home of Watteau's childhood, but also the old house of Florian Deleal which, like the church, became a trap for the bird-soul.

Marie-Marguerite's love for Antony provides her what success she has in furnishing her time, but hers remains an unfulfilled love, for Antony is to her, and to everyone else, "distant and preoccupied" (*IP*, 20). As a substitute, she participates vicariously in his career. It was she who arranged, without Antony's knowing it, for his departure to Paris (a move she later came to rue), and it was she who planned to finance secretly his much desired Italian trip. She tells us that hers is "a tame, unambitious soul" (*IP*, 8) and accordingly she will "follow his fortunes (of which I for one feel quite sure) at a distance" (*IP*, 9). But after launching him on his career, she realizes that following him even "at a distance" will be demanding: "Certainly, great heights of achievement would seem to lie before him; access to regions whither one may find it increasingly hard to follow him even in imagination, and figure to one's self after what manner his life moves therein" (*IP*, 15). So it is that Watteau, from time to time, descends meteor-like upon Valenciennes while Marie-Marguerite continues to follow his career through her younger brother, Jean-Baptiste, who goes almost as her spy, she hopes, to study in Paris under the tuition of his great idol, Watteau. "I have made him promise to write often to us," she notes in her journal, and adds: "With how small a part of my whole life shall I be really living at Valenciennes!" (*IP*, 18).

---

which is unknown to us, like to the swift flight of a sparrow through the hall where you sit at supper in winter, with your chiefs and men, while the fire blazes, and the hall is warmed, but outside the wintry storms of rain or snow are raging. The sparrow, flying in at one door and immediately out at another, while he is within, is safe from the wintry tempest; but after a short space of fair weather, he immediately vanishes out of your sight, passing from winter into winter again. So this life of man appears for a little while, but of what is to follow or what went before we know nothing at all. If, therefore, this new doctrine tells us something more certain, it seems justly to deserve to be followed.' "

As his death approaches, Watteau returns full circle to the world of his youth. His Parisian friends "have become to him nothing less than insupportable" (*IP*, 42), and he summons Jean-Baptiste to be with him in his last days. Watteau's turn to Jean-Baptiste represents his final acceptance of his native Valenciennes heritage. It is this "new interest in an old friend" (*IP*, 43), together with sheer exhaustion, that leads Watteau, Marie-Marguerite says, to "tranquility at last, a tranquility in which he is much occupied with matters of religion. Ah! it was ever so with me" (*IP*, 43). But to underline the fact that Antony's whole life prior to his dying had been without this final achievement of tranquility, she adds: "And one *lives* also most reasonably so.—With women, at least, it is thus, quite certainly." Resting at the estate of the Abbé Haranger, Watteau spends his last days fashioning a crucifix for him and dies a Christian, having received Communion.

It is evident that at first Marie-Marguerite had hoped to marry Watteau but that in the end she learned resignation instead. In a poignant passage—it almost seems Pater himself is speaking—she writes that "there are good things, attractive things, in life, meant for one and not for another—not meant perhaps for me; as there are pretty clothes which are not suitable for every one" (*IP*, 28). She discovers in religion a holy love which is beyond or above its secular counterpart, as Apollo is above and beyond the prettiness of the summer Dionysus. The vision that all one's days and hours are held in some divine continuity, that all the rags and shreds of time lie as burning seeds upon the divine hand—this vision gives tranquility to her restless life.

As the embodiment of religious sorrow, Marie-Marguerite is to be associated with Demeter herself. Like the mother goddess in search of Persephone, she attempts to follow Watteau "at a distance." But Watteau is beyond her reach; they are in separate worlds, each trapped in the winter prison. The fact that Watteau is intensely mobile, whereas she is more of a pure spectator—"I find a certain immobility of disposition in me, to quicken or interfere with which is like physical pain" (*IP*, 28)—is another indication of her role as mother-goddess and of Watteau's cyclic, Dionysian alternations. Indeed, even Marie-Marguerite's name suggests the *Magna Mater*, for it has the same alliterative *M*, and the significance of her being "Mary" is obvious; the Great Mother was, so Pater says, "our Lady of Sorrows, the *mater dolorosa* of the ancient world" (*GS*, 114).

Only by suffering the sting of death can Watteau awake from the mortality of that wintry life-in-death to become one with

Marie-Marguerite in a joyous and creative immortality. Here at the end one finds the same relation between Marie-Marguerite and Watteau as existed between Cecilia and Marius. In both instances the same masculine, priestly dedication and feminine chastity and religious tranquility are disclosed, and as in *Marius*, the union or marriage of priest and *Magna Mater* is expressed in terms of a religious love. The crucifix which Watteau fashions has a three-fold significance. First, it represents his discovery of that visible church which he joins by taking Communion, a larger, yet concrete, order in which his own limited self can find freedom. Second, the crucifix represents an art form in every way superior to the rococo triviality of Paris. It is large enough to encompass the soul and its dreams of a world of immortal love; in it we do not see the forms of sense struggling vainly to contain in the narrow sensuousness of the present moment some unmanageable vision. Finally, the crucifix represents Watteau's own role as year-daimon, for he quite literally sacrificed his life to his ideal world, his death a visible manifestation of his love. The last sentence of Marie-Marguerite's journal expresses her deepest insight into Watteau's character: "He was," she says, "always a seeker after something in the world that is there in no satisfying measure, or not at all" (*IP*, 44). But Watteau's victory lay precisely in this world, for in the hour of his death he gave visible expression to that ideal religion, art, and love for which he had striven all his life.

"DENYS L'AUXERROIS" (1886)

In the thirteenth century, while building the great cathedral of Saint Etienne at Auxerrois, the masons unearthed "a finely-sculptured Greek coffin of stone, which had been made to serve for some later Roman funeral. . . . Within the coffin lay an object of a fresh and brilliant clearness among the ashes of the dead—a flask of lively green glass, like a great emerald" (*IP*, 56). The contrast between the flask and the ashes in the coffin is obvious: the ashes are dead; the flask, Phoenix-like, glows with new life— "and whether or not the opening of the buried vessel had anything to do with it, from that time a sort of golden age seemed indeed to be reigning there for a while, and the triumphant completion of the great church was contemporary with a series of remarkable wine seasons" (*IP*, 57). The medieval craftsman, with his heavy-handed "seriousness of conception lacking in the old Greek" (*IP*, 56), suddenly reached a level of art to which he had aspired but which he had never before realized, coming "nearer than the art of that age was used to do to the expression of life; with a feeling for reality, in no ignoble form, caught, it might seem, from the ardent and full-veined existence then current in these actual streets and houses" (*IP*, 55). This rebirth of the Golden Age centered around the person of Denys, for the lad was in reality, though he was quite unaware of it, the old wine-god Dionysus, whose appearance was heralded by the discovery of the flask within the tomb.

Eleven years before writing this story, Pater had quoted, in a review of Symonds' *Renaissance in Italy*, a passage from that book which told how in the fifteenth century some workmen "had discovered a Roman sarcophagus while digging on the Appian Way, . . . and inside the coffin lay the body of a most beautiful girl of fifteen years, preserved by precious unguents from corruption and the injury of time." The story, said Symonds, is a sort of "parable of the ecstatic devotion which prompted the men of that age to discover a form of unimaginable beauty in the tomb of the classic world" (*UE*, 8–9). Pater is drawing on Symonds' passage here, although he fuses it with Heinrich Heine's theme of the gods in exile, the story of Denys being "a quaint legend," Pater says, of the "return of a golden or poetically-gilded age (a denizen of old Greece itself actually finding his way back again among men)" (*IP*, 47). Naturally, then, the similarities between the myth of Dionysus and Pater's parable of the classical revival are numerous; in fact, almost everything that happens to Denys is dictated by the events in the Dionysus legend.[8] Further, almost every event in Denys' life had its counterpart in real-life Auxerre; Pater investigated his background as thoroughly as did any writer of historical fiction of his day.[9] Despite Pater's obvious virtuosity, however, "Denys L'Auxerrois" would still be far from artistically satisfying if the events which Pater narrates did not do more than combine the traditional legend and the historical facts, if they did not offer insight into Pater's own unique world-view, his myth of art. In this portrait Pater dramatizes the idea of "renaissance"

---

[8] Numerous parallels of this sort have been pointed out by Harrison, *PMLA*, XXXIX, 655–86. Mr. Harrison, however, contents himself with pointing to such parallels and fails to demonstrate their meaning and relevance.

[9] Friedrich Staub, in *Das Imaginäre Porträt Walter Paters* (Zurich, 1926), has listed several events in Auxerre which Pater utilized in the portrait. While none of Pater's portraits has ever received treatment in depth and few have received any significant treatment at all, "Denys L'Auxerrois" has probably attracted more attention than any other short story by Pater, and one can say that Staub's few pages are the most intelligent. But Staub, too, though to a lesser degree than Harrison, often fails to point out the *relevance* of the events which the historical facts parallel.

in a series of imagistic triads which embody the summer-winter cycle of Dionysus and its Apollonian synthesis. In effect, this pattern gives the story its structure as well as its meaning.

"Denys L'Auxerrois" has sometimes been criticized by readers for its lengthy introduction by the narrator, whose tone is that of a cultivated English gentleman expanding the perfunctory remarks of his guide book as he tours leisurely through the summer countryside of France. Undoubtedly, such criticism would be valid if the descriptive material were not organically related to the story that follows. As a matter of fact, the three towns of Troyes, Sens, and Auxerre, described in the introduction, are made to serve metaphorically as Pater translates the mythic pattern behind the story into actual geographical localities. Troyes, says our cultivated traveler, is a town of gay and warm restlessness set off to best advantage by "the rich, almost coarse, summer colouring of the Champagne country" (*IP*, 48). It is the city of the summer Dionysus, and it contrasts with Sens much as, in *Marius*, Pisa contrasts with White-nights. Sens belongs to the winter Dionysus; it is "a place of far graver aspect. . . . Here all is cool and composed, with an almost English austerity" (*IP*, 50). The melancholy of its "cleanly quiet" (*IP*, 50) reflects a northern temperament, just as the gaiety and warmth of Troyes reflect the southern character. Auxerre is the "perfect type of that happy mean between northern earnestness and the luxury of the south, for which we prize midland France" (*IP*, 51). Auxerre, says our English traveler, "is perhaps the most complete realisation to be found by the actual wanderer" of the town "in which the products of successive ages, not without lively touches of the present, are blended together harmoniously, with a beauty *specific*—a beauty cisalpine [on the Roman side, southern] and northern" (*IP*, 48).

At this point our English tourist lays aside his Baedeker and creates for us a tale far beyond the imaginative capabilities of the ordinary Victorian gentleman-traveler. His story turns on the familiar pattern of the sense-spirit antithesis, Auxerre being the synthesis of a *Streben* between the summer sensuousness of Troyes and the winter spirituality of Sens. This triadic image of the towns serves only to introduce us to the greater triad embodied in the figure of Denys. Denys, like the god Dionysus, has a "*Doppelgänger*" (*GS*, 44), for Denys is a two-sided figure who is closely linked with the natural cycle of the seasons, the embodiment both of summer vitality and of winter death. In the portrait Pater has divided Denys' life into three parts presented in three separate years. In the first year he is the summer Dionysus; in the second year he is the winter Dionysus; in the third year he is not really Dionysus at all—he is Dionysus transposed into timeless, Apollonian terms.

But before we can define the Apollonian qualities of Denys, we must examine the career of the lad in his first two years. Denys is the illegitimate eighteen-year-old son of the Count of Auxerre, and like the English poet in Pater's second portrait, he is born after the manner of Dionysus himself—from the union "of a god with a mortal woman," the mother dying "in childbirth, and ignorant of the glory of her son" (*GS*, 44). Denys is seen "for the first time" (*IP*, 58) in public at the cathedral ball-playing on Easter Day. His appearance at his stall in town occurs at about this time also, for Pater tells us that he first brought the produce from his cliff-side cottage garden to market when he was "grown to manhood" (*IP*, 59). That Easter should be the date of the general appearance of the old wine-god Dionysus hardly needs comment. Indeed, throughout the story Denys is a type of Christ-Dionysus. With the appearance of the lad there is simultaneously a *renouveau* of all life and activity which he touches. We are told that "the sight of him made old people feel young again" (*IP*, 60), and Denys' influence at the ball game in the cathedral dramatically bears this out.[10] Politically, too, a "new spirit was abroad everywhere" (*IP*, 61), seen particularly in "the movement then on foot at Auxerre, as in other French towns, for the liberation of the *commune* from its old feudal superiors" (*IP*, 60–61). There were also processions and bacchanalian revels "with swarming troops of dishevelled women and youths with red-stained limbs and faces, carrying their lighted torches over the vine-clad hills, or rushing down the streets, to the horror of timid watchers, towards the cool spaces by the river" (*IP*, 61). A pagan morality play, centering around Dionysus, "was presented, amid an intolerable noise of every kind of pipe-music, with Denys in the chief part, upon a gaily-painted chariot, in soft silken raiment, and, for a headdress, a strange elephant-scalp with gilded tusks" (*IP*, 63–64). Even the Christmas-New Year's *festum stultorum*, the most obvious remnant of pagan Rome in the church calendar,[11] was undertaken with

---

[10] See *Ibid.*, pp. 81–82. And E. K. Chambers in *The Medieval Stage* (Oxford, 1903) also has a lengthy note on this custom of ball-playing—a custom not restricted to Auxerre. Chambers tells us that "often the ball play was outside the church, but the canons of Evreux on their return from the *procession noire* of May 1, played '*ad quillas super voltas ecclesiae*'; and the Easter *pilota* of Auxerre which lasted to 1538, took place in the nave before vespers." I, 128–29, n. 4.

[11] Staub, *Imaginäre Porträt*, pp. 82–83; see also Chambers, *Medieval Stage*, I, 325, 329–30.

new enthusiasm. All things are so infused with the joy of the summer Dionysus that "it seemed there would be winter no more" (*IP*, 62), and indeed, the winter of that year is not described. Pater simply tells us that Denys "had fled to the south from the first forbidding days of a hard winter which came at last" (*IP*, 65).

The second year opens with the reappearance of Denys on Easter, bringing back from the south exotic oriental "wares, exposed now for sale, to the wonder of all, at the Easter Fair" (*IP*, 65). But in this second year Denys is different. Upon his return "he ate flesh for the first time, tearing the hot, red morsels with his delicate fingers in a kind of wild greed" (*IP*, 64–65). Just as in the first year when Denys had charmed the artists who "caught what they could" (*IP*, 62) of his vitality, so now again "the artists were more delighted than ever" (*IP*, 65) with him. It was not so, however, with everyone:

Strange motiveless misdeeds had happened; and, at a loss for other causes, not the envious only would fain have traced the blame to Denys. He was making the younger world mad. Would he make himself Count of Auxerre? The lady Ariane, deserted by her former lover, had looked kindly upon him; was ready to make him son-in-law to the old count her father, old and not long for this world. . . . A kind of degeneration, of coarseness—the coarseness of satiety, and shapeless, battered-out appetite—with an almost savage taste for carnivorous diet, had come over the company. (*IP*, 66)

The darker side of the wine-god now appears. This is the moment when the visions of the expanding soul can no longer find an external outlet in sensuous nature. All is infused with the delirium of the trapped and unrelieved dreams of the winter Dionysus. "The wise monk Hermes," writes Pater, "bethought him of certain old readings in which the wine-god, whose part Denys had played so well, had his contrast, his dark or antipathetic side; was like a double creature, of two natures, difficult or impossible to harmonise" (*IP*, 66). In the *Greek Studies*, as was pointed out in Chapter I, Pater had dwelt at length on this duality in the nature of the god. In his "Study of Dionysus," for example, he speaks of

a certain darker side of the double god of nature, obscured behind the brighter episodes of Thebes and Naxos, but never quite forgotten, something corresponding to this deeper, more refined idea, really existed—the conception of Dionysus Zagreus . . . and discernible, not as a late afterthought, but as a tradition really primitive, and harmonious with the original motive of the idea of Dionysus. (*GS*, 42–43)

Later in this essay Pater says that the figure of Dionysus Zagreus, the hunter of life, concentrates "into itself all men's forebodings over the departure of the year at its richest, and the death of all sweet things in the long-continued cold, when the sick and the old and little children, gazing out morning after morning on the dun sky, can hardly believe in the return any more of a bright day" (*GS*, 47).

So the second winter comes to Auxerre: "Those fat years were over. It was a time of scarcity. . . . And then, one night, the night which seemed literally to have swallowed up the shortest day of the year, a plot was contrived by certain persons to take Denys as he went and kill him privately for a sorcerer" (*IP*, 67–68). But the attempted murder is mysteriously transformed into its opposite—a feast in his honor. The reason, as we can learn in the "Study of Dionysus," is that the winter solstice was the traditional date for the propitiation of the god and the beginning of his return:

> Yearly, about the time of the shortest day, just as the light begins
> to increase, and while hope is still tremulously strung, the priestesses
> of Dionysus were wont to assemble with many lights at his shrine,
> and there, with songs and dances, awoke the new-born child after
> his wintry sleep, waving in a sacred cradle, like the great basket
> used for winnowing corn, a symbolical image, or perhaps a real infant.
> (*GS*, 43–44)

A critical point has now been reached in the life of the people of Auxerre. It is the point at which death begins to yield to life.

The third year opens with a ghastly prelude to resurrection— exhumation:

> At last the clergy bethought themselves of a remedy for this evil
> time. The body of one of the patron saints had lain neglected some-
> where under the flagstones of the sanctuary. This must be piously
> exhumed, and provided with a shrine worthy of it. The goldsmiths,
> the jewellers and lapidaries, set diligently to work, and no long time
> after, the shrine, like a little cathedral with portals and tower complete,
> stood ready, its chiselled gold framing panels of rock crystal, on the
> great altar. (*IP*, 68)

Because the winter Dionysus "is hollow and devouring, an eater of man's flesh—*sarcophagus*" (*GS*, 44), we have a ritual in which the macabre spectacle of death is invoked for the purpose of the renewal of life. Only when the grave is made to yield up its contents can the hoped-for dawn of new life replace the darkness of death. The cathedral-like cradle stands ready for the body of the saint, shrunken to the size of the Dionysian infant:

> Many bishops arrived, with King Lewis the Saint himself accompanied
> by his mother, to assist at the search for and disinterment of the
> sacred relics. In their presence, the Bishop of Auxerre, with vestments
> of deep red in honor of the relics, blessed the new shrine, according
> to the office *De benedictione capsarum pro reliquiis*. The pavement
> of the choir, removed amid a surging sea of lugubrious chants, all
> persons fasting, discovered as if it had been a battlefield of mouldering
> human remains. Their odour rose plainly above the plentiful clouds
> of incense, such as was used in the king's private chapel. The search
> for the Saint himself continued in vain all day and far into the night.
> At last from a little narrow chest, into which the remains had been
> almost crushed together, the bishop's red-gloved hands drew the dwin-
> dled body, shrunken inconceivably, but still with every feature of
> the face traceable in a sudden oblique ray of ghastly dawn. (*IP*, 68–69)[12]

This gruesome spectacle has an almost traumatic effect on the de-ranged lad: "that shocking sight . . . seemed indeed to have cured the madness of Denys, but certainly did not restore his gaiety. He was left a subdued, silent, melancholy creature" (*IP*, 69). Denys has now reached the third stage of his development: first gay, then mad, and now subdued, silent, melancholy. He is like the town of Auxerre itself, "its physiognomy is not quite happy—attractive in part for its melancholy" (*IP*, 51).

For the Greeks, Dionysus was a seasonal god whose nature changed from gaiety to madness and then back to gaiety. In the story of Denys we never go beyond the certain knowledge that life is returning. During the third year, time stops at the instant of renewal, "while hope is still tremulously strung." We are conscious, however, that where there had been only the flux of summer yielding to winter and winter yielding to summer, there is now a reconciliation of these opposites, and the natural order seems about to give birth to a summertime which is more than merely physical. In this third period Denys abandons vine-dressing and turns his whole effort toward a single great project—building the first organ. His greatest artistic creativity coincides with this third period, for Denys is no longer merely the primitive seasonal Dionysus; he is now also the priest of Apollo, the symbol of cultural rebirth.

Pater twice invokes the three-stage development in Denys' artistic career. His influence may be traced, says Pater,

[12] "*Wiederum taucht Historisches auf*," writes Staub, *Imaginäre Porträt*, p. 83.

in three successive phases or fashions. . . . There was first wild gaiety, exuberant in a wreathing of life-like imageries, from which nothing really present in nature was excluded. That, as the soul of Denys darkened, had passed into obscure regions of the satiric, the grotesque and coarse. But from this time there was manifest, with no loss of power or effect, a well-assured seriousness. . . . It was as if the gay old pagan world had been *blessed* in some way; with effects to be seen most clearly in the rich miniature work of the manuscripts of the capitular library,—a marvellous Ovid especially, upon the pages of which those old loves and sorrows seemed to come to life again in medieval costume, as Denys, in cowl now and with tonsured head, leaned over the painter, and led his work, by a kind of visible sympathy, often unspoken, rather than by any formal comment. (*IP*, 70–71)

This triad is reflected also in Denys' career as a musician. "There was," Pater notes,

a desire abroad to attain the instruments of a freer and more various sacred music than had been in use hitherto—a music that might express the whole compass of souls now grown to manhood. . . . Here, too, there had been evident those three fashions or "modes":—first, the simple and pastoral, the homely note of the pipe, like the piping of the wind itself from off the distant fields; then, the wild, savage din, that had cost so much to quiet people, and driven excitable people mad. Now he would compose all this to sweeter purposes; and the building of the first organ became like the book of his life: it expanded to the full compass of his nature, in its sorrow and delight. (*IP*, 71–72)

This organ, to the building of which the whole of the third year is devoted, is the great symbol of Apollonian order in chaotic flux: "It was the triumph of all the various modes of the power of the pipe, tamed, ruled, united" (*IP*, 72). And the organ is given its first trial on "a notable public occasion" that following winter at the third year's end.

As Pater tells it:

The old count of Chastellux was lately dead, and the heir had announced his coming, according to custom, to claim his ecclesiastical privilege. There had been long feud between the houses of Chastellux and Auxerre; but on this happy occasion an offer of peace came with a proposal for the hand of the Lady Ariane. (*IP*, 75)[13]

At the marriage, a transformation of hate into love, the organ, a symbol of the diverse united, is played. In Greek myth—as Pater

[13] And again Staub supplies us with an historical note: *Ibid.* While Pater never insists, he yet hints that Denys may be the half brother of Ariane and tells us that he very nearly became her husband. Denys is, then, truly involved with the marriage and becomes, almost, assimilated into the persons of both the bride and bridegroom.

tells us in his "Study of Dionysus" (*GS*, 22)—Ariadne is a seasonal goddess similar in nature to Demeter. The marriage exemplifies the continuity of life, of "rebirth" itself, and as is usual in the *Magna Mater* myth, the fructifying of nature by the year-daimon is conceived after the manner of sacramental communion. The occurrence at the civic celebration which followed is, on the surface only, in contrast to the gaiety and joy of the religious ceremony:

The festival was to end at nightfall with a somewhat rude popular pageant, in which the person of Winter would be hunted blindfold through the streets. It was the sequel to that earlier stage-play of the *Return from the East* in which Denys had been the central figure. The old forgotten player saw his part before him, and, as if mechanically, fell again into the chief place, monk's dress and all. (*IP*, 75–76)

His scratched lip bleeds, the blood drives the people to a frenzy, and the mob tears his flesh to shreds, the men sticking pieces of it into their caps.

The mob in its fury is the incarnation of the winter Dionysus, the hunter of life, fully as much as is Denys, who plays the part. However, in his discussion of the frenzied disciples of the winter god in "The Bacchanals of Euripides," Pater had pointed out that with respect to the figure of Dionysus

a certain transference, or substitution must be made—much of the horror and sorrow . . . of the whole tragic situation, must be transferred to him, if we wish to realise in the older, profounder, and more complete sense of his nature, that mystical being of Greek tradition to whom all these experiences—his madness, the chase, his imprisonment and death, his peace again—really belong. . . . Dionysus *Omophagus*—the eater of raw flesh, must be added to the golden image of Dionysus *Meilichius*—the honey-sweet, . . . if we are to catch, in its fulness, that deep undercurrent of horror which runs below, all through this masque of spring, and realise the spectacle of that wild chase, in which Dionysus is ultimately both the hunter and the spoil. (*GS*, 78–79)

So, too, in the mad frenzy of the mob we have the spectacle of death destroying itself, transforming itself into its opposite. In the suffering victim who, for the sake of purgation, takes upon himself the guilt of his destroyer, the eucharistic overtones are unmistakably present. In his "Study of Dionysus," Pater had written that

the tradition of human sacrifice lingered on in Greece, in connexion with Dionysus, as a thing of actual detail, and not remote, so that Dionysius of Halicarnassus counts it among the horrors of Greek religion. That the sacred women of Dionysus ate, in mystical ceremony, raw flesh, and drank blood, is a fact often mentioned, and commemorates, as it seems, the actual sacrifice of a fair boy deliberately torn to pieces, fading at last into a symbolical offering. (*GS*, 47–48)

Denys becomes the god whose flesh is eaten, whose blood is drunk; and the ghastly end of this "fair boy" stands as the guarantee of the renewal of life. Indeed, this was a sacrificial role which Denys very nearly filled some time previously when the citizens of Auxerre built a bridge across the Yonne. They almost chose Denys as successor to the little child who had been placed alive at the core of the old structure in the belief that, "by way of vicarious substitution, its death would secure the safety of all who should pass over" (*IP*, 73). But Denys escaped the townsmen until, several months later, in the midst of the third winter, they succeeded in their third attempt upon his life.

The portrait of Denys ends not in chaotic despair but in hope, a hope which arises from the knowledge that out of the natural cycle of the seasons, out of the ceaseless flux between life and death, there springs the perpetual summertime of Apollo himself, belonging not to the space-time world of vegetation but to the eternal world of the Logos. As a direct result of this cyclic pattern of the god who lives, dies, and is reborn, the legend of Dionysus in antiquity was able to embody

a peculiar message for a certain number of refined minds, seeking, in the later days of Greek religion, such modifications of the old legend as may minister to ethical culture, to the perfecting of the moral nature. A type of second birth, from first to last, he opens, in his series of annual changes, for minds on the look-out for it, the hope of a possible analogy, between the resurrection of nature, and something else, as yet unrealized, reserved for human souls; and the beautiful, weeping creature, vexed by the wind, suffering, torn to pieces, and rejuvenescent again at last, like a tender shoot of living green out of the hardness and stony darkness of the earth, becomes an emblem or ideal of chastening and purification, and of final victory through suffering. (*GS*, 49–50)

Denys symbolizes this "type of second birth," and the "shoot of living green" which springs from the "stony darkness of the earth" reminds us of the green flask in the ashes of the stone coffin. He is like the Christ of which Isaiah prophesied, a root out of dry ground, like the vine itself, springing "out of the bitter salts of a smitten, volcanic soil, . . . a wonder of freshness, drawing its everlasting green and typical coolness out of the midst of the ashes"

(GS, 26). And all of this, of course, becomes an emblem not of mere seasonal alternation but of the renewal of the human soul and the transcendent order which it reflects.

"Almost every people," Pater wrote at the opening of the portrait of Denys, "has its legend of a 'golden age' and of its return. And yet," he says,

since we are no longer children, we might well question the advantage
of the return to us of a condition of life in which, by the nature
of the case, the values of things would, so to speak, lie wholly on
their surfaces, unless we could regain also the childish consciousness,
or rather unconsciousness, in ourselves, to take all that adroitly and
with the appropriate lightness of heart. (*IP*, 47)

The idea of the impossibility of a return to the Golden Age is the same here as it was in the Watteau portrait or in *Marius* or "The Child in the House." Man cannot go back to his racial childhood, for cultural maturity has destroyed his primitive unconsciousness. He must go forward, and individuals such as Denys are the ones who point the way by exhibiting in their lives the profounder significance underlying the figure of Dionysus, by showing us that the old wine-god may also be the herald of Apollo. Out of the perpetual seasonal cycle, out of the mounded ashes of the youth of mankind, arose a nobler ideal of immortality through death. Surely this is why Pater writes that the representation of Dionysus in ancient sculpture "may seem to have waited for the hand of Michelangelo before it attained complete realisation" (*GS*, 19).

"SEBASTIAN VAN STORCK" (1886)

Even as a school boy, Sebastian van Storck distinguished himself from others by a strong speculative mentality and by a corresponding tendency to make the day-by-day conduct of his life conform to his rigorously deduced conclusions. As his thought matured, Sebastian took for his premise the sole reality of the One and threw in his lot with that long and illustrious line of philosophical idealists which began in antiquity with Parmenides. "It was a tradition," Sebastian realized,

a constant tradition—that daring thought of his; an echo, or haunting
recurrent voice of the human soul itself, and as such sealed with
natural truth, which certain minds would not fail to heed; discerning
also, if they were really loyal to themselves, its practical conclusion.
—The one alone is: and all things beside are but its passing affections,
which have no necessary or proper right to be. (*IP*, 107)

In the spirit of this single premise Sebastian molded his life so that it resembled nothing so much as the cold, impassive nature of the Emperor Aurelius in *Marius*. Obviously, Sebastian's rejection of the life around him is based on a logic too rigorously applied, a failing which extends even to his method of composition. What dull reading that Spinozistic journal of his is, with its ideas set down by "a rigid intellectual gymnastic, which was like the making of Euclid" (*IP*, 108). But, of course, Sebastian's foibles as a writer are small compared with his failure as a thinker.

There is a passage in Pater's *Plato and Platonism* which not only admirably introduces us to the illustrious antecedents of Sebastian's philosophy but also lets us see just what sort of a judgment Pater would pass upon Sebastian were he called upon to do so. Pater derisively writes here that as a result of Parmenides' idealism, with its overwhelming interest in the One,

the European mind . . . will never be quite sane again. It has been put on a quest (vain quest it may prove to be) after a kind of knowledge perhaps not properly attainable. Hereafter, in every age, some will be found to start afresh quixotically, through what wastes of words! in search of that true Substance, the One, the Absolute, which to the majority of acute people is after all but zero, and a mere algebraic symbol for nothingness. . . . It is assumed, in the words of Plato, that to be colourless, formless, impalpable is the note of the superior grade of knowledge and existence, evanescing steadily, as one ascends towards that perfect (perhaps not quite attainable) condition of either, which in truth can only be attained by the supression of all rule and outline of one's own actual experience and thought. (*PP*, 40–41)[14]

This doctrine of the One extended from Elea, through the neo-Platonists and the Middle Ages, to the seventeenth-century Nether-

[14] Another description applicable to Sebastian is found in *PP*, pp. 37–38. Further, Pater's chapter on "Coleridge" in *Ap.* is also a portrait of a Sebastian-like personality. Coleridge's effort to " 'apprehend the absolute' " is, says Pater, "an effort of sickly thought, that saddened his mind, and limited the operation of his unique poetic gift" (*Ap*, pp. 68–69). And later in the essay Pater says of Coleridge that there was "some tendency to disease in the physical temperament, something of a morbid want of balance in those parts where the physical and intellectual elements mix most closely together" (*Ap*, p. 83). Giordano Bruno's pantheism seems to be of a more satisfactory kind than Parmenides' or Coleridge's or Sebastian's: "To unite oneself to the infinite by largeness and lucidity of intellect, to enter, by that admirable faculty, into eternal life—this was the true vocation of the spouse, of the rightly amorous soul" (*GdL*, p. 147). With Sebastian, the "eternal life" became an "eternal death," for his mysticism excluded the phenomenal world as Bruno's did not. Bruno's mysticism seems to be of the kind described in *IP*, p. 110. But even Bruno may fall short, for since the Bruno chapter follows the St. Bartholomew's Day Massacre chapter, Pater appears to raise the question as to whether his mysticism is really capable of acknowledging the existence of evil.

lands. Here it found expression in the philosophy of Sebastian's hero, "in the hard and ambitious intellectualism of Spinoza; a doctrine of pure repellent substance—substance 'in vacuo,' to be lost in which, however, would be the proper consummation of the transitory individual life. Spinoza's own absolutely colourless existence was a practical comment upon it" (*PP*, 41).

Pater's philosophy, as it is expressed, for example, in his Conclusion to *The Renaissance*, was meant to serve as a corrective to this tradition of "the literal negation of self, by a kind of moral suicide" (*PP*, 41). If, perhaps, the Conclusion "might possibly mislead some of those young men into whose hands it might fall" (R, 233), then there are others, one would certainly suppose, for whom it "might possibly" prove a benefit. And surely Sebastian van Storck would have been one such. Sebastian is Pater's example of the individual who has almost destroyed his life by this not-quite-sane philosophy of Parmenides. And it is of primary importance that Sebastian, unlike Pater's other heroes, is neither an artist nor, it is quite evident, a truly creative personality. This is the direct result of that One-sided, sterile philosophy which so directly shaped his manner of life.

In sharp contrast to Sebastian's self-annihilating philosophy of the impalpable is the tremendously active world of the Dutch people. After the Congress of Munster, which ended the Eighty Years' War and accorded to the Dutch full independence, the Netherlands entered upon a mercantile expansion which brought it to the period of greatest prosperity and power it had ever known. Sebastian's environment, typified by his father, was busy with this purposeful, active life:

"My Son!" said his father, "be stimulated to action!" . . . The heroism by which the national wellbeing had been achieved was still of recent memory—the air full of its reverberation, and great movement. There was a tradition to be maintained; the sword by no means resting in its sheath. The age was still fitted to evoke a generous ambition; and this son, from whose natural gifts there was so much to hope for, might play his part, at least as a diplomatist, if the present quiet continued. (*IP*, 95; 85)

Life was successful self-assertion against the Spaniards in the Eighty Years' War, against the sea in a war without beginning or end, and against hostile religious factions in a conflict just then beginning.

Concomitant with this material prosperity came the culmination of an artistic development which reflected this life in unexcelled painting.[15] In the Netherlands of the seventeenth century, art was a way of life. "The Dutch," Pater tells us, "had just begun to see what a picture their country was—its canals, and *boompjis*, and endless, broadly-lighted meadows, and thousands of miles of quaint water-side: and their painters, the first true masters of landscape for its own sake, were further informing them in the matter" (*IP*, 87). Sebastian has no choice but to be an unwilling witness to this love of art. At one of Burgomaster van Storck's arts-and-letters gatherings, the names of the guests sound as if they had been lifted straight from the catalogue of the Rijksmuseum (which is probably not far from the fact): Willem van Aelst, Gerard Dow, Thomas and Peter de Keyser, Albert Cuyp, Peter de Hooch, Willem van de Velde, and the three Hondecoeters—Giles, Gybrecht, and Melchior. One and all, they reflect the warm, busy life of Holland, whether they paint exotic flower arrangements (van Aelst) or sunshine summer scenes (Cuyp) or everyday household life (de Hooch) or seascapes (van de Velde) or domestic birds and wild game (the Hondecoeters, who arrived at the Burgomaster's party early in order to watch the poultry go to roost!). The van Storck's home was the perfect setting for the gathering since "the family mansion of the Storcks—a house, the front of which still survives in one of those patient architectural pieces by Jan van der Heyde—was, in its minute and busy well-being, like an epitome of Holland itself with all the good-fortune of its 'thriving genius' reflected, quite spontaneously, in the national taste" (*IP*, 86).

In this preoccupation with material well-being, which was the essence of Dutch art and life, Sebastian's personality is very much out of place:

The contrast was a strange one between the careful, the almost petty fineness of his personal surrounding—all the elegant conventionalities of life, in that rising Dutch family—and the mortal coldness of a temperament, the intellectual tendencies of which seemed to necessitate straight-forward flight from all that was positive. He seemed, if one

---

[15] Because the Dutch were primarily Protestant, such traditional areas as religion, myth, and history were generally ignored. "Dutch painting . . . was and could be only the portrait of Holland, its exterior image, faithful, exact, complete, with no embellishments. Portraits of men and places, citizen habits, squares, streets, countryplaces, the sea and the sky—such was to be . . . the programme followed by the Dutch school, and such it was from its first day to the day of its decline." Eugène Fromentin, *The Old Masters of Belgium and Holland* (*Les Maîtres d'autrefois* [Paris, 1876]) trans. M. Robbins (New York, 1963), p. 131. Recent work in art history has rather radically reversed this judgment, Dutch still life painting, for example, being apparently full of symbolism. Yet Fromentin's estimate probably would have been Pater's own, and this is what is important to us.

may say so, in love with death; preferring winter to summer; finding only a tranquillising influence in the thought of the earth beneath our feet cooling down for ever from its old cosmic heat; watching pleasurably how their colours fled out of things, and the long sand-bank in the sea, which had been the rampart of a town, was washed down in its turn. (*IP*, 98–99)

The abstract Absolute to which Sebastian had pledged himself is not the warm sunshine of Apollo; rather, it recalls Marie-Marguerite's "glacial point in the motionless sky." For Sebastian

that one abstract being was as the pallid Arctic sun, disclosing itself over the dead level of a glacial, a barren and absolutely lonely sea. The lively purpose of life had been frozen out of it. What he must admire, and love if he could, was "equilibrium," the void, the *tabula rasa*, into which, through all those apparent energies of man and nature, that in truth are but forces of disintegration, the world was really settling. (*IP*, 108)

Just as the Dutch *deftige gezelligheid* reflects the warm, busy world of the summer Dionysus, so Sebastian himself embodies the somber winter god. Not surprisingly, the time of year that Sebastian prefers is winter, with "its expression of a perfect impassivity, or at least of a perfect repose" (*IP*, 81).

This world of the *tabula rasa* is symbolized for Sebastian by the sea, the eternal washing of which reduces all the signs of life to a dead level. The country that Pliny despised "as scarcely dry land at all" (*IP*, 92) is on this account a most congenial surrounding for Sebastian:

In his passion for *Schwindsucht*—we haven't the word—he found it pleasant to think of the resistless element which left one hardly a foot-space amidst the yielding sand; of the old beds of lost rivers, surviving now only as deeper channels in the sea; of the remains of a certain ancient town, which within men's memory had lost its few remaining inhabitants, and, with its already empty tombs, dissolved and disappeared in the flood. (*IP*, 93)

A passage in the early 1868 Conclusion adumbrates this image of the sea and defines it for us. Speaking of "that strange perpetual weaving and unweaving of ourselves," Pater says:

Such thoughts seem desolate at first; at times all the bitterness of life seems concentrated in them. They bring the image of one washed out beyond the bar in a sea at ebb, losing even his personality, as the elements of which he is composed pass into new combinations.

Struggling, as he must, to save himself, it is himself that he loses at every moment.[16]

Sebastian happily accepted this fate, for he believed it was the way to the One. But ultimately his yearning toward dissolution is only another manifestation of the excess of the romantic spirit. Instead of desiring to find the counterpart to his expanding soul in that concrete object of space and time in which for a moment the Absolute is concentrated, Sebastian prefers to watch the diffusion of all energy back into undifferentiated nothingness. The artwork in his room is indicative of his desire to pass out beyond the objective focal point of the One, for though he

refused to travel, he loved the distant—enjoyed the sense of things seen from a distance, carrying us, as on wide wings of space itself, far out of one's actual surrounding. His preference in the matter of art was, therefore, for those prospects *à vol d'oiseau*—of the caged bird on the wing at last—of which Rubens had the secret, and still more Philip de Koninck, four of whose choicest works occupied the four walls of his chamber; visionary escapes, north, south, east, and west, into a wide-open though, it must be confessed, a somewhat sullen land. (*IP*, 89)

What Sebastian fails to see is that the "caged bird" of the soul must find its freedom in some concrete objective world, not in the self-annihilation of the winter Dionysus.

"From time to time," says Pater, "the mind of Sebastian had been occupied on the subject of monastic life, its quiet, its negation. . . . But what he could not away with in the Catholic religion was its unfailing drift towards the concrete—the positive imageries of a faith, so richly beset with persons, things, historical incidents" (*IP*, 97–98). So, instead, Sebastian withdrew by a winding staircase and a long passage to a room that seemed "as if shut off from the whole talkative Dutch world. . . . A kind of empty place! Here, you felt, all had been mentally put to rights by the working-out of a long equation, which had zero is equal to zero for its result. Here one did, and perhaps felt nothing; one only thought" (*IP*, 89–90). This is, again, an image of the Dionysian prison. That it should be a sort of tower room is significant; it not only resembles the upper room where Marius had his interview with Aurelius, but it is also related to the myth of the winter Dionysus, who was "shut in a strong tower" (*GS*, 51).

Sebastian was not necessarily fated by some inevitable consequence of his personality to withdraw to the prison of the winter

[16] Pater, *Westminster Review*, XXXIV, 311.

Dionysus, for from his Catholic mother he had inherited Spanish blood, and both this Catholicism and southern temperament tended to involve him in an active life. He had, we are told, a good eye for art and was able to comment upon it acutely. Yet he despised his heritage, and one of the subtlest ways in which Pater portrays Sebastian's rejection is by showing us his refusal to be painted. In seventeenth-century Holland all things and all people were painted—except Sebastian. Only as a boy was he sufficiently indifferent to allow Isaac van Ostade to paint his portrait from a sketch made at a skating party. And even here there is a certain indirection, for the portrait itself was not made from life. Perhaps it was Sebastian's failing health or perhaps his maturing philosophy, but upon his return home from school to recover "a certain loss of robustness, something more than that cheerful indifference of early youth had passed away" (*IP*, 82), and when Thomas de Keyser saw Sebastian skating and asked permission to paint him, "the young man declined the offer; not graciously, as was thought" (*IP*, 84).

Unlike Sebastian, the other members of the van Storck family certainly have no aversion whatsoever to portraiture. Sebastian's father "had assisted at the Congress of Munster, and figures conspicuously in Terburgh's picture of that assembly" (*IP*, 85). And for one of the panoramic de Konicks which hung in his room, Sebastian heartlessly "exchanged with his mother a marvellously vivid Metsu, lately bequeathed to him, in which she herself was presented" (*IP*, 89). Even the family residence found its way into a picture by van der Heyde, and the friends who visited the house seemed only to need a heavy Baroque frame to be ready for the museum wall: "Grave ministers of religion assembled sometimes, as in the painted scene by Rembrandt, in the Burgomaster's house" (*IP*, 97). Sebastian, however, is painted only in his father's ambitious imagination: "Admiral-general of Holland, as painted by Van der Helst, with a marine background by Backhuizen:—at moments his father could fancy him so" (*IP*, 96–97). If his picture is to be recorded, it must be done so without his knowledge. Thomas de Keyser visited the home and hoped "to catch by stealth the likeness of Sebastian the younger" (*IP*, 91), and Baruch de Spinoza did likewise; Sebastian "did not know that his visitor, very ready with the pencil, had taken his likeness as they talked on the fly-leaf of his note-book" (*IP*, 97). That Spinoza does not share Sebastian's aversion undoubtedly is significant, for it shows that the master had not carried his uncongenial philosophy to abnormal extremes as had his disciple.

The climactic incident of the story, the rejection of Mademoiselle van Westrheene, is closely interwoven with Sebastian's obsessive determination not to be painted. Sebastian's rejection of her is foreshadowed by his attitude toward the family portrait: "all his singularities appeared to be summed up in his refusal to take his place in the life-sized family group (*très distingué et très soigné*, remarks a modern critic of the work) painted about this time" (*IP*, 100). If Sebastian is unwilling even to appear in the picture of his family, then most certainly he is not going to establish a family of his own; and almost immediately after this refusal we are told of the letter to Mademoiselle van Westrheene. There will be no marriage, no future generations. Just as Sebastian withdrew to his lonely tower by the sea, never to be seen alive again by his parents, so his almost-bethrothed "never appeared again in the world" (*IP*, 102). And to make the sterility complete, Sebastian slashes to fragments, just before he leaves, "the one portrait of him in existence" (*IP*, 103).

The significance of Sebastian's aversion to portraiture is obvious; he does not want to be painted, for he does not want to be caught in the web of the material world. So great was his distaste of entanglement in the world that, when he wrote to anyone, he "left his letters unsigned" (*IP*, 100). Dutch paintings, as Sebastian knew, had very little of the other-wordly quality of, for example, the "Quattrocento"; they are, rather, as Pater takes pains to point out, especially this-worldly: "Of the earth earthy—genuine red earth of the old Adam—it was an ideal very different from that which the sacred Italian painters had evoked from the life of Italy, yet, in its best types, was not without a kind of natural religiousness" (*IP*, 87–88). Sebastian prided himself on his realization that "this picturesque and sensuous world of Dutch art and Dutch reality all around that would fain have made him the prisoner of its colours, its genial warmth, its struggle for life, its selfish and crafty love, was but a transient perturbation of the one absolute mind" (*IP*, 106). For Sebastian, "the arts were a matter he could but just tolerate" (*IP*, 88).

Sebastian's state of mind was not a healthy one; it brought him only an intolerable burden of "black melancholy," aggravating his consumption, a physical counterpart to his mental state: "Is it only the result of disease? he would ask himself sometimes with a sudden suspicion of his intellectual cogency—this persuasion that myself, and all that surrounds me, are but a diminution of that which really is?—this unkindly melancholy?" (*IP*, 112) But the most telling objection to an "intellectual cogency" which he himself was beginning to suspect was one that had not yet occurred to him:

> Bent on making sacrifice of the rich existence possible for him, as
> he would readily have sacrificed that of other people, to the bare
> and formal logic of the answer to a query (never proposed at all
> to entirely healthy minds) regarding the remote conditions and ten-
> dencies of that existence, he did not reflect that if others had inquired
> as curiously as himself the world could never have come so far at
> all—that the fact of its having come so far was itself a weighty excep-
> tion to his hypothesis. (*IP*, 111)

Pater's gentle irony prepares us for a denouement in which Sebastian, finally realizing his mistake, suddenly reverses his whole logic of action. Isolated in his tower by the sea, Sebastian is suddenly plunged willy-nilly into the flux: "a sudden rising of the wind altered, as it might seem, in a few dark tempestuous hours, the entire world around him" (*IP*, 114). The wind continued to blow for a fortnight, and

> when the body of Sebastian was found, apparently not long after death,
> a child lay asleep, swaddled warmly in his heavy furs, in an upper
> room of the old tower, to which the tide was almost risen; though
> the building still stood firmly, and still with the means of life in
> plenty. And it was in the saving of this child, with a great effort,
> as certain circumstances seemed to indicate, that Sebastian had lost
> his life. (*IP*, 114)

This is undeniably the sacrifice of self for the sake of another, and though it might be argued that Sebastian did not care whether he lived or died, he certainly did not sacrifice the existence of another human being for the sake of his system. When the imperative need for action was laid upon him, he ceased inquiring so "curiously" and acted instinctively in order that the child, who is a symbol of the continuity of humanity, might live.

Despite the radical inconsistency with his previously held doctrines, Sebastian's action is one for which we are not totally unprepared. It is essentially an act of love for mankind expressed in terms of a concern for the life of a particular individual, and much has been said on this subject of love throughout the portrait. There was first of all "the cold precept of Spinoza, that great reassertor of the Parmenidean tradition: That whoso loves God truly must not expect to be loved by Him in return" (*PP*, 49; *IP*, 104). Then there is another kind, something more tangible than this loveless love: the "selfish and crafty love" (*IP*, 106) of Mademoiselle van

Westrheene's mother, who would weave a web about Sebastian in her climb to status, it being a mere convenience from the mother's point of view that the daughter "was one of the few who, in spite of his terrible coldness, really loved him for himself" (*IP*, 101). Sebastian preferred the *amor intellectualis* to this human love so often tainted with imperfection. He had, however, heard of a purer type of love—the almost sacred love of the wife of Grotius for her husband, and here, for once, "Sebastian was forcibly taken by the simplicity of a great affection" (*IP*, 96). It is through the love of his wife that Grotius effects his escape from the total isolation of his prison, an event which becomes for Sebastian a symbol of the escape that love can offer from the desolation of subjectivity. But it is not through the usual man-woman relationship of secular love that Sebastian escapes; it is through the divine love of the Dionysian priest who gives himself for the life of humanity that he finds his immortality. It is clear that Mademoiselle van Westrheene, because of Sebastian's priest-like dedication to humanity, has retired from the world to join Cecilia and Marie-Marguerite as chaste women who are associated with the sorrowing *Magna Mater* herself.

Sebastian's death cannot be held to be ironic, as some have asserted. It is no more ironic than the martyrdom of Marius. Neither can his death be regarded as a natural consequence of his rejection of the world and the love of Mademoiselle van Westrheene, the final step in a steady progress toward annihilation. His death comes, rather, as his witness to the fact that it is not some disembodied Absolute which is of supreme value, but one's fellow men, among whom at every moment, touched by the One, "some form grows perfect in hand or face" (*R*, 236). In such love Sebastian found freedom from the intolerable prison of subjectivity without having to deny either his or anyone else's individuality. He discovered in the ideal of self-sacrifice the true value of the romantic spirit, the necessary role which his individual soul played in the progress of humanity. And because Sebastian discovered his own value and that of others as well, his priest-like dedication is not sterile and the sorrow of his "intended" not without final joy. In death, hope has been born, and this new world that Sebastian discovered in his last moments is symbolized by the child found safe in the tower of the house built "amid the sands" (*IP*, 113). When the rain descended and the floods came and the winds blew and beat upon that house, it stood; for a new foundation had been provided which was not of sand, but was the rock of love.

"DUKE CARL OF ROSENMOLD" (1887)

In this portrait Pater takes us back to the time in the history of German thought which has sometimes been called *Spätrenaissance-Kultur*—the late Renaissance culture. One of the most important sources for the general idea of the story, then, is the "Winckelmann" essay in *The Renaissance*. Winckelmann, says Pater,

coming in the eighteenth century, really belongs in spirit to an earlier age. By his enthusiasm for the things of the intellect and the imagination for their own sake, by his Hellenism, his life-long struggle to attain to the Greek spirit, he is in sympathy with the humanists of a previous century. He is the last fruit of the Renaissance, and explains in a striking way its motive and tendencies. (*R*, xiv–xv)

Winckelmann and Duke Carl are kindred souls, the last fruit of the Italian Renaissance and the first fruit of a German enlightenment which did not culminate until the age of Goethe. Both are Germans of the eighteenth century who long for the spirit of antiquity in an alien environment, and both Winckelmann and Carl died tragically before the desired *Aufklärung* arrived. In the presentation of the young Duke's character, Pater has, of course, allowed himself greater imaginative latitude than in the historical portrait of Winckelmann, but his essential aim in the story as in the essay was the same: to define the spirit of the German Renaissance as it was created in the aspirations of the artistic soul.

It is in the lumber-room of the castle that Carl, "escaped from that candlelight into the broad day of the uppermost windows" (*IP*, 122–23), discovers Conrad Celtes' *Art of Versification and Song* (1486). Celtes was one of the leading German humanists of his century—poet laureate, librarian of the Imperial University, a friend of the great Albrecht Dürer, whose picture, so Pater says, formed a frontispiece for the book; and Celtes' home city of Heidelberg, with its imposing castle rising above the jumble of gables and roofs of the town below, may well have played a substantial part in creating the courtly city of the Rosenmolds.[17] Celtes' Sap-

---

[17] The most readable history of Heidelberg is Elizabeth Godfrey's *Heidelberg: Its Princes and its Palaces* (New York, 1906). Undoubtedly memories of visits to the city were still vividly present in Pater's mind, for his aunt and sisters had resided there for several summers during his undergraduate days at Queens. And if we accept Heidelberg as the home of the Rosenmold dynasty, then, when Pater speaks of the sudden surge of prosperity of the Duchy some centuries before the time of Duke Carl, we recall the history of the city under the two sons of Philip the Upright, Ludwig and Friedrich. They inherited the weakened Palatinate at a moment of disadvantageously concluded peace, and weathering the vicissitudes of restless peasants and Reformation doctrine, they strengthened the Duchy and embarked on the extensive

phic "Ode to Apollo," only the title of which is given by Pater in the portrait, reads as follows:

Phoebus, who the sweet-noted lyre constructed,
Leave fair Helicon and depart your Pindus,
And by pleasant song designated, hasten
*   To these our borders.*

You perceive how joyous the Muses gather,
Sweetly singing under a frozen heaven;
Come yourself, and with your melodious harp-strings,
*   Gaze on these wastelands.*

So must he, whom sometime a rude or rustic
Parent fostered, barbarous, all unknowing
Latium's splendors, choose you now as his teacher
*   At writing verses.*

Just as Orpheus sang to the old Pelasgians,
Orpheus, whom swift stags, beasts of savage custom,
Whom the lofty trees of the forest followed,
*   Charmed by his plectrum.*

Swift and joyous, once you forswore, and gladly,
Greece for Latium, passing the mighty ocean;
There you wished your delectable arts to broadcast,
*   Leading the Muses.*

Thus it is our prayer you may wish to visit
Our abode, as once those Italian reaches.
May wild tongue take flight, and may all of darkness
*   Come to destruction.*[18]

and often extravagant building program which saw the main design of Heidelberg Castle completed. One of the two, Frederick, friend and supporter of Emperor Charles V, married the daughter of the King of Denmark in 1535 and further added to the prosperity of the region—though this marriage was not the sole reason for the prosperity of the Duchy, as Pater seems to hint. Under the enlightened rule of Philip the Upright, Heidelberg became a great humanistic center. The names of its scholars are a veritable roll call of the choice and master spirits of the age: Johann Dalberg, Dietrich von Plenningen, Johann Reuchlin, and the great Rudolf Agricola, whose successor was Conrad Celtes.

A brief biography of Celtes can be found in Godfrey's book, pp. 163–64. There is a full study of Celtes by Lewis W. Spitz: *Conrad Celtis: The German Arch-Humanist* (Cambridge, 1957). Spitz tells us (p. 10) that "Celtis [or Celtes] was twenty-eight when, in the summer of 1487, he crossed the Alps for the first and only time. He went not just to admire the land of ancient Rome, but to bring its muses like the Imperium northward. In his 'Ode to Apollo' he expressed this thought beautifully and thereby laid down the program for the northern humanists."

[18] I use the translation which Spitz provides at the end of his first chapter of *Conrad Celtis*, p. 10. Spitz, however, does not give the Latin itself, which was printed in the usual fifteenth-century manner and was difficult to straighten out. (In my rendering I have regularized somewhat the spelling of the original

Around this ode Pater constructed his portrait of Duke Carl, for it is Carl's function as the German Apollo, the bringer of light to northern darkness, that constitutes the essential imaginative idea of the story. Indeed, Carl's whole life becomes patterned after the actual incidents found in the classical and Teutonic myths of the sun god.

The plight of Duke Carl, like that of all of Pater's heroes, is that he finds himself in a world that does not understand him, in an alien and hostile environment. The sleepy duchy of Rosenmold is a relic of the Middle Ages, stiff, dark, and dead, with only the minimum of activity—"a sleepy ceremonial, to make the hours just noticeable as they slipped away" (*IP*, 122). In the god Apollo, the young Duke catches a glimpse of a new ideal of freedom and happiness and a rebirth of the arts. Carl's vision was of

the hyperborean Apollo, sojourning, in the revolutions of time, in the sluggish north for a season, yet Apollo still, prompting art, music, poetry, and the philosophy which interprets man's life, making a sort of intercalary day amid the natural darkness; not meridian day, of course, but a soft derivative daylight, good enough for us. (*IP*, 132)

This idea was first presented to him by the ode of Celtes, and the similarity of his function to the hyperborean Apollo strikes Carl the moment he has finished reading the poem: "To bring Apollo with his lyre to Germany! It was precisely what he, Carl, desired to do—was, as he might flatter himself, actually doing" (*IP*, 124). But, says Pater,

the daylight, the Apolline aurora, which the young Duke Carl claimed to be bringing to his candle-lit people, came in the somewhat questionable form of the contemporary French ideal, in matters of art and

---

sin; for example, "*lira*" in the title was changed to "*lyra*"—thus saving a few pennies.) The meter (lesser Sapphic) is technically correct, but, of course, it sounds medieval and artificial; it should not be read like classical Latin but should be given an Italianate pronunciation. Nevertheless, like the young Duke himself, the ode is primitive but impressive. Celtes managed fairly well even if he was *Germanus barbarusque:* "Ode ad Apollinem repertorem poetices: ut ab Italis cum lyra ad Germanos veniat. Phoebe qui blandae citharae repertor/ Linque delectos Heliconque Pindum/ Et veni nostris vocitatus oris/ Carmine grato.// Cernis ut laetae properent Camenae/ Et canant dulces gelido sub aere/ Tu veni incultam fidibus canoris/ Visere terram.// Barbarus quem olim genuit vel acer/ Vel parens hirtus; laeti leporis/ Nescius: nunc sit duce te ducendus/ Pangere carmen.// Quod ferunt dulcem cecinisse Orpheum/ Quem ferae atroces agilesque cervi/ Arboresque altae celeres secutae/ Plectra moventem.// Tu celer vastas aequoris per undas/ Laetus a Graecia Latium videre/ Invehens Musas voluisti gratas/ Pandere et artes.// Sic velis nostras rogitamus oras/ Italas ceu quondam aditare terras/ Barbarus sermo fugiatque ut atr-[itat]um/ Subruat omne."

literature—French plays, French architecture, French looking-glasses—Apollo in the dandified costume of Lewis the Fourteenth. Only, confronting the essentially aged and decrepit graces of his model with his own essentially youthful temper, he invigorated what he borrowed; and with him an aspiration toward the classical ideal, so often hollow and insincere, lost all its affectation. (*IP*, 124)

Even if Pater does laugh a little at the young Duke so enthusiastically imitating the imitation, yet, oddly enough, there is something genuine in what he is doing:

People had in Carl, could they have understood it, the spectacle, under those superficial braveries, of a really heroic effort of mind at a disadvantage. That *rococo* seventeenth-century French imitation of the true Renaissance, called out in Carl a boundless enthusiasm, as the Italian original had done two centuries before. He put into his reception of the aesthetic achievements of Lewis the Fourteenth what young France had felt when Francis the First brought home the great Da Vinci and his works. (*IP*, 129–30)

In this spirit the Mansard style of architecture was introduced and Marivaux's *Death of Hannibal* presented at court, where "Duke Carl himself, attired after the newest French fashion, played the part of Hannibal" (*IP*, 125). A Raphael is bought and eagerly awaited, though when it arrives its cool medieval piety proves a disappointment; Carl's "youthful and somewhat animal taste" (*IP*, 127) preferred the southern gaiety and sensuousness of Rubens. The young Duke even went so far as to contemplate introducing Dresden china factories.

Under the impact of his success, Carl tends progressively to identify himself with Apollo. At first he had been conscious only of performing the same function as the god, but gradually he is led to conceive of himself as an Apollo: " 'You are the Apollo you tell us of, the northern Apollo,' people were beginning to say to him" (*IP*, 128). Carl accepts this idea and actually fancies "that he must really belong by descent to a southern race, that a physical cause might lie beneath this strange restlessness, like the imperfect reminiscence of something that had passed in earlier life" (*IP*, 133). Carl's musings remind us here of the passage in "Diaphaneitè" which tells of "the reminiscence of a forgotten culture," the mind "beginning its spiritual progress over again, but with a certain power of anticipating its stages" (*IP*B, 211). Already by this time Duke Carl had taken to acting in order to perform the major idea of the reincarnated god, becoming, in short, a conscious imitator of specific events in the hyperborean myth. What the friend of the young Duke, the court organist, had conceived as light entertainment in the form of a musical satire on the Duke himself—*Balder, an Interlude,* as he called it—becomes recast, under the prompting of Carl, into a serious musical drama. Carl had perceived that although many of the arts in Germany were not of a high order, music did rate well: "In music, it might be thought, Germany had already vindicated its spiritual liberty. . . . The first notes had been heard of a music not borrowed from France, but flowing, as naturally as springs from their sources, out of the ever musical soul of Germany itself" (*IP*, 130–31). The subject of the Celtes ode, then, is cast in the form of serious operatic music, and Carl's "proposed part" (*IP*, 133) is that of Balder himself—the hyperborean Apollo.

Balder offers an instructive contrast to Marivaux's play, in which Carl had previously acted the chief role. *Annibal* was Marivaux's first and only attempt at writing tragedy. Marivaux composed his tragedy along classical lines, following all the time-honored rules. Undoubtedly part of the reason why *Annibal* failed at the Théâtre Français, where it was first given, was that it ran a poor second to the classical tragedies of Racine and Corneille. If the play was artificial in France, it seemed doubly out of place in Germany. It differed radically from *Balder,* for *Balder* was written according to the Teutonic, not the classical, formula. *Balder* was a native theme handled by native Germans. Carl does not sufficiently recognize the value of "home-born German genius" (*IP*, 147) at this point in his development, but the reader surmises that Carl is slowly closing the gap between himself and Apollo, for if there was one thing which kept Carl from being a true bringer of light, it was that he was derivative rather than original. He, like his contemporary Watteau, must break free from the rococo world of Paris.

It is interesting to speculate on Pater's source for the Balder legend. Possibly Matthew Arnold's "Balder Dead," a poem with which Pater was no doubt familiar, was his source, since it is well known that Pater was a close student of Arnold. Although Arnold's is only one of many versions of the myth, it provides us with the main outline for and some interesting verbal parallels to Pater's work. Balder, of course, is the young god of light who dwells in the golden city of Asgard among the other gods and heroes of the Teutonic pantheon. The god Loke, who in the quasi-Manichaean cosmology of the Teutons is the personification of the evil forces, destroys him, and Balder can only be rescued from the grip of hell if all nature weeps without exception for him.

Because one aged hag refuses, Balder must wait in hell until the
coming of the new Golden Age, when the heavenly city of Asgard,
after destruction, will be reconstituted on a higher ethical and
moral plane:

> . . . I attend the course
> Of ages, and my late return to light,
> In times less alien to a spirit mild,
> In new-recover'd seats, the happier day. . . .
> Far to the south, beyond the blue, there spreads
> Another Heaven, the boundless—no one yet
> Hath reach'd it; there hereafter shall arise
> The second Asgard, with another name.
> Thither, when o'er this present earth and Heavens
> The tempest of the latter days hath swept,
> And they from sight have disappear'd, and sunk,
> Shall a small remnant of the Gods repair;
> Hoder and I shall join them from the grave.
> There re-assembling we shall see emerge
> From the bright Ocean at our feet an earth
> More fresh, more verdant than the last, with fruits
> Self-springing, and a seed of man preserved,
> Who then shall live in peace, as now in war.
> But we in Heaven shall find again with joy
> The ruin'd palaces of Odin, seats
> Familiar, halls where we have supp'd of old;
> Re-enter them with wonder, never fill
> Our eyes with gazing, and rebuild with tears.[19]

No doubt this theme of death, return, and the rebuilding of the
city was the burden of Duke Carl's opera, *Balder*.

Surely the young Duke could not have helped sensing a certain
parallel between his situation and that of the "exiled" god Balder.
Carl's city was a once-golden, now somewhat tarnished, Asgard,
a city which has "a kind of golden architectural splendour"
(*IP*, 121) but which at the same time is covered with a "venerable
dark-green mouldiness" (*IP*, 121). This mouldiness was especially
noticeable in the vicinity of the burial vaults. These loom large
in the eyes of the sensitive young boy because, like Marius in
a similar situation, he is literally the last of his line:

The whole body of Carl's relations, saving the drowsy old grandfather,
already lay buried beneath their expansive heraldries: at times the
whole world almost seemed buried thus—made and re-made of the
dead—its entire fabric of politics, of art, of custom, being essentially
heraldic "achievements," dead men's mementoes such as those. You

[19] *The Poems of Matthew Arnold*, ed. Tinker and Lowry (London, 1950),
p. 128, ll. 510–36.

see he was a sceptical young man, and his kinsmen dead and gone
had passed certainly, in his imaginations of them, into no other world,
save, perhaps, into some stiffer, slower, sleepier, and more pompous
phase of ceremony—the last degree of court etiquette—as they lay
there in the great low-pitched, grand-ducal vault, in their coffins,
dusted once a year for All Souls' Day, when the court officials descended thither, and Mass for the dead was sung, amid an array of
dropping crape and cobwebs. (*IP*, 136–37)

Undoubtedly Carl is envisioning the grand-ducal burial vaults as
not unlike "Hela's mouldering realm," where Balder lay
imprisoned among the weak:

> *Yet dreary, Nanna, is the life they lead*
> *In that dim world, in Hela's mouldering realm;*
> *And doleful are the ghosts, the troops of dead,*
> *Whom Hela with austere control presides.*
> *For of the race of Gods is no one there,*
> *Save me alone, and Hela, solemn queen;*
> *And all the nobler souls of mortal men*
> *On battle-field have met their death, and now*
> *Feast in Valhalla, in my father's hall;*
> *Only the inglorious sort are there below,*
> *The old, the cowards, and the weak are there—*
> *Men spent by sickness, or obscure decay.*[20]

Here, with the spiritually and physically dead, Balder waited until
he could return victorious.

Obviously the "drowsy," "sleepy" court of the Rosenmolds,
centering on the coffins of the deceased, is in reality the counterpart
to the realm of the Chthonian gods. The Rosenmold world is in-
habited by those "with that fulness or heaviness in the brow, as
of sleepy people," which, says Pater in the *Greek Studies*, "distinguish the infernal deities from their Olympian kindred"
(*GS*, 150). And Duke Carl, too, is one of the shades of Hades,
for his precise role is not that of Apollo. He is Balder, the god
whose life follows that of Dionysus in his death and resurrection.
The young Duke fulfills his Apollonian task as the priest of Apollo,
not as the eternal god himself. Balder's cycle of death and resurrection accompanied by a spiritual rejuvenation of the golden city
must have appealed immensely to the young Duke, who undoubtedly incorporated the whole scheme in his opera as a not-too-subtle
comment upon the conditions of his time.

Having perceived the similarity of function between himself
and the god, having been told he actually was the god, and having

[20] *Ibid.*, p. 104, ll. 314–25.

then played the god-role in *Balder*, Duke Carl now turns his whole life into an actual re-enactment of the Apollo-Balder myth. After the manner of his illustrious namesake, he will stage a mock funeral and then reappear:

> In that complex but wholly Teutonic genealogy lately under research,
> lay a much-prized thread of descent from the fifth Emperor Charles,
> and Carl, under direction read with much readiness to be impressed
> all that was attainable concerning the great ancestor, finding there
> in truth little enough to reward his pains. One hint he took, however.
> He determined to assist at his own obsequies. (*IP*, 135–36)

There is, now, a growing spontaneity in Carl's playing the Dionysus role, an authenticity which shows him to be not so much imitating Dionysus as actually being the god himself, and for this reason he seems almost unconscious of the relation between the mock funeral and his Apollonian function. Although the mock funeral would test the sincerity of those who told him he was the German Apollo, its idea goes beyond this simple motive of exposing flattery; it also enables Duke Carl to escape the death-like atmosphere of the Rosenmold court. Critics have pointed to the young Duke as a prime example of the morbid Paterian hero. Granted that Carl was subject to periods of gloom. Who would not be in such an environment with such a soul? But his funeral, it should be obvious, was undertaken by him in order to escape from the Chthonian atmosphere of the place: "The lad, with his full red lips and open blue eyes, coming as with a great cup in his hands to life's feast, revolted from the like of that, as from suffocation" (*IP*, 137). And just as the thoughts of death

> sent him back in the rebounding power of youth, with renewed appe-
> tite, to life and sense, so, grown at last familiar, they gave additional
> purpose to his fantastic experiment. Had it not been said by a wise
> man that after all the offence of death was in its trappings? Well!
> he would, as far as might be, try the thing while, presumably, a
> large reversionary interest in life was still his. He would purchase
> his freedom, at least of those gloomy "trappings," and listen while
> he was spoken of as dead. (*IP*, 137–38)

Carl utilized his new-found freedom to escape the confines of the court and to take his long-desired humanistic pilgrimage to the sources of culture, after which he would be fit to return as the bringer of a totally new way of life. This rationale behind his "death" clearly shows us how Carl's funeral fits his Dionysian-Apollonian role as the herald of cultural renewal: the old having died, the new is about to be born.

The center of Duke Carl's deception is the empty coffin, a symbolic object. It remains long after Carl was forgiven the scheme of burial "and his still greater enormity in coming to life again . . . to the dismay of court marshals" (*IP*, 139–40). The idea of the young Duke as the priest of Apollo invests the empty coffin, emblazoned with the motto, *Resurgam* ("I shall rise again"), with meaning. It is the coffin of one who has already risen, who cannot die in any absolute sense. Indeed, Pater actually speaks of "the empty coffin remaining as a kind of symbolical 'coronation incident'" (*IP*, 140). The empty coffin crowns Carl as the initiator of the German Renaissance, and his whole life falls into the Dionysian pattern as he acts out this awakening. He had "died" in the autumn of the year and traveled south during the winter, and when spring comes he returns north. His travels, then, reflect the seasonal cycle itself, and we are told that after the episode of the funeral Carl "would never again be quite so near people's lives as in the past—a fitful, intermittent visitor—almost as if he had been properly dead" (*IP*, 140).

Duke Carl had planned to descend, like Balder, into the realm of the dead and then reappear, after an absence in which he assimilated the culture of Greece and Rome, in a blaze of splendor to rebuild the golden city along grander lines. The Duke, however, never goes beyond the extreme limits of the German cultural sphere. As he evolves progressively closer to the nature of Apollo, he simultaneously becomes more truly himself, less imitative of others. He makes the vital discovery that he is German and that Germany itself carries the seeds of its own awakening. At long last, with this discovery, originality and true genius are assured. Gradually there has taken place a total identification of the young Duke with Balder, the mask of the player having become the reality. The German Renaissance is at hand, the dawn of the new age has come:

Straight through life, straight through nature and man, with one's own self-knowledge as a light thereon, not by way of the geographical Italy or Greece, lay the road to the new Hellas, to be realised now as the outcome of home-born German genius. At times, in that early fine weather, looking now not southwards, but towards Germany, he seemed to trace the outspread of a faint, not wholly natural, aurora over the dark northern country. And it was in an actual sunrise that the news came which finally put him on the directest road homewards. (*IP*, 147)

The old Grand Duke is dead; Carl is the new sovereign—an auspicious moment, surely, for the advent of the *Aufklärung*. Carl resolves to take for his bride the peasant girl who had wept for him at his "death." But on his marriage night, he is betrayed by his old counsellors, and the invading army tramples him and his bride into the earth. General destruction follows, "the tempest of the latter days" that Balder had foreseen. Now that Carl has become the god in reality, he must also undergo an actual death. It is not Carl who effects the German Renaissance, for Carl, like Balder, is early dead. He revives not in his own person, but in the beautiful skating figure of Goethe fifty years later, who is " 'like a son of the gods' " (*IP*, 153).

Carl becomes, then, the seed-bed out of which the German Renaissance arises, as his name, Rosenmold, indicates: *Rosen* is German for *roses*, and roses are a metaphor for works of art. Carl's importation of works of art, often merely imitations, are described in such images:

> Meantime, its more portable flowers came to order in abundance. That the roses, so to put it, were but excellent artificial flowers, redolent only of musk, neither disproved for Carl the validity of his ideal nor for our minds the vocation of Carl in these matters. . . . It was but himself truly, after all, that he had found, so fresh and real, among those artificial roses. (*IP*, 129–30)

The last part of the Duke's surname seems to embody multiple levels of meaning. First, and most obviously, as a family name it stands for what the family represents in relation to the artistic roses: mouldiness. The roses are mouldy; the gold of art is tarnished. Then, too, *mould* can mean *grave*, where all of Carl's relations are. There is, however, a positive meaning: *humus*. Carl is the mould out of which all the roses will eventually grow. In the opening of the portrait we are told of the yew-tree which came down "exposing, together with its roots, the remains of two persons" (*IP*, 119). Two trees in the portrait loom large, and Carl's relation to them is all-important: the great tree under which he lies and the genealogical tree which asserted that Carl was as indigenous "as the old yew-trees asquat on the heath" (*IP*, 134). Carl is the end of the genealogical tree and the source of the natural tree. He stands, precisely as Marius stood, at the transitional point between sterility and vitality, between the burial vaults and the new order about to be born.

As Winckelmann, Lessing, Herder, and Goethe insisted, true German roses can only grow from native German soil, and Carl becomes fit *Rosenmold* only after he discovers the value of "home-born" genius.[21] Carl's discovery, not unlike the discovery made by the English poet who eventually found poetic beauty in the stern Cumberland mountains, is symbolized by his love for Gretchen, who is the soul of Germany itself and a child of the native soil. As is quite evident, Gretchen is the *Magna Mater*. Carl senses something of the mystic body of the earth about her: she was "like clear sunny weather, with bluebells and the green leaves, between rainy days, and seemed to embody *Die Ruh auf dem Gipfel*—all the restful hours he had spent of late in the wood-sides and on the hill-tops" (*IP*, 148-49). She was, too, "capable of sorrow" like the mother goddess; hence, it was she who shed tears at the funeral of Carl, her divine consort. Carl's love of the artificial is incompatible with his love of the peasant girl, and the decision to marry her, by "our lover of artificial roses, who had cared so little hitherto for the like of her," brings him into true contact with the vital source of all art: " 'Go straight to life!' said his new poetic code; and here was the opportunity;—here, also, the real 'adventure,' in comparison of which his previous efforts that way seemed childish theatricalities, fit only to cheat a little the profound *ennui* of actual life" (*IP*, 149).

Carl's death, which comes as a kind of consummation of his marriage, reminds us of the marriage-deaths of the Christian martyrs in *Marius*. Indeed, two other obvious parallels to the novel prepare us for the Dionysian end. Like Marius, Carl feared death, the "enemy" which "dogged one's footsteps" (*IP*, 137), and, like Psyche, Gretchen feared the "aged wizard" (*IP*, 150) on her wedding night. Significantly, neither Carl nor Gretchen's body is found and placed in the grand-ducal vaults—a sterile place. In the Balder legend a distinction was made between the cowards, the weak,

---

[21] This German renaissance of which Carl was the precursor belonged in special measure to Heidelberg, for here, between the appearance of the *Athenaeum* and the Battle of Leipzig, romantic vitality brought new life to the old classicism, restoring to the city the literary prominence it had enjoyed once before in the days of Conrad Celtes. Revolting against the rococo of the seventeenth century, Carl's successors directed German literature away from its pseudo-classicism and toward the true antique; and by their insistence that literature be national and sincere, they also emancipated German art from the French influence. In "Aesthetic Poetry" Pater wrote: "The end of the eighteenth century, swept by vast disturbing currents, experienced an excitement of spirit of which one note was a reaction against an outworn classicism severed not more from nature than from the genuine motives of ancient art; and a return to true Hellenism was as much a part of this reaction as the sudden preoccupation with things medieval. The medieval tendency is in Goethe's *Goetz von Berlichingen*, the Hellenic in his *Iphigenie*" (*Ap* [1889], p. 214).

and the inglorious who are kept in the sterile realm of Hela and those who heroically die on the battlefield. In a sense, Carl dies on a battlefield, for he is destroyed by the trampling of the army in his fight to bring light to Germany. He thus merges with the earth, with nature, the *Magna Mater* which is the source of all vitality. Here again new life means a martyr's death, but with this death the German Renaissance has begun. In the figure of Goethe, writes Pater, "I seem to see the fulfillment of the *Resurgam* on Carl's empty coffin—the aspiring soul of Carl himself, in freedom and effective, at last" (*IP*, 153).

V

GASTON DE LATOUR (1888)
AND RELIGIOUS BELIEF

Pater's life-long friend and literary executor, Charles Shadwell, gives us the publication history of the unfinished *Gaston
de Latour*, Pater's second novel-length imaginary portrait. Shadwell
writes in the Preface to the Macmillan Library Edition the
following:

"Gaston de Latour" was probably begun by Mr. Pater not long after
the completion of "Marius." Five chapters appeared successively in
Macmillan's Magazine in the months of June to October 1889 [1888].
One more chapter appeared, as an independent article, in the *Fortnightly Review* for August 1889, under the title "Giordano Bruno."
This article was afterwards largely revised, and marked Chapter VII.,
as it is here printed. Some portions of other chapters, intended to
form part of the romance, have been found among Mr. Pater's manuscripts. . . . The sixth Chapter, so entitled by Mr. Pater, is now
printed from this source. (*GdL*, v)[1]

Shadwell further states that "the work, if completed, would have
been a parallel study of character to 'Marius the Epicurean,' the
scene shifted to another age of transition, when the old fabric of
belief was breaking up, and when the problem of man's destiny
and his relations to the unseen was undergoing a new solution"
(*GdL*, vi). Shadwell's assertion that *Gaston* parallels *Marius* has
been reinforced by a recently discovered letter of Pater to an Ameri-

---

[1] Actually, the seventh chapter is entitled "The Lower Pantheism" and
is perhaps a conscious echo of Tennyson's "The Higher Pantheism" and Swin-
burne's parody, "The Higher Pantheism in a Nut-Shell." Despite the fact
that seven chapters only were written, *Gaston* would, indeed, have at least
run to three books if finished. (A MS fragment is headed "Book III, Chapter
XIII.") *Gaston*, then, was conceived on a scale as great as that of *Marius*.
Just why or when Pater abandoned the work is uncertain. According to the
journal of Michael Field (ed., T. and D. C. S. Moore [London, 1933], p.
119), Pater was still at work on it in 1890 and actually hoped to finish
it that summer.

can correspondent. Pater, in his reply to a query about his work and writings generally, had written: "I may add that 'Marius' is designed to be the first of a kind of a trilogy, or triplet, of works of a similar character; dealing with the same problems, under altered historical conditions. The period of the second of the series would be at the end of the 16th century, and the place France: of the third, the time, probably the end of the last century— and the scene, England."[2] The unfinished *Gaston* was the second novel; there is no trace of the third. Because *Gaston* is incomplete, it cannot be the subject of any thorough-going structural analysis, but it does lend itself to a comparison with *Marius* and, in particular, to a consideration of their common subject, the struggle toward religious faith.

The narrative of *Gaston* itself does not get very far at all. The action of the story was planned to encompass the last half of the sixteenth century, with Gaston dying in 1594. However, the story as Pater tells it never gets much beyond 1572, the year of the St. Bartholomew's Day Massacre. The action begins at Gaston's home of Deux-manoirs, located in "the pleasant level of La Beauce, the great corn-land of central France" (*GdL*, 1). Gaston moves from there to service as a young boy at Notre-Dame de Chartres and lives through the siege of the town in 1567. Pater then tells us of visits which Gaston makes to Ronsard and Montaigne, the latter visit lasting for some nine months. After that, Gaston goes to Paris and, though a Catholic, marries a Huguenot girl. On the eve of the massacre, Gaston, all-unknowing, leaves the city for the bed of his dying grandfather, and in the terrible events that follow, his wife dies in labor "in the belief that she had been treacherously deserted, like many another at that great crisis" (*GdL*, 130). At this point the narrative sequence ends, and the novel itself breaks off entirely after the chapter on Giordano Bruno.

Undeniably, the parallelism between *Marius* and *Gaston* extends to a considerable degree beyond that of a common problem or subject. For example, Gaston's childhood home, just like Marius', embodies a rural, dreamy way of life, and, again like Marius, Gaston fulfills in this environment the function of the boy-priest (*GdL*, 8)—his nature, we are told, was "instinctively religious" (*GdL*, 22). Then, too, Gaston's mind, like Marius', had a "native

---

[2] Quoted in *IP*B, p. 4. Perhaps the line in *Marius* where Pater apologizes for "passing from Marius to his modern representatives—from Rome, to Paris or London" (*ME*, II, 14) is an indication of the proposed trilogy and Pater's comments on the "isolating narrowness" of Marius' philosophy at this point an indication that whoever the hero of the third novel might be, his "difficulties and hopes" would be analogous to those of Marius and Gaston.

impressibility to the sorrow and hazard that are constant and necessary in human life" (*GdL*, 19); it was a nature that understood beauty in terms of suffering: "Sorrow came along with beauty, a rival of its intricate omni-presence in life" (*GdL*, 23). In a passage which recalls not only *Marius*, but also the last paragraphs of "The Child in the House," Pater writes of Gaston:

> The beauty of the world and its sorrow, solaced a little by religious faith, itself so beautiful a thing; these were the chief impressions with which he made his way outwards, at first only in longer rambles, as physical strength increased, over his native plains, whereon, as we have seen, the cruel warfare of that age had aggravated at a thousand points the everyday appeal of suffering humanity. (*GdL*, 24–25)

And in this warfare (Gaston's life, so Pater tells us (*GdL*, 15), coincided with the duration of the religious wars) one can see the counterpart to the plague which racked the second-century world of Marius. Indeed, the Saint Bartholomew's Day Massacre may perhaps find its parallel in the slaughter of the Christians at Lyons and Vienne. And, like Marius, who from childhood trained himself for "some great occasion of self-devotion" (*ME*, I, 18), so Gaston, too, in this era of painful transition, feels within himself "the appetite for some great distinguishing passion" (*GdL*, 21).

Individual episodes in the lives of Gaston and Marius are also parallel. In Gaston's removal from home to serve as a clerk in the Bishop of Chartres' retinue, we see Marius' journey as a young lad to Pisa. In both instances the boys encounter a modernity which clashes, not unpleasantly, with their former way of life. Of Gaston's reaction to Chartres, Pater writes:

> What was of the past there—the actual stones of the temple and that sacred liturgical order—entered readily enough into Gaston's mental kingdom, filling places prepared by the anticipations of his tranquil, dream-struck youth. It was the present, the uncalculated present, which now disturbed the complacent habit of his thoughts, proposing itself, importunately, in the living forms of his immediate companions, in the great clerical body . . . as a thing, alien at a thousand points from his preconceptions of life. (*GdL*, 32–33)

But in the world of the centrifugal there is inevitably the suffering and the terror. One is reminded of the episode of the fall of rock which nearly killed Marius; its counterpart in Gaston's life is the collapsing church:

> Gaston, the last lingerer, halting to let others proceed quietly before him, turned himself about to gaze upon the deserted church, half tempted to remain, ere he too stepped forth lightly and leisurely,

when under a shower of massy stones from the *coulevrine*s or great cannon of the besiegers, the entire roof of the place sank into the empty space behind him. But it was otherwise in a neighbouring church, crushed, in a similar way, with all its good people, not long afterwards. (*GdL*, 46)

And just as the death of Flavian seemed totally to destroy Marius' childhood ideas, so the death of a beloved grandmother (perhaps a detail from Pater's own biography) ended the childhood of Gaston: "That broken link with life seemed to end some other things for him. As one puts away the toys of childhood, so now he seemed to discard what had been the central influence of his earlier youth, what more than anything else had stirred the imagination and brought the consciousness of his own life warm and full" (*GdL*, 47). Finally, there was with Gaston, as with Marius, an eventual return after much wandering through the world of Paris, the Renaissance counterpart of Rome, to the childhood home, for we are told that Gaston effected considerable architectural change at Deux-manoirs (*GdL*, 2, 6) before his death in 1594. Interestingly, although both Gaston and Marius, like most of Pater's heroes, are the last of their line (*GdL*, 5, 9), they differ from all the other Pater heroes in that they live much longer. Marius, we are told, was as old as his father when he died, and Gaston, who was ten years old in 1562, dies only six years before the close of the century.

The major similarity between *Gaston* and *Marius* is, however, the structure of dialectical opposition, of the summer and winter Dionysus, whose narrow worlds of sense and spirit crave the harmony of the Apollonian order. Pater writes of Gaston—and we recall here Marius' response to Pisa—the following:

A nature with the capacity of worship, he was straightway challenged, as by a rival new religion claiming to supersede the religion he knew, to identify himself conclusively with this so tangible world, its suppositions, its issues, its risks. . . . Two worlds, two antagonistic ideals, were in evidence before him. Could a third condition supervene, to mend their discord, or only vex him perhaps, from time to time, with efforts towards an impossible adjustment? (*GdL*, 38–39)

And again:

For a moment, amid casuistical questions as to one's indefeasible right to liberty of heart, he saw himself, somewhat wearily, very far gone from the choice, the consecration, of his boyhood. If he could but be rid of that altogether! Or if that would but speak with irresistible decision and effect! Was there perhaps somewhere, in some penetrative mind in this age of novelties, some scheme of truth, some science about men and things, which might harmonise for him his earlier and later preference, "the sacred and the profane loves," or, failing that, establish, to his pacification, the exclusive supremacy of the latter? (*GdL*, 71–72)

This opposition is obviously fundamental to the work, and perhaps Shadwell was personally told by Pater that this was to be the structure of the portrait, for Shadwell writes that in *Gaston* "the interest would have centered round the spiritual development of a refined and cultivated mind, capable of keen enjoyment in the pleasures of the senses and of the intellect, but destined to find its complete satisfaction in that which transcends both" (*GdL*, vi).

But if the tracing of the Dionysian alternation in the unfinished *Gaston* is impossible, we can, however, still discuss the idea of "spiritual development." *Gaston*, like *Marius*, would have been a novel in which Pater attempted to formulate a solution to the problem of religious belief in a world of doubt. That he considered his projected trilogy as an excursus into religion is evident in a letter he wrote to Violet Paget. In referring to her article "The Responsibilities of Unbelief," Pater told Miss Paget that he considered the writing of *Marius* to be "a sort of duty," because, as he said, "I think there is a . . . sort of religious phase possible for the modern mind, . . . the conditions of which phase it is the main object of my design to convey."[3] Just what that "religious phase" is which *Marius* and *Gaston* embody has rarely been considered with much success. The chapter on *Marius* attempted to explain in terms of the book's structure what Pater's religious beliefs were. In this chapter the same problem will be considered from the philosopher's point of view, utilizing Pater's non-fictional writings. This should cast a great deal of light back not only on *Marius* and *Gaston* but on all of the imaginary portraits, for Pater's philosophy is, so to speak, the raw material out of which he creates the metaphors of his art.

Since maturity is always the ripening of youth, the best way to begin such a consideration is to look closely at the early religious ideal of the young Pater. As we know from "The Child in the House," from *Marius*, and from *Gaston*, the boy had a deep religious sensitivity and a desire even to join the clergy. Indeed, much

---

[3] Quoted in Benson, *Pater*, p. 90. See Evans, *Letters of Pater*, p. 64, for a correct rendering of the letter. Paget's article appeared under the pseudonym of Vernon Lee in the *Contemporary Review*, XLIII (May, 1883), 685–710. It was, as the subtitle has it, "a conversation between three rationalists"—an "optimistic Voltairean," an "aesthetic pessimist," and a "militant, humanitarian atheist." Pater believed in a fourth phase, over and above those presented here, which was religious and by implication not wholly rationalistic.

of this stayed with him throughout life: "that first, early boyish ideal of priesthood, the sense of dedication, survived through all the distractions of the world, when all thought of such vocation had finally passed from him, as a ministry, in spirit at least, towards a sort of hieratic beauty and orderliness in the conduct of life" (*ME*, I, 25). That unique quality of bouyancy which characterized Pater's early religious sense is especially evident in a poem which he wrote in his sixteenth year, one that is well worth attention because of the interesting insight which it gives us into young Pater's mind.

In imitation of Goethe, Pater burned most of his early poetry because of its naïve religiosity. However, "The Chant of the Celestial Sailors" and a half dozen or so more poems survived. Obviously part of Pater's juvenilia, "The Chant" is, nevertheless, considerably more than the "jingle of musical words" which Thomas Wright believed it to be.[4] It is evident that the young poet had been reading his contemporaries, for the tone and even some of the imagery are markedly Tennysonian. The celestial sailors seem to be a Christianized version of the long-wandering Greeks who gave up wind, wave, and oar to listen to sweet music in the land of the Lotos-

---

[4] *Life of Pater*, I, 101. Actually, in my estimation it is one of the best of Pater's poems. Since it cannot easily be found, it is here given: "The Chant of the Celestial Sailors. Homeward! Homeward! thro' the glowing/ Wavelets of the violet sea,/ As the western breezes blowing/ Waft us on mysteriously./ Every wave behind us glancing/ Wears a crest of snow-white foam,/ Like the matin clouds advancing/ In the blue ethereal dome./ Soon the stars will shine above us,/ Daughters of the silent night—/ Like the peaceful saints who love us,/ Dwelling in eternal light./ Homeward to the shore celestial! onward to the silver strand!/ Homeward! Homeward! gentle brothers, to the tranquil morning land.// Now no need of oarsmen urging/ All their strength at port to be,/ Angels speed us o'er the surging/ Bosom of the billowy sea./ Far above, our banner pendent/ Lifts the wondrous sign on high,/ Sacred ensign, thrice triumphant,/ Purple in the purple sky./ In the stillness, tall and stately/ Soars our mast in solitude,/ Steadfast as the mountain pine-tree,/ Solemn like the holy Rood./ Homeward to the shore celestial! onward to the silver strand!/ Homeward! Homeward! gentle brothers, to the tranquil morning land.// Now, behold the crystal morning/ Paves the East with rosy dyes;/ All the hues of heavenly dawning/ Rise to our expectant eyes;/ And amid these shades terrestrial,/ O'er the rushing waves afar,/ Come the Angels' songs celestial,/ Singing to the Morning Star./ Chanting in the golden valleys/ Watered by the living rills,/ Where above the woodland valleys/ Rise the everlasting hills./ Homeward to the shore celestial! onward to the silver strand!/ Homeward! Homeward! gentle brothers, to the tranquil morning land." The poem was privately printed in Winchester, England, by the Reverend Edward H. Blakeney in 1928 in an edition of only thirty copies. The word *celestial* may be Bunyanesque or it may have Swedenborgian connotations. Swedenborg exercised an influence on Pater and is mentioned in *ME*, II, 93 and *Ap*, p. 26. The word *homeward* is, of course, invested with all the usual Paterian overtones.

Eaters.[5] Somewhat less pagan than Tennyson's, Pater's poem is an allegory of life, death, and rebirth dramatically presented in the form of the boat sailing east toward the dawn, the region of the Holy Land.[6] The song of the men in the boat becomes the chant of humanity itself moving toward its heavenly home. As the "celestial sailors" head toward the night, their boat is propelled by sails ("breezes") and oars. But in the mystery of the darkness, human and natural causes cease and the supernatural takes over. The boat moves without "oarsmen" and without sails ("our mast in solitude"). The men in the boat look up, and what they see in the dim starlight is perfectly predictable—the ship's flag. Perhaps Wright is correct in assuming Pater had a "very elementary knowledge of boating," but Pater is nevertheless true to his situation, for the flag is British, and it is a "sacred ensign, thrice triumphant" because it bears three crosses: St. George's, St. Andrew's, and St. Patrick's. The cross, then, appears as the central symbol at the climax of the poem—temporal (the present bracketed by past and future), spatial (up, rather than back or ahead), thematic (middle stanza of the night section, the darkest part), and structural (middle stanza of the middle section).[7]

[5] Tennyson's "Hesperides," in addition to his "Lotos-Eaters," probably also added to Pater's total conception. And, of course, if we jump back to the metaphysicals of whom Pater was very fond, we are rather reminded of Andrew Marvell's "Bermudas," in which we have a similar situation—the boat on the sea of life, the men on their way to the New Jerusalem. Marvell's men, too, sing in their small boat as they row toward their Holy Land. But Marvell's poem is not quite as obvious as Pater's. Pater simply calls his Holy Land "the shore celestial"; Marvell, on the other hand, gently tells us, by planting there all the fruits mentioned in the Bible, that his paradise of the New World is the Holy Land. Marvell's men, of course, were sailing west to the New World, and Tennyson's Hesperides was also west; Pater is, however, true to his initial facts, and his men sail in the geographically correct direction.

[6] The poem is balanced in three sections of three stanzas each. Each of the three sections is ended with the same refrain, while the second and third sections are introduced by the same word: "Now." This word calls our attention from the mechanical structure to the temporal structure of the poem. The three sections are devoted to sunset, night, and morning, respectively—or to light which wanes to extinction and then grows once again. There is, further, a spatial or directional structure implied in the three sections. In the first section, the sailors are looking west, back toward the waves "behind" them. In the third section, they are looking ahead with "expectant eyes" toward the east. In the middle section, they are looking neither behind nor before, but up, "on high."

[7] The cross image is continued in the following stanza, in which the naked mast is compared to the holy Rood—the Cross of Crucifixion which in the standard cruciform church is positioned at the juncture of the nave and choir—and in relation to the church the Rood is the same distance forward as the mast is in the boat. There is a hint, though only a hint, that Pater is seeing the physical church as analogous to the boat, as he does many years later in *Gaston de Latour* (p. 26).

It comes as a surprise to the alert reader to perceive that already at the age of sixteen Pater had worked out the pattern of his future thought. Take it any way one wishes, the dialectical structure of day, night, and dawn is an obvious adumbration of the mythic pattern of the summer Dionysus who is past, the winter Dionysus whose agony fills the present, and the hope of Apollo which lies in the future. It is, of course, cast in Christian rather than mythic terms, but it is certainly complete. The cross in the night section, representative of the suffering and death of Christ, has an inescapable relation to the winter Dionysus, whose death issues in the Apollonian world. This Apollonian realm of the timeless is described here by Pater in Christian terms as the dawning of a light not physical, a chanting of praise and adoration no longer wholly mortal, and a description of things that human eye hath not seen nor ear heard. The angels "singing to the Morning Star" recall the image in Revelation of Christ as "the root and the offspring of David, the bright morning star" (Rev. 22:16). The whole of the language is infused with the apocalyptic vision of John on Patmos, who "saw a new heaven and a new earth, . . . the holy city, a new Jerusalem, coming down out of heaven from God" (Rev. 21:1–2). And, indeed, here for the first time, in the last stanza, we have a description of stable land, not the perpetual flux of the sea.

But somehow Pater could not always believe so easily in this vision of the land of hope. "Our pilgrimage is meant indeed to end in nothing less than the *vision* of what we seek," says Pater in *Plato*. "But can we ever be quite sure that we are really come to that? By what sign or test?" (*PP*, 192). It is, of course, to religious myth that Pater turns for help, for myth is the natural creation of man's search for meaning, and it, more perfectly than anything else, embodies his universal and recurrent ideas on the subject. Pater felt that these mythic patterns owe their inextinguishable hold upon the imaginations of men to that empirically real counterpart which they reflect—the dying of the old year and the birth of the new. Yet it was only gradually that through myth Pater discovered in the physical universe this concrete expression of the Christian hope of resurrection. As he so touchingly narrated in "The Child in the House," the boy's sudden realization of the reality of death shattered his early paradise and brought him into the turbulence of maturity. Only two years after "The Chant" Pater wrote the following lines in a poem entitled "Watchman, what of the Night?":

> *. . . Where are the dead?*
> *Nowhere!—a voice replies. Yet Thou hast died,*
> *O Christ Redeemer! Let me cling to Thee,*
> *Hold me from yon abyss; with frenzied glide*
> *Down, down, I sink. Oh let me live in Thee,*
> *Or deep in hell; it seems so awful not to be.*
>
> *And yet in dreams at night, in wakeful dreams*
> *When thought is free and flings her bonds away,*
> *The soul untrammeled like a prophet seems*
> *To tell how all things verge to their decay;*
> *Herself, that seems immortal, in the round*
> *Of nature—mistress stern—shall one day fall*
> *Back whence she came, nor hear the trumpet sound*
> *Awakening, nor the high Archangel's call*
> *And chaos grim once more supremely rule o'er all.*[8]

But the poem does not end on such a pessimistic note; the young poet calls to Christ as the God of Light to dispel with his Truth the dark shadows of doubt which haunt his mind, and the poem concludes, much like *Marius*, with the confident assertion that the moment of death will prove once and for all that "Thou lovest and art just."

Still the doubts are there, and Pater's religious struggle reminds one of Pascal, who is seen in his *Thoughts* "as if at the very centre of a perpetually maintained tragic crisis holding the faith steadfastly, but amid the well-poised points of essential doubt all around him and it. It is no mere calm supersession of a state of doubt by a state of faith; the doubts never die, they are only just kept down in a perpetual *agonia*" (*MS, 77*). Intellectually the "abyss" was ever at Pascal's side, and because of an accident in which he was nearly killed, Pascal came to imagine the gulf as actually real: "As he walked or sat he was apt to perceive a yawning depth beside him; would set stick or chair there to reassure himself" (*MS, 89*). For Pater, as for Pascal, it was the impact of the relative spirit of modern science upon the old moral absolutes which was the disturbing element in religious faith, and he, like Pascal, was ever searching for some ground of certainty in doubt's boundless sea.

What Pater has to say in his essay on Sir Thomas Browne is interesting, for Browne was a scientist, born in a religiously skeptical age. Yet for all of Browne's so-called doubt, writes Pater, his faith never really came to grips with the unsettling implications of modern science:

[8] Quoted in d'Hangest, *Walter Pater*, I, 343, n. 25.

147

Certainly Browne has not, like Pascal, made the "great resolution,"
by the apprehension that it is just in the contrast of the moral world
to the world with which science deals that religion finds its proper basis.
It is from the homelessness of the world which science analyses so
victoriously, its dark unspirituality, wherein the soul he is conscious of
seems such a stranger, that Pascal "turns again to his rest," in the
conception of a world of wholly reasonable and moral agencies. For
Browne, on the contrary, the light is full, design everywhere obvious,
its conclusion easy to draw, all small and great things marked clearly
with the signature of the "Word." (*Ap*, 137–38)

Browne was a scientist, but not a modern one; his religion, then,
is rather limited in its significance for the modern man who, lost
in the vastness of the universe and unable to find any objective
criterion for moral action or religious belief, is imprisoned in his
own subjectivity. "The adhesion, the difficult adhesion, of men
such as Pascal," says Pater, "is an immense conbribution to religious controversy; the concession, again, of a man like Addison,
of great significance there. But in the adhesion of Browne, in spite
of his crusade against 'vulgar errors,' there is no real significance.
The *Religio Medici* is a contribution, not to faith, but to piety,
. . . a help not so much to religious belief in a world of doubt,
as to the maintenance of the religious mood amid the interests
of a secular calling" (*Ap*, 138). Still, as Pater later in the essay
points out, the bare fact that Browne could so effectively ignore
the implications of science in favor of belief is perhaps a valuable
testimony to the power of certain religious temperaments.

One might reasonably expect Pascal to be an important influence on Pater's thought. Unfortunately, Pater's essay on Pascal
is rather disappointing. Aside from the few lines quoted and some
appreciative remarks on "the wholeness of Pascal's assent, the entirety of his submission, his immense sincerity, the heroic grandeur
of his achieved faith" (*MS*, 79), there is little that is helpful. Perhaps this is due to the fact that the study is unfinished, but whatever the reason, the most significant discussion of Pascal is to be
found in another unfinished essay entitled "Art and Religion,"[9]
in which Pater takes a significant step forward in his analysis
of the modern religious temperament. There is a class of persons
in the Christian community, says Pater, in whom the faculty of
conscience is evoked by the sense of thankfulness to some divine

[9] I have utilized as background material for this discussion three Pater
essays lent to me in typescript by Mr. Evans, with his kind permission to
paraphrase. These three are titled "Art and Religion," "The Writings of
Cardinal Newman," and "Moral Philosophy." (I am also in Mr. Evans' debt
for two story fragments which I shall consider in the following chapter.)

personage who sustains and preserves one in the turmoils of life. Pascal is one such, certainly, but he is not the only one who belongs to that class of persons. Pater, too, places himself among those who have experienced this sense of appreciation to some divine person. And Pater's hero, Marius, also has this feeling of "personal gratitude and the sense of a friendly hand laid upon him amid the shadows of the world" (*ME*, II, 71). Pater writes of Marius that "he hardly knew how strong that old religious sense of responsibility, the conscience, as we call it, still was within him—a body of inward impressions, as real as those so highly valued outward ones—to offend against which, brought with it a strange feeling of disloyalty, as to a person" (*ME*, I, 155–56).

It is precisely this loyal conscience which constitutes religious belief, though neither Pascal nor Marius nor Pater can offer any logical explanation of why he should have this sense of gratitude. Religious belief is non-logical by nature, and Pater, in his essay on "The Writings of Cardinal Newman," sees temperament as a factor in this capacity to believe. In the *Sermons* and in his *Grammar of Assent*, says Pater, Newman works out the psychological notion of a faith conditioned by certain temperamental qualities. Faith, according to Newman, is a matter of the whole man— heart as well as head, a lifetime of experience as well as an hour of logic. It is an act of the imaginative reason, of what Newman called the "illative sense," and resembles nothing quite so much as Napoleon's strategy or the intuitions of a poet. Even the most skeptical intellect, if rigorously fair, will of necessity be forced to admit that belief goes beyond the formulae of the syllogism. Montaigne, says Pater, is perhaps the most characteristic example of the man who illustrates the extreme degree of skepticism, yet nonetheless does make the all-important concession to the inadequacy of logic in such matters. In Montaigne certain definite acts and admissions seem to betray momentarily his all-pervasive attitude of *que sçais-je*. Pater represents this imaginatively in his novel when he has Gaston recall, upon hearing of Monsieur de Montaigne's death, "a hundred, always quiet but not always insignificant, acts of devotion, noticeable in those old days, on passing a church, or at home, in the little chapel—superstitions, concessions to others, strictly appropriate recognitions rather, as it might seem, of a certain great possibility which might lie among the conditions of so complex a world" (*GdL*, 112–13). And those concessions which Montaigne's manner of life makes implicitly, others, such as J. S. Mill in his essays on religion, concede explicitly. But whether the concessions are implicit or explicit, the skeptical thinker nonetheless admits that the matter of belief is still *sub judice* and that there is a certain amount of evidence for the truth of those facts to which belief testifies.

Pater points out in "Art and Religion" that the individual with the loyal conscience stands in a significant relation to such skeptical thinkers as Montaigne and Mill. For Montaigne and Mill, of course, the concessions or possibilities admitted by intellectual skepticism merely lead to a suspension of judgment or to a cold preference, but for those with the sense of the loyal conscience, such concessions become all-important, become, indeed, sufficient evidence for enthusiastic belief. In his review of Mrs. Humphry Ward's novel *Robert Elsmere*, Pater says that Elsmere was one of those who "cannot be sure that the sacred story is true." There is, however, another, more interesting and significant, class of minds who

cannot be sure it is false—minds of very various degrees of conscientiousness and intellectual power, up to the highest. They will think those who are quite sure it is false unphilosophical through lack of doubt. For their part, they make allowance in their scheme of life for a great possibility, and with some of them that bare concession of possibility (the subject of it being what it is) becomes the most important fact in the world. The recognition of it straightway opens wide the door to hope and love; and such persons are, as we fancy they always will be, the nucleus of a Church. (*EG*, 67–68)

Pascal is, for Pater, the foremost representative of this class who, though completely scrupulous intellectually and fully aware of the laws of evidence, nevertheless on the bare concession, which in others is just powerful enough for suspension of judgment, reach a buoyant, enthusiastic belief, an indefectible certitude.

The one element, then, that gives continuing validity to all expressions of the Christian community, no matter how inadequate its own rational explanations of its views may be, is that throughout the history of the church, in a sufficient number of lives, there has been a consciousness of some divine personage in contact with life. Pascal's magnificent achievement of faith becomes itself a kind of valuable evidence for those who do not have the sense of the loyal conscience. In a world so obscure, the majority would do well to accept the testimony of experts such as he. Even Apuleius' wild guesses at the truth "witness, at least, to a variety of human disposition, and a consequent variety of mental view, which might—who could tell?—be correspondent to, be defined by and define, varieties of facts, of truths just 'behind the veil'"

(*ME*, II, 91). And Pater had exactly the same thing to say about Browne, who "represents, in an age, the intellectual powers of which tend strongly to agnosticism, that class of minds to which the supernatural view of things is still credible" (*Ap*, 159). What does one do with a man like Browne or Apuleius who fails to draw the obvious skeptical conclusion? This indeed is

a fact worth the consideration of all ingenuous thinkers, if (as is certainly the case with colour, music, number, for instance) there may be whole regions of fact, the recognition of which belongs to one and not to another, which people may possess in various degrees; for the knowledge of which, therefore, one person is dependent upon another; and in relation to which the appropriate means of cognition must lie among the elements of what we call individual temperament, so that what looks like a pre-judgment may be really a legitimate apprehension. "Men are what they are," and are not wholly at the mercy of formal conclusions from their formally limited premises. (*Ap*, 160)

Yet, of course, the evidence which an Apuleius or a Browne supplies is limited, for neither offers any empirical proof beyond that of his own temperamental predilections.

The personal loyalty of a Pascal, on the other hand, has a more concrete form of evidence to recommend it because the object of his loyalty has an embodiment which can be seen. The transcendent Judaeo-Christian God, the Hegelian Absolute, the Platonic One—all of these seem to Pater too abstract to inspire such warm and personal loyalty. It is toward all good men, the better part of humanity itself, that the sense of loyalty is directed. "The moral order," says Pater in *Marius*,

is, in reality, the total product and effect of all the higher moral experience of many generations, and all their aspirations after a more perfect world: it expresses the moral judgment of the honest dead—a body so much more numerous than the living. . . . And the moral development of the individual may well follow the tendency of that larger current, and permit its flights and heats, its *élans*, as the French say, only so much freedom of play as may be consistent with full sympathy with, and a full practical assent to, the moral preferences of that "great majority," which exercises the authority of humanity; and is actually a vast force all around us.[10]

Pater gives this same explanation of the object of loyalty in his unfinished essay "Moral Philosophy." No moral philosophy, says Pater, has proved itself an adequate standard for modern man in

[10] This section was cut from Chap. XVI, "Second Thoughts," in later editions of *Marius*.

the face of the relativity of human knowledge and the diminished hold of religious authority. The problem, then, which Pater takes up in "Moral Philosophy" is identical with that which Cornelius Fronto's lecture on the *Nature of Morals* had approached in *Marius*. It is the problem of the young man who, says Pater in the novel, is

> in search after some principle of conduct (and it was here that he seemed to Marius to be speaking straight to him) which might give unity of motive to an actual rectitude, a cleanness and probity of life, determined partly by natural affection, partly by enlightened self-interest or the feeling of honour, due in part even to the mere fear of penalties; no element of which, however, was distinctively moral in the agent himself as such, and providing him, therefore, no common ground with a really moral being like Cornelius, or even like the philosophic emperor. (*ME*, II, 7–8)

This "isolating narrowness" (*ME*, II, 14), as Pater called it in the following chapter, is the problem shared by Roman and Victorian alike, and it is the direct result of man's failure to find a common empirical basis for moral action. Every system that transcends the individual seems to lose touch with the concrete world. Yet flawed as all the abstract moral systems are, they nevertheless attest to the fact that man is still actively searching for some principle of conduct broad enough to sum up the whole complex and diverse sphere of actual experience. And humanity will continue its search because it is an inescapable fact that, when one considers individual cases, particular acts are judged to have moral significance; some are unqualifiedly believed to be good (acts such as those of sincerity or love) and others bad (acts of ingratitude and treachery). Clearly, moral values are not relative.

In "Moral Philosophy" and in *Marius*, Pater distinguishes one comprehensive and distinctly moral principle which, because it is not as abstract as all the others, may serve to direct conduct. This is "custom." It is this external authority of humanity which is able to free us from our own capricious subjectivity. Just as philosophers, despite all their theoretical doubts, act on unprovable assumptions in the light of common sense, so in the sphere of morals, says Pater, we act by faith when we occasionally concede to traditional ideas of morality. This faith is a kind of sympathy with all honest men, living and dead, whom we cannot bear to betray, so to speak, in our daily actions. As Pater noted in *Marius*, the searcher after a principle of morality may notice that, over and above "practical rectitude . . . determined by natural affection or self-love or fear, . . . there is a remnant of right conduct, what he does, still more what he abstains from doing, not so much through his own free election, as from a deference, an 'assent,' entire, habitual, unconscious, to custom—to the actual habit or fashion of others, from whom he could not endure to break away" (*ME*, II, 9). Deference to custom, far from being an ethical system for unoriginal, weak men, actually becomes the system for powerful and gifted persons who, by the transparency of their character, both give expression to the great consensus and also partly lead it. And once again, "Moral Philosophy" has its parallel in *Marius*, in which Pater writes:

An assent, such as this, to the preferences of others, might seem to be the weakest of motives, and the rectitude it could determine the least considerable element in a moral life. Yet here, according to Cornelius Fronto, was in truth the revealing example, albeit operating upon comparative trifles, of the general principle required. There was one great idea associated with which that determination to conform to precedent was elevated into the clearest, the fullest, the weightiest principle of moral action; a principle under which one might subsume men's most strenuous efforts after righteousness. (*ME*, II, 9)

It is to the bygone heroes of the past, who were an expression of the principle of morality, that we defer in matters of conduct, whose authority over us is like parental authority idealized. Our personal loyalty to them preserves some sort of continuity in moral behavior in the face of the liberalizing tendencies of modern thought. It is too great a price to pay for personal liberty or some slight improvement in the present system, says Pater, to have the great men of the past—Dante or Augustine or others like them— against us, for these men constitute "a visible or invisible aristocracy . . . whose actual manners, whose preferences from of old, become now a weighty tradition as to the way in which things should or should not be done, are like a music, to which the intercourse of life proceeds—such a music as no one who had once caught its harmonies would willingly jar" (*ME*, II, 10). It was precisely this "loyal conscience, . . . deciding, judging himself and every one else, with a wonderful sort of authority" (*ME*, I, 241), which enabled Marius to escape his subjectivity, to transcend his immediate environment, and to see the unique point of moral blindness in the Emperor Aurelius and the Roman Empire.

Pater extends to Pascal the credit for being the first explicitly to conceive of the moral mind of humanity as the Logos. And for his own century, Pater says that the two opposite schools which have divided speculative activity between them—Hegelian Idealism and Comtean Positivism—are at one in this conception of humanity. In Comte's "Grand-être," which is the society of the dead, and in Hegel's "Absolute," which is the collective life of the whole human race, two opposite philosophical schools meet half-way. We see how very close to this Hegelian Absolute Marius' sense of the loyal conscience actually comes when Pater writes in the novel

> That divine companion figured no longer as but an occasional way-farer beside him; but as the unfailing "assistant," without whose in-spiration and concurrence he could not breathe or see, instrumenting his bodily senses, rounding, supporting his imperfect thoughts. . . . How had he longed, sometimes, that there were indeed one to whose boundless power of memory he could commit his own most fortunate moments . . .—one strong to retain them even though he forgot, in whose more vigorous consciousness they might subsist for ever, beyond that mere quickening of capacity which was all that remained of them in himself! . . . Today . . . he seemed to have apprehended that in which the experiences he valued most might find, one by one, an abiding-place. And again, the resultant sense of companionship, of a person beside him, evoked the faculty of conscience—of conscience, as of old and when he had been at his best, in the form, not of fear, nor of self-reproach even, but of a certain lively gratitude. (*ME*, II, 70–71)[11]

Actually, says Pater, this idea of the Logos as embodied in persons is far older even than Roman philosophy. It has been present in philosophy from the time of Heraclitus' belief in a universal intelli-gence in things—in terms of Pater's favorite metaphor, it is "the harmony of musical notes" (*ME*, I, 131) or "antiphonal rhythm" (*PP*, 17) within the perpetual flux—and it has been one of the most enduring of ideas since. Throughout history, Pater says, there have been certain recurrent ideas which, because they persistently reappear, must have an irresistible attraction for the human imagi-nation. Such ideas must surely some day find their vindication in practical experience, must have some concrete and observable counterpart, otherwise how could we explain their persistence?[12]

---

[11] The autobiographical equivalent to this concept is found in "The Child in the House," in which the young boy's fear of ghosts, the spirits of the dead, became, under the impact of biblical ideas, the vision of "heavenly companionship" (*MS*, p. 194).

[12] In *ME*, I, 144; *IP*, p. 107; *Ap*, pp. 75–77; *PP*, pp. 40–41, 72–73; and elsewhere, Pater writes of those philosophical traditions which have been con-stantly present from the time of the Greeks. There appear to be three such traditions—the belief that the One alone is real, the belief that only the Many are real, and the belief that there is some Absolute which embodies both the One and the Many. The first two traditions owe their persistence to the fact that they reflect one side of the actual truth.

In the long progress of man's cultural history, the concrete equivalent of Heraclitus' old idea of the Logos has finally been identified with the ethical and religious spirit of collective humanity itself. And precisely because the Logos is thus recognizable in a concrete and almost bodily form, it becomes something which it is possible to know, love, and serve.

Pater does not present his own philosophical position with precision, but, broadly speaking, he was an idealist, although he believed that the palpable world of sensuous "forms" and "selves" was never to be transmuted into thought. In this respect he sympathizes more with the philosophies of Kant, Leibniz, and Lotze, who held to a pluralistic view of the universe, than with the philosophy of Hegel, whose rational Absolute is literally a Universe of Mind, a totally mental, super-personal reality. The cardinal thesis which Lotze had asserted we find re-echoed in Pater. Lotze had argued, as against Hegel, that thought can manipulate the so-called independent material world, can be valid of this world, but that the world itself never "reduces" to thought. Moreover, it is man's practical and aesthetic nature, rather than his intellectual faculty, which fundamentally determines his experience. Lotze's first and foremost concern was to preserve the inner individuality of things and selves. The Kantian "categories of the understanding" are never, Lotze points out, a mere inclination of uninterested understanding, but the inspiration of a reason appreciative of worth. This is, of course, the perfect springboard for the Oxford Personalists, the most notable of which was Pater's good friend Thomas Hill Green. The Personalists simply extended Lotze's argument to say that there is no neutral, non-human thinking, no impersonal reasoning. Hence, Kant's "Transcendental Self" has no meaning, says Green, except in experienceable qualities of human selves; it is a kind of world-consciousness, the source of the real or unalterable relations which are the external world of nature. By explicating the meaning of the terms further, the inference is that the Absolute is both immanent and transcendent, both the here-and-now and the yet-to-be, both finite and infinite, both fact and ideal, both matter and form, the One in the Many. Green made great efforts to show that the Absolute, far from negating finite selves, human aims and desires, human values and ideals, and personal freedom, is itself the fusion, the crystallization, as it were, of all these contrary elements. The Absolute came to be thought of not simply as a single being, but as the Person over and including all finite persons in whom they "live and move and have their being." Insofar as each human person gains true wisdom, vision, ethical purpose, fulfills his own duties in life, enjoys his best desires for his own happiness, exercises his own true freedom, outgrows his own limitations—just to that extent each person reflects in his own way the one all-inclusive Person, the personal Absolute. The more intensely each finite person refracts the brilliance, as it were, of the Absolute, the more interrelated with all others, the more of a "person" he will become.

One has no trouble at all in fitting Pater into this context. That aspiration toward the true union of all the parts of our broken existence, that yearning for "wholeness," goodness, and beauty is expressed by what Pater calls the Logos. If Pater's theories differed from Green's, it was because Pater often preferred to cast his thought in the form of myth—in terms of Dionysus, Apollo, and the Perfect City. These become the metaphors of his thought. The Apollonian brightness which surrounds the Paterian hero is the light of the Absolute Self which underlies and includes all the narrow, limited selves and constitutes their relatedness. Small wonder, then, that the subjective self should have intuitions of the overarching divinity of which it is the expression. The soul's sense of loyalty is largely a measure of its sensitivity to who and what it is, the ground of its being. At times one wonders if the image of the *Beata Urbs* really derived from Plato at all. It did undoubtedly. But just as "the somewhat visionary towers of Plato's *Republic* blend . . . with those of the *Civitas Dei* of Augustine" (*PP*, 243), so the City of God finds itself identified with the ideal community of selves as conceived by nineteenth-century Personalism.

Mankind's ideas, says Pater, grew slowly, like a plant; they were not ready-made, and the idea of the collective mind of humanity as the Logos, as significant as it has become in the present era, evolved but gradually in philosophic thought. Pater implies that the great contribution of Christianity and modern philosophy is the empirical reality which it bestows upon the "visionary" ideals of antiquity. In particular, the Christian understanding of the nature of the historic church has been of inestimable value in locating the Logos in a visible, personal form. Like Pater, Marius could not believe that that which can not be experienced, at least in part, is real. Certainly of primary importance, then, is Marius' discovery of the Christian community and the bringing of his vague sense of personal loyalty to some "divine companion" (*ME*, II, 70) into identification with Cornelius and this society. The physical manifestation of the divine companion, whose presence Marius had felt, was first realized in the incarnation of Christ, and it is the Christian society, as the "body of Christ," which is a continuation of that incarnation. Not surprisingly, then, the historic role that the Christian church has played is of great importance to Pater. In 1885, the year, significantly, that *Marius* was published, Pater had written to Mrs. Ward apropos of her translation of Henri-Frederic Amiel's *Journal Intime* that, in his opinion,

there was still something Amiel might have added to those elements of natural religion, (so to call it, for want of a better expression,) which he was able to accept, at times with full belief, and always with the sort of hope which is a great factor in life. To my mind, the beliefs, and the function in the world, of the historic church, form just one of those obscure but all-important possibilities, which the human mind is powerless effectively to dismiss from itself; and might wisely accept, in the first place, as a workable hypothesis.[13]

A few months later, in March of 1886, Pater wrote a review of the translation for the *Guardian,* in which he noted, among other things, that Amiel's failing was a "metaphysical prejudice for the 'Absolute' " (*EG*, 32), the wholly transcendent and abstract God. Analyzing this shortcoming of Amiel, Pater considers

what might have been the development of his profoundly religious spirit, had he been able to see that the old-fashioned Christianity is itself but the proper historic development of the true "essence" of the New Testament. There, again, is the constitutional shrinking, through a kind of metaphysical prejudice, from the concrete—that fear of the actual—in this case, of the Church of history; to which the admissions, which form so large a part of these volumes, naturally lead. Assenting, on probable evidence, to so many of the judgments of the religious sense, he failed to see the equally probable evidence there is for the beliefs, the peculiar direction of men's hopes, which complete those judgments harmoniously, and bring them into connection with the facts, the venerable institutions of the past—with the lives of the saints. By failure, as we think, of that historic sense, of which he could speak so well, he got no further in this direction than the glacial condition of rationalistic Geneva. "Philosophy," he says, "can never replace religion." Only, one cannot see why it might not replace a religion such as his: a religion, after all, much like Seneca's. "I miss something," he himself confesses, "common worship, a positive religion, shared with other people. Ah! when will the Church to which I belong in heart rise into being?" To many at least of those who can detect the ideal through the disturbing circumstances which belong to all actual institutions in the world, it was already there. Pascal, from considerations to which Amiel was no stranger, came to the large hopes of the Catholic Church; Amiel stopped short at a faith almost hopeless; and by stopping short just there he really

---

[13] Benson, *Pater*, p. 200. See also Mary Ward's *A Writer's Recollections* (London, 1918), II, 39–40.

failed, as we think, of intellectual consistency, and missed that appeasing influence which his nature demanded as the condition of its full activity, as a force, an intellectual force, in the world—in the special business of his life. "Welcome the unforeseen," he says again, by way of a counsel of perfection in the matter of culture, "but give to your life unity, and bring the unforeseen within the lines of your plan." Bring, we should add, the Great Possibility at least within the lines of your plan—your plan of action or production; of morality; especially of your conceptions of religion. (*EG*, 33–35)

In these sentences, Pater seems to be creating his own variation upon the natural religion of Amiel by insisting that the actual church is, itself, a kind of evidence.[14]

Marius' failure to make some sort of formal declaration of belief, then, is seen to be irrelevant once we have made Pascal's discovery, for the important thing is Marius' relation to the moral body of humanity, and in terms of this, his position is definite. This is why Marius feels that in human love there is "a touching of that absolute ground amid all the changes of phenomena" (*ME*, II, 184). In our sympathy with others we "seem to touch the eternal" (*ME*, II, 184), though we do not know it completely. For Pater's Marius, the final revelation can come only after death. Yet one can go a long way toward that Apollonian light outside the cave of human experience by joining the society of men who have answered religious questions in the affirmative. What Augustine or Dante or Pascal or Newman—or even the skeptics, even Montaigne or Mill—had to say will be of great importance to those like Marius, for it leaves the way open to hope. While the facts of Christianity cannot be proved, says Pater, nevertheless the very existence of a historical church seems to attest to some ideal order, and hope and love are immediately present in life whenever one is willing to make allowance for that possibility. Certainly, the duty of those who are innately skeptical yet loyal is to assent and accept, and out of this may grow a religion and a church to console and minister. The Church Universal has that

[14] By "natural religion," of course, Pater meant the adherence to any given religious belief—the existence of God, the immortality of the soul—entirely on the basis of the evidence which human experience and reason supply. As J. S. Mill had said, natural religion treats any doctrine "as a strictly scientific question," and its claims are to be tested "by the same scientific methods, and on the same principles as those of any of the speculative conclusions drawn by physical science" (*Three Essays on Religion* [New York, 1874], pp. 128–29). If Mill speaks for the Pater who demanded visual proof, there is also the Pater who acknowledged as significant those imponderables of temperamental variation. Something there remains in Pater's religion which cannot be weighed directly—that sense of dependence upon Someone who inspires the trust and loyalty which constitutes faith.

height and depth in which the single individual may find the freedom he so much desires. It extends beyond and breaks up the *flammantia moenia mundi*, says Pater. Aristippus of Cyrene, Montaigne, Mill, and the others had left off in "suspense of judgment as to what might really lie behind . . . the flaming ramparts of the world" (*ME*, I, 134), but with Pater and his heroes there is an insatiable desire to know, for even if this life were pleasant, which it certainly is not, even so, age and death will come.

Undoubtedly, Pater's projected trilogy of novels would have reflected this same concern with the intense desire of the hero to find freedom in a larger Apollonian world beyond himself. Perhaps the novels would have mirrored successive stages of the evolving idea that the Logos is the visible expression of the Self in the human race. It is this idea which supplies intellectual history with a thread of unity in the midst of the flux of opinion, and Pater may have planned to string his trilogy on this thread. But we shall never know. Certainly the trilogy would have occupied a unique place in Pater's fiction, for since the novels are longer than the other portraits, they would have permitted a more systematic and detailed analysis of these ideologies. But all of the fiction, regardless of length, turns around the single ideal of the Apollonian society, and it radiates a Utopian hope for a Perfect City that is far from being a "Nowhere." It is an ideal which rests on the past, but is nevertheless to be realized by "the human spirit on its way to perfection" (*Ap*, 65) only at the end of a long intellectual and moral evolution.

One comes to the conclusion that T. S. Eliot's appraisal of Pater as "just the cultivated Oxford don and disciple of Arnold, for whom religion was a matter of feeling, and metaphysics and not much more" greatly misses the mark. And when Eliot continues by saying of Pater that "being incapable of sustained reasoning, he could not take philosophy or theology seriously," he not only misses the mark, but shoots in the wrong direction entirely.[15] Undeniably, Pater liked ritual, but this is not to say that his religion was merely an aesthetic or humanistic pleasure in ceremony. "Roman religion," says Pater in *Marius*, "had, indeed, been always something to be done, rather than something to be thought, or believed, or loved" (*ME*, I, 181). For Pater and Pater's hero Marius, however, religion was not mere ritual, but "vision, the *seeing* of a perfect humanity, in a perfect world . . . —he had always set that above the *having*, or even the *doing*, of anything. For such vision, if received with due attitude on his part, was,

[15] *Selected Essays*, pp. 390–91.

in reality, the *being* something" (*ME*, II, 218). Christian ritual was, for Pater, an outward, visible sign of that inward and spiritual Love which renews the soul and creates the Perfect City of men. Indeed, Pater's religion differed from the religion of *Literature and Dogma*, for example, precisely by its realistic sacramentalism— as it is present to Marius, for example, in the "Divine Service," in which it is seen to be a revelation of God:

> *Let us then before him bending*
> *This great sacrament revere,*
> *Types and shadows have their ending*
> *For the newer rite is here.* (*ME*, II, 127)

Of course, Pater did not accept any strict evangelical approach to religion. On this point, at least, he was one with Arnold and the broad churchmen. He writes to Mrs. Ward that "the supposed facts on which Christianity rests, utterly incapable as they have become of any ordinary test, seem to me matters of very much the same sort of assent we give to any assumption, in the strict and ultimate sense, moral. The question whether those facts were real will, I think, always continue to be what I should call one of the *natural* questions of the human mind."[16] But precisely here the older mythic patterns proved helpful. Pater saw the Eucharist, celebrating the death of Christ, as having grown from some forgotten but still valid mythic pattern (*ME*, II, 126), and Dionysus, Demeter, and all the other mythic types and shadows of the newer rite had not been without their real spiritual significance. They bestowed on the event of the Crucifixion, which lies at the heart of the historic church, the reality of the analogous seasonal death and renewal of nature, making the church and its rites the proper continuation of the concrete expression of the Logos in history.

Certainly Pater's religion, while not an easy one, was genuine. He chose a harder faith, perhaps, than that of Arnold or Carlyle or Ruskin, for his was a religion without rest—restless not because flux and the relativity of knowledge are inevitably the human lot but because mankind is forever moving on to higher plateaus of religious vision. The historic church is like a ship carrying humanity on toward some distant goal. It is precisely this metaphor which occurs to Gaston when he first sees Chartres far off across the wheat fields, "like a ship for ever a-sail in the distance" (*GdL*, 26). Pater may have had in mind that passage in the *Phaedo* in which Simmias says,

[16] Benson, *Pater*, p. 200.

It is our duty to do one of two things. We must learn, or we must discover for ourselves, the truth of these matters; or, if that be impossible, we must take the best and most irrefragable of human doctrines, and embarking on that, as on a raft, risk the voyage of life, unless a stronger vessel, some divine word, could be found, on which we might take our journey more safely and more securely.[17]

That stronger vessel the Greek mind could later have found in Christianity—"in the Gospel of Saint John, perhaps, some of them might have found the kind of vision they were seeking for; but not in 'doubtful disputations' concerning 'being' and 'not-being,' knowledge and appearance" (*ME*, I, 140). Yet the Greek had used his single talent well, says Pater; he had been faithful "in what comparatively is perhaps little—in the culture, the administration, of the visible world; and he merited, so we might go on to say—he merited Revelation, something which should solace his heart in the inevitable fading of that" (*GS*, 298). Surely Pater is the Greek of which he writes, and his voyage of life was, he hoped, ultimately to prove a journey undertaken on a stronger vessel than abstract and doubtful doctrine. Precisely there, in the visible world, Pater found the promise of a Revelation to come. In humanity and in the historic church, the manifest expression of God, Pater discovered "something to rest on, in the drift of mere 'appearances'" (*ME*, I, 156). The celestial sailor did find land and home, after all.

[17] Plato, *Phaedo* 85ᵈ, trans. by F. J. Church in *The Trial and Death of Socrates* (London, 1959), pp. 156–57.

VI

THE UNCOLLECTED IMAGINARY PORTRAITS

After the publication of the *Imaginary Portraits*, no new editions of it appeared, although this was the book that Pater himself preferred above all his others. Toward the end of his life, however, Pater told both Benson and Symons that he intended to bring out a new collection of imaginary portraits which was to include "Hippolytus Veiled," "Apollo in Picardy," and a modern study—perhaps "An English Poet"—which Symons took to be "Emerald Uthwart." Further, Symons writes that Pater "had another subject in Moroni's *Portrait of a Tailor* in the National Gallery, whom he was going to make a Burgomaster; and another was to have been a study of life in the time of the Albigensian persecution."[1] No trace of the former exists; the latter, however, is probably the fragment "Tibalt the Albigense." There is also a second unfinished portrait, "Gaudioso, the Second." Neither Symons nor Benson mentions this portrait, but it, too, was probably destined for the second volume of *Imaginary Portraits*. "Hippolytus Veiled" is the earliest of these uncollected portraits.[2]

"HIPPOLYTUS VEILED" (1889)

Among the lost plays of Euripides, *Hippolytus Veiled* has attracted from classicists more than its share of attention, in part, no doubt, because of the unquestioned merit of the extant *Hippolytus* (or *Hippolytus Crowned*, as it is sometimes called) which followed it. Interestingly, *Hippolytus Veiled* was not well

---

[1] *Study of Pater*, p. 105; see also Benson, *Pater*, p. 123.
[2] Pater's literary critics have been slow to concede that "Hippolytus Veiled" deserves to be considered as an authentic portrait. Despite the fact that Pater himself called it an "Imaginary Portrait," Eugene Brzenk's otherwise excellent collection of the portraits has excluded it. What is obviously needed now is a reading of the portrait which will demonstrate its essentially imaginative character.

received, though with the rewritten version Euripides won first prize the year he brought it out. Undoubtedly what the literary critics of antiquity objected to in the earlier play was the manner in which Euripides treated Phaedra's passion for Hippolytus. In the revised version, Phaedra, the helpless victim of Aphrodite, nobly refrains from disclosing her passion to Hippolytus; it is only through the meddling of the nurse that Hippolytus discovers Phaedra's love for him. But in the *Hippolytus Veiled,* as we know from Seneca and Ovid, who both wrote books inspired by Euripides' lost drama, Phaedra forthrightly offers herself to the young man. It is this version which we find in Pater's portrait.

Why Pater should be drawn to this lost play is not hard to guess. First, he liked it because it was lost. Pater is here working in the realm of classical scholarship, but the absence of positive facts gives him freedom to improvise. Also, he undoubtedly preferred the more dramatic confrontation found in the plot of the first play. The story of the woman who offers herself and is rebuffed throws the whole chastity-lust conflict into high relief. Finally, another appealing feature of the lost play perhaps lies in what would have been for Pater its very metaphoric title, for his portrait of Hippolytus deals with the Greek awakening, the lifting of the veil from the origins of Western culture. What Pater wrote about the "exquisite early light" of that other awakening, the Italian one, is important in this connection. He tells us that "the choice life of the human spirit is always under mixed lights, and in mixed situations; when it is not too sure of itself, is still expectant, girt up to leap forward to the promise."[3] The world of Hippolytus, we note, is a "twilight" world—Pater uses the word a number of times—and this veiled or twilight quality is indicative of the "mixed lights" in the first moments of promise just before the break of day.

Indeed, the opening of Pater's "Hippolytus Veiled" is devoted to an elaborate parallel between the dawning of the Italian Renaissance and the first Greek cultural flowering. Pater tells us that

[3] *Westminster Review,* XXXIV, 307. In its revised form in "Aesthetic Poetry," in *Ap*(1889), p. 224, the phrase "exquisite early light" becomes "exquisite first period"—not nearly so meaningful, I think.

Certainly one can point to numerous other possible, though not quite so probable, explanations of the significance of the title. Germain d'Hangest, *Walter Pater,* II, 357–58, points out that Euripides' meaning, or what he takes to be Euripides' meaning—that of the hero veiling his face in a gesture of horror before a stepmother who is too provocative—is certainly not Pater's primary meaning. D'Hangest fancifully suggests that the old myth of Hippolytus is "veiled" in the thick shadows of hazy conjecture and that Pater will clear the cobwebs for us.

the "early Attic deme-life" offered "many a relic of primitive religion, many an early growth of art parallel to what Vasari records of artistic beginnings in the smaller cities of Italy" (*GS*, 153). Of the youth of the arts in Greece, Pater writes:

Overbeck's careful gleanings of its history form indeed a sorry relic
as contrasted with Vasari's intimations of the beginnings of the Renaissance. Fired by certain fragments of its earlier days, of a beauty,
in truth, absolute, and vainly longing for more, the student of Greek
sculpture indulges the thought of an ideal of youthful energy therein,
yet withal of youthful self-restraint; and again, as with survivals of
old religion, the privileged home, he fancies, of that ideal must have
been in those venerable Attic townships, as to a large extent it passed
away with them. The budding of new art, the survival of old religion,
at isolated centres of provincial life, where varieties of human character
also were keen, abundant, asserted in correspondingly effective incident—this is what irresistible fancy superinduces on historic details,
themselves meagre enough. (*GS*, 157–58)

And that which "irresistible fancy" superinduced on the "historic details" of Euripides' lost drama is nothing less than Pater's imaginary portrait of Hippolytus in which "the budding of new art" springs from a revitalizing encounter between the cold world of "old religion" and the "youthful energy" of the summer Dionysus.

Evoking the poignant scene of a soldier from one of those deme-towns nostalgically recalling the days of his youth, gone now forever in the chaos of the Peloponnesian war, Pater takes the reader back to an even earlier period of transition: "in those crumbling little towns, as heroic life had lingered on into the actual, so, at an earlier date, the supernatural into the heroic" (*GS*, 160). Our story begins soon after Theseus' seduction of Antiope, the Amazon queen. Theseus, who has already tired of his stolen mistress and new son, has placed mother and child in one of those "doomed, decaying villages, . . . hidden, yet secure, within the Attic border, as men veil their mistakes or crimes. They might pass away, they and their story, together with the memory of other antiquated creatures of such places, who had had connubial dealings with the stars" (*GS*, 163). This place of exile is one of the most crucial aspects in the story of Hippolytus as Pater tells it. The locus of the action is neither primarily at Troezen nor at Athens, as it was in Euripides' dramas, but on a by-path leading to Eleusis, the stone house Hippolytus and Antiope inhabit not far from the Eleusian shrine. Pater describes this house, and "its cubicle hewn in the stone" (*GS*, 164) in which the young Hippolytus slept, as invested with an aura of mystery:

In these highland villages the tradition of celestial visitants clung fondly, of god or hero, belated or misled on long journeys, yet pleased to be among the sons of men, as their way led them up the steep, narrow, crooked street, condescending to rest a little, as one, under some sudden stress not clearly ascertained, had done here, in this very house, thereafter for ever sacred. The place and its inhabitants, of course, had been something bigger in the days of those old mythic hospitalities, unless, indeed, divine persons took kindly the will for the deed—very different, surely, from the present condition of things, for there was little here to detain a delicate traveller, even in the abode of Antiope and her son, though it had been the residence of a king. Hard by stood the chapel of the goddess, who had thus adorned the place with her memories. (*GS*, 167)

The essay on "Demeter and Persephone" which Pater had written some years before "Hippolytus" acquaints us with the scene of Hippolytus' childhood home, for it reveals that the deity who veiled her godhead in human form to dwell in the crude stone house was none other than the goddess Demeter:

In her anger against Zeus, she forsook the assembly of the gods and abode among men, for a long time veiling her beauty under a worn countenance, so that none who looked upon her knew her, until she came to the house of Celeus, who was then king of Eleusis. In her sorrow she sat down at the wayside by the virgin's well, where the people of Eleusis come to draw water, under the shadow of an olive-tree. (*GS*, 85)

Sorrowing for her lost Persephone, Demeter nevertheless accepts the invitation to nurse the son of one of Celeus' daughters. But her identity revealed by herself after a time, she leaves to live in the chapel which she commanded the king to build for her over the well. Now, Hippolytus and Antiope share a home located at Eleusis, once owned by a king and once visited by a goddess. It is a house surrounded by olive trees and situated near the chapel dedicated to the goddess. Even the well-spring next to which Demeter rests is found in the story of Hippolytus, who unstops it when he returns to its rightful place the image which belonged in the chapel.

But the curious fact is that Hippolytus worships this goddess under the name of Artemis, not Demeter. The nature of this new and strange Artemis gradually becomes clear to the young lad in the course of his meditations:

Through much labour at length he comes to the veritable story of her birth, like a gift direct from the goddess herself to this loyal soul. There were those in later times who, like Aeschylus, knew Artemis as the daughter not of Leto but of Demeter, according to the version of her history now conveyed to the young Hippolytus, together with some deepened insight into her character. The goddess of Eleusis, on a journey, in the old days when, as Plato says, men lived nearer the gods, finding herself with child by some starry inmate of those high places, had lain down in the rock-hewn cubicle of the inner chamber, and, certainly in sorrow, brought forth a daughter. (*GS*, 169–70)[4]

Hippolytus' Artemis, then, is fully as much the double of Demeter's Persephone—"the late birth into the world of this so shadowy daughter was somehow identified with the sudden passing into Hades of her first-born, Persephone" (*GS*, 170)—as she is the sister of Apollo. And just as Persephone was in early myth identified with her mother—"in the mythical conception, as in the religious acts connected with it, the mother and the daughter are almost interchangeable; they are the *two* goddesses, the twin-named" (*GS*, 108–9)—so Artemis also is identified with Demeter. She was, in her "ambiguous" (*GS*, 170), paradoxical nature, a "virgin mother" (*GS*, 169):

At once a virgin, necessarily therefore the creature of solitude, yet also . . . the assiduous nurse of children, and patroness of the young. Her friendly intervention at the act of birth everywhere, her claim upon the nursling, among tame and wild creatures equally, among men as among gods, nay! among the stars (upon the very star of dawn), gave her a breadth of influence seemingly coextensive with the sum of things. Yes! his great mother was in touch with everything. (*GS*, 168)

That she is actually Demeter explains her "lighted touch" and "long straight vesture rolled round so formally" (*GS*, 169):

Here was the secret at once of the genial, all-embracing maternity of this new, strange Artemis, and of those more dubious tokens, the lighted torch, the winding-sheet, the arrow of death on the string—of sudden death, truly, which may be thought after all the kindest, as prevenient of all disgraceful sickness or waste in the unsullied limbs. (*GS*, 170)

Hippolytus has pledged himself, in Pater's version of the old legend, to the *Magna Mater*, to the sorrowing mother who is a virgin

[4] When Pater tells us that the dramatist Aeschylus "knew Artemis as the daughter not of Leto but of Demeter," he undoubtedly had in mind the passage in the first choral speech of the *Agamemnon*: "Artemis the undefiled is angered with pity at the flying hounds of her father eating the unborn young in the hare and the shivering mother. She is sick at the eagles's feasting. Sing sorrow, sorrow: but good win out in the end. Lovely you are and kind to the tender young of ravening lions. For sucklings of all the savage beasts that lurk in the lonely places you have sympathy."

because she has lost her lover. Her sterility can only be cured by the return of Persephone from the grave, a return which is symbolized by the fructifying death of the year-daimon. Both Hippolytus and his goddess are in a state of life-in-death, and only by breaking through death can the two be reunited in an immortal world. That he must undergo death in order to escape from it accounts for Hippolytus' "awful surmise" that "his divine patroness moves there as death, surely" (GS, 170).

Clearly Pater's rendering of the Hippolytus story is much closer to the original form of the myth than Euripides' version. One modern classicist writes:

It would not be going too far if we said that a goddess known as Hippolyta had had a priest-attendant who, becoming her masculine counterpart, took on a masculine form of her name. In doing so he was identifying himself also with a divine consort of the type usually associated with the pre-Greek vegetation goddesses. Possibly in the beginning the goddess was served by an actual eunuch who, as time softened the myth, became priest or worshiper merely bound by a vow of chastity. . . . If we are to say that originally he was a consort of a primitive goddess, then immediately he takes his place with other "year-gods," all of whom represented the annual cycle of vegetation. As the year itself grows from infancy to full maturity and then declines to make way for the new year, so the year-god grows to adulthood, makes fertile and thus renews the creative powers of the earth goddess, then dies (often is torn apart), and is later resurrected.[5]

Pater undoubtedly suspected that this was the original pre-Euripidean form of the myth and realized how effectively he could employ it to his ends. His portrait of Hippolytus, then, cannot be regarded as a mere reconstruction of Euripides' lost play; it is a great deal more than this. Like a deity of vegetation, all the impressions of natural things are condensed into Pater's figure of Hippolytus. He, like Dionysus, is the "spiritual form" of nature: "healthily white and red, he had a marvelous air of discretion about him, as of one never to be caught unaware, as if he could never by anything but like water from the rock, or the wild flowers of the morning, or the beams of the morning star turned to human flesh" (GS, 181).

Having recognized the fact that Hippolytus worships Artemis-Demeter, we can now plunge directly to the heart of the story. In Hippolytus' relation to Demeter, we discover a clear similarity to the daimon-mother relationship found in the other portraits by

[5] Donald Sutherland and Hazel Barnes, *Hippolytus in Drama and Myth* (Lincoln, Nebraska, 1960), pp. 116–17.

Pater, although perhaps it is most similar to the Marius-Cecilia relation. Saint Cecilia had early in life vowed perpetual virginity, and upon her marriage she induced her husband to respect her vow. When Marius sees her, she is without a husband (history tells us he was martyred); although surrounded by children like a mother, she is a virgin mother. Cecilia, then, corresponds exactly to the Demeter whom Hippolytus worships. Marius, of course, corresponds to Hippolytus; he loves Cecilia, but as a priest, not as physical man. There were incidents which Marius noted in his relations with Cecilia "warning a susceptible conscience not to mix together the spirit and the flesh, nor make the matter of a heavenly banquet serve for earthly meat and drink" (*ME*, II, 187). Such chaste love follows the usual mythic pattern. The year-daimon takes from the *Magna Mater* his origin, being called her son, though he is simultaneously raised to divine status as her consort. This explains Hippolytus' son-husband relation to Demeter, which Pater records as follows:

Phaedra's young children draw from the seemingly unconscious finger
the marriage-ring, set it spinning on the floor at his feet, and the
staid youth places it for a moment on his own finger for safety. As
it settles there, his step-mother, aware all the while, suddenly presses
his hand over it. He found the ring there that night as he lay; left
his bed in the darkness, and again, for safety, put it on the finger
of the image, wedding once for all that so kindly mystical mother.
(*GS*, 179)

The familial relationships are curious, but not indicative of "aesthetic decadence" on Pater's part. Hippolytus is merely portrayed here in the usual manner of the year-daimon, as the virile generative force seen in nature, but ultimately dependent upon the goddess.

Small wonder that Hippolytus, as the priest of Demeter, should prove difficult to seduce! Phaedra, who "explains the delights of love, of marriage, the husband once out of the way; finds in him, with misgiving, a sort of forwardness, as she thinks, on this one matter, as if he understood her craft and despised it" (*GS*, 179). Hardly naïve, he seems "a wily priest rather, skilfully circumventing her sorceries, with mystic precautions of his own" (*GS*, 181). Hippolytus recommends to the rather startled Phaedra the possibility of finding children in the temple or of buying them "as you could buy flowers in Athens" (*GS*, 179). So the blandishments of the whore are withstood, and her love turns to fury. In a passage designed to show the high moral quality of Hippolytus' chastity, Pater draws a parallel between his expulsion and that of the biblical Joseph: "What words! what terrible words! following, clinging to him, like acrid fire upon his bare flesh, as he hasted from Phaedra's house, thrust out at last, his vesture remaining in her hands. The husband returning suddenly, she tells him a false story of violence to her bed, and is believed" (*GS*, 182).[6] Theseus then expends "one of three precious curses (some mystery of wasting sickness therein) with which Poseidon had indulged him" (*GS*, 182) upon the unfortunate Hippolytus.

The "wasting sickness" comes upon Hippolytus, and the world around him seems to become part of Phaedra's chapel: "his wholesome religion seeming to turn against him now, the trees, the streams, the very rocks, swoon into living creatures, swarming around the goddess who has lost her grave quietness. He finds solicitation, and recoils, in the wind, in the sounds of the rain; till at length delirium itself finds a note of returning health" (*GS*, 183–84). In a passage in "Aesthetic Poetry," already quoted in Chapter I, Pater speaks of this "wild, convulsed sensuousness . . . in which the things of nature begin to play a strange delirious part" (*Ap* [1889], 218). Hippolytus has begun to outgrow the summer world of the year-daimon, and his soul, imprisoned, descends to the delirium of winter death. But then, with a "sharp rebound" to the "broad daylight" (*Ap* [1889], 221), there comes the awakening. With his recovery, Antiope thinks the curse on Hippolytus is past: "her misgivings, arising always out of the actual spectacle of his profound happiness, seemed at an end in this meek bliss, the more as she observed that it was a shade less unconscious than of old" (*GS*, 184–85). But this recovery is only symptomatic of the greater awakening; Hippolytus in reaching maturity has lost his own youthful unconsciousness, and the consummation of his marriage to the Great Mother is celebrated by his death. The two remaining curses of Theseus take effect, and Hippolytus is dragged home to die by the horses and chariot that had been his ruin.

Pater's last few perfunctory remarks on the seeming afterthought of Hippolytus' resurrection are of great importance. They call attention to the pre-Euripidean form of the myth which included, in its earliest, mystical state, a resurrection.[7] Pater tells

---

[6] The syncretic mythologists had often implied a common origin between the biblical story and the Hippolytus myth. Sometimes the Egyptian "Tale of Two Brothers" was also included here.

[7] Even Euripides did not completely escape overtones of the resurrected Hippolytus; there are traces of the original Dionysian drama of death and rebirth or deification. In the play, Euripides has Artemis tell the audience of the cult of Hippolytus in her last speech: "And to thee, poor sufferer, for

us at the end that to the desolate Antiope, "counting the wounds, the disfigurements, telling over the pains which had shot through that dear head now insensible to her touch among the pillows under the harsh broad daylight" (*GS*, 186), all the posthumous healing of "the kindly Asclepius" (*GS*, 186) or the fancies of Ovid in later years could not console her, for her son lay dead. Pater dismisses the help of Ovid and Asclepius, who heal the mortal man, a crude form of the idea of the renewal of life in an immortal state. They fail to see that beyond the resurrection of nature there lies the Apollonian world of immortality freed from the eternal cycle of the primitive seasonal god. Central to all of Pater's thought is the idea that mortality is not renewed but that there occurs a rebirth into immortality. The physical Hippolytus does not return, but the great Greek intellectual awakening comes as an indication of the renewal of life which has taken place within the soul itself. Certainly Antiope's grief is real, but it is a tragedy not without a certain measure of hard, astringent joy. She is like the statue of Demeter, the seeker, an antique Pieta, with "something of the pity of Michelangelo's *mater dolorosa*, in the wasted form and marred countenance, yet with the light breaking faintly over it from the eyes . . . looking upward" (*GS*, 145). In the tremendous silence as she sits beside the torn body, one fancies one can hear, even beyond the dance music of the old Dionysian *Sacar Laudus*, the chant of the *Kyrie Eleison*.

"EMERALD UTHWART" (1892)

As in so many of Pater's portraits, the narrator of "Emerald Uthwart" is once again the well-traveled Victorian man of letters. Seemingly an inveterate reader of epitaphs, our narrator yearns to flesh the bare bones of the inscriptions with a life history. He recalls the epitaphs of the German students in the Dominican church at Siena. One of these in particular, on which the dates were left out, seems to testify, somehow, by its peculiar atemporality, to that sense of immortality which is so strong when death comes to the young. At the present moment, however, the epitaph which has struck our narrator's fancy is not that of some student who has died far from home, but rather that of a young man

---

thy anguish now will I grant high honors in the city of Troezen; for thee shall maids unwed before their marriage cut off their hair, thy harvest through the long roll of time of countless bitter tears." Pausanias, in the second century A.D., corroborates Euripides, telling us of the annual sacrifices at Troezen and the ritual of hair-cutting. See Jane Harrison in *Themis: A Study of the Social Origins of Greek Religion* (Cambridge, 1912), pp. 336–37.

who died in the local parish where he was born. He was, however, as student and soldier, one who had spent the major part of his life away from home. Bit by bit the details of Emerald Uthwart's life are filled in before our eyes.

Much of Pater's own life, of course, enters one way or another into his story of Emerald.[8] Certainly the particular direction of Pater's studies at this time were of primary importance in the creation of the world which surrounds Emerald. In 1892 Pater was absorbed in writing the last three chapters of *Plato and Platonism*, in which, for the most part, he concerned himself with Plato's vision of the ideal society, "the Republic." Emerald's environment, both in school and in the army, has as its background the Dorian ideal of discipline and *ascêsis*, and much that is said in *Plato* of the ideal city is pertinent to an analysis of Emerald's world.[9]

In most of Pater's portraits, home is conceived to be an ideal environment. Emerald's home, however, is not ideal, although if the average child were to be consulted, he would probably say that it is the very embodiment of perfection. Emerald, says Pater, enjoyed

all the freedom of the almost grown-up brothers, the unrepressed noise, the unchecked hours, the old rooms, all their own way, he is literally without the consciousness of rule. Only, when the long irresponsible day is over, amid the dew, the odours, of summer twilight, they roll

---

[8] The small Sussex village, home of the Uthwarts, resembles Chailey, where Pater had often visited his friend McQueen, while the Uthwart house itself recalls the old Pater residence at Enfield. Germain d'Hangest has also suggested that the name "Uthwart" may have been derived from an actual family known to Pater, from that of the Uthwatts who visited Pater's grandfather at Olney (*Walter Pater*, II, 361). In addition, one can hardly escape noticing that Emerald's preparatory school is remarkably like King's School in Canterbury, which Pater attended. Indeed, the portrait itself may have been the direct result of a visit which Pater made to Canterbury just at the time of his writing. May Ottley says, "It was written soon after Mr. Pater's last visit to his old school, in the summer of 1891, a visit which revivified faded memories, and evoked an eager response to the impressions of the moment" (*IPB*, p. 9).

[9] This portrait of Emerald, then, is a typical instance of the crossing of lines in Pater's fiction and criticism, Pater undertaking the one because of his interest in the other. The essays on Rossetti and Lemaître, for example, were in all probability stimulated by parallel interests in *Marius*, the subject of Roman euphuism and ballads suggesting the former, thoughts about the nature of true religious conversion producing the latter. In "Emerald Uthwart" (as in "Denys" and the two last unfinished portraits) the current obviously runs in the opposite direction, from criticism to fiction. The lack of imaginary portraits between 1889 and 1892 was directly due to Pater's preoccupation with *Plato and Platonism*, and the appearance of "Emerald Uthwart" was in a sense the fictional embodiment of themes already worked out in *Plato*.

their cricket-field against to-morrow's game. So it had always been
with the Uthwarts; they never went to school. In the great attic he
has chosen for himself Emerald awakes;—it was a rule, sanitary, almost medical, never to rouse the children—rises to play betimes; or,
if he choose, with window flung open to the roses, the sea, turns
to sleep again, deliberately, deliciously, under the fine old blankets.
(*MS*, 201)

Yet this environment falls short of the ideal in two ways: Emerald
was a neglected child, and there was very little in this life to
call out the intellectual side of his nature. This lack of maternal
love and intellectual challenge results in a complete absence of
environmental cohesion; all falls apart into the little unrelated
units of the centrifugal world. Pater very carefully points to this
"littleness" in the Uthwart's vegetative way of life:

The very mould here, rich old black gardener's earth, was flower-seed;
and beyond, the fields, one after another, through the white gates
breaking the well-grown hedge-rows, were hardly less garden-like;
little velvety fields, little with the true sweet English littleness of
our little island, our land of vignettes. Here all was little; the very
church where they went to pray, to sit, the ancient Uthwarts sleeping
all around under the windows, deposited there as quietly as fallen
trees on their native soil, and almost unrecorded, as there had been
almost nothing to record. (*MS*, 200)

This is the littleness, of course, of the summer world of Dionysus—
quite satisfactory to the Uthwarts, apparently, who seem not to
have outgrown the narrow confines of the vegetative cycle. It calls
to mind the same sort of littleness which Marie-Marguerite saw
in the petty life of Paris.

Emerald, like a flower, is "plucked forth" (*MS*, 203) from
this carefree existence and sent off to a school different in every
way from his home:

The Uthwarts had scarcely had more memories than their woods, noise-
lessly deciduous; or their pre-historic, entirely unprogressive, unrecord-
ing fore-fathers, in or before the days of the Druids. Centuries of
almost "still" life—of birth, death, and the rest, as merely natural
processes—had made them and their home what we find them. Centuries of conscious endeavour, on the other hand, had builded, shaped,
and coloured the place, a small cell, which Emerald Uthwart was
now to occupy; a place such as our most characteristic English education has rightly tended to "find itself a house" in—a place full, for
those who came within its influence, of a will of its own. Here everything, one's very games, have gone by rule onwards from the dim
old monastic days, and the Benedictine school for novices with the
wholesome severities which have descended to our own time.
(*MS*, 203–4)

Emerald's "wild-growth must now adapt itself" (*MS*, 204) to the discipline of the school, whose buildings are "beautifully proportioned," but "hard" and "cold" (*MS*, 204): "From his native world of soft garden touches, carnation and rose (they had been everywhere in those last weeks), where every one did just what he liked, he was passed now to this world of grey stone; and here it was always the decisive word of command" (*MS*, 204–5).

By going to school, Emerald has allied himself with something larger than the small and disparate elements of the Uthwart world: "If at home there had been nothing great, here, to boyish sense, one seems diminished to nothing at all, amid the grand waves, wave upon wave, of patiently-wrought stone" (*MS*, 209). The ocean, as an image of a larger order external to oneself, is here seen in the architectural waves of the school buildings. It is an ocean of almost infinite extension, but without Dionysian lawlessness. The hardness of a stone form gives it an Apollonian outline. One is reminded of what Pater had written in *Marius*, as Marius, too, moved from his centrifugal Epicureanism toward the more centripetal Christian system:

A wonderful order, actually in possession of human life!—grown inextricably through and through it; penetrating into its laws, its very language, its mere habits of decorum, in a thousand half-conscious ways; yet still felt to be, in part, an unfulfilled ideal; and, as such, awakening hope, and an aim, identical with the one only consistent aspiration of mankind! (*ME*, II, 27)

Like Marius, Emerald joins the one great and continuous system of mankind, pagan and Christian:

The old heathen's way of looking at things, his melodious expression of it, blends, or contrasts itself oddly with the everyday detail, with the very stones, the Gothic stones, of a world he could hardly have conceived, its medieval surroundings, their half-clerical life here. Yet not so inconsistently after all! The builders of these aisles and cloisters had known and valued as much of him as they could come by in their own un-instructed time; had built up their intellectual edifice more than they were aware of from fragments of pagan thought, as, quite consciously, they constructed their churches of old Roman bricks and pillars, or frank imitations of them. (*MS*, 215)

In this great system where every part has its function, where even the stones are made of minute dead bodies, Emerald, too, has his little place, his "narrow cubicle" (*MS*, 206–7). Beyond doubt, the coherence lacking at home is present at school.

Pater's study of Plato's ideal society is of great importance here. The whole tendency of the perfect Platonic society is toward the centripetal ideal of order, rule, and intellect. Pater tells us that Plato in his *Republic* envisions the subordination of the individual to the whole as the supreme virtue in society. Public life is regimented in a military manner, war itself, indeed, occupying an important place in the total pattern. This ideal, says Pater, was perhaps most closely approximated in antiquity by the Spartans. Pater utilizes the material in his chapter on "Lacedaemon" when he writes in "Emerald Uthwart":

The aim of a veritable community, says Plato, is not that this or that member of it should be disproportionately at ease, but that the whole should flourish; though indeed such general welfare might come round again to the loyal unit therein, and rest with him, as a privilege of his individual being after all. The social type he preferred, as we know, was conservative Sparta and its youth; whose unsparing discipline had doubtless something to do with the fact that it was the handsomest and best-formed in all Greece. (*MS*, 210)

The Dorian spirit that reigned at Canterbury expressed itself as a type of military monasticism, just as the Spartan ethos was "half-military, half-monastic" (*PP*, 218): "Uniforms and surplices were always close together here, where a military garrison had been established in the suburbs for centuries past, and there were always sons of its officers in the school" (*MS*, 222). This asceticism of the rigorously disciplined military-monastic life reflects that Apollonian principle of order which tames the chaos. "*Ascêsis*" is a word we need, says Pater—need, perhaps, because *asceticism* too often connotes a contempt for the individuality and beauty of physical things certainly not found in the true Dorian community.

This Spartan regimen had its impact on the youth. Emerald is mistakenly called, by those who go so far as to identify him with the principle of order itself, "golden-haired, scholar Apollo" (*MS*, 221). Certainly the physical form of Emerald seems to have been inspired with the Apollonian ideal:

A musical composer's notes, we know, are not themselves till the fit executant comes, who can put all they may be into them. The somewhat unmeaningly handsome facial type of the Uthwarts, moulded to a mere animal or physical perfection through wholesome centuries, is breathed on now, informed, by the touches, traces, complex influences from past and present, a thousandfold, crossing each other in this late century, and yet at unity in the simple law of the system to which he is now subject. (*MS*, 221)

We are reminded of Lucius Verus' physiognomy, described in *Marius:* "healthy-looking, cleanly, and firm, which seemed unassociable with any form of self-torment, and made one think of the muzzle of some young hound or roe, such as human beings invariably like to stroke—a physiognomy, in effect, with all the goodliness of animalism of the finer sort, though still wholly animal" (*ME,* I, 195). Verus' physical perfection is strictly limited to the narrow sphere of the summer Dionysus and does not get beyond that "littleness" reflected in the Uthwart world. Marius, observing Verus, thought for a moment that his own life "might have been fulfilled by an enthusiastic quest after perfection;—say, in the flowering and folding of a toga" (*ME,* I, 197). Pater had again indicated this ironic limitation of the Dionysian in his portrait of Duke Carl, where the old Grand Duke desires to have his Apollo-like grandson "a *virtuoso* in nothing less costly than gold—gold snuff boxes" (*IP,* 128). But Emerald, Marius, and the young Duke all rise beyond the unconsciousness of this superficial summer world into a really perfect and golden world of Apollo.

Inspired not only by the military atmosphere of the school but also by his memory of "that old warrior Uthwart's record in the church at home" (*MS,* 205), Emerald moves by a natural transition from the world of the school to that of the army. We should not be surprised at Emerald's great success in adapting to his Spartan environment nor even at his eventual enlistment in the army, for his name tells us a great deal about him, a clear instance of Pater's characterization by nomenclature. The greenness of the emerald reminds us, as does the "emerald" (*IP,* 56) green flask in "Denys," of the shoot of new life, Dionysian vitality of the summer-time. The emerald, as a gem, has traditionally signified immortality, incorruptibility, and the conquest of sin and trial; Pater opened his portrait with this theme of immortality, and he will return to it again at the conclusion. Emerald's last name is equally revealing. We are told by Pater that Emerald has descended from an "old-English" (*MS,* 202) family; thus, if we open the *Oxford English Dictionary* to *uthe,* we discover that its Anglo-Saxon meaning is *harmony,* the word being derived from an older world meaning *poetry* or *melody.* Emerald, says Pater, "seemed, in short, to harmonise by their combination in himself all the various qualities proper to a large and varied community of youths of nineteen or twenty, to which, when actually present there, he was felt from hour to hour to be indispensable" (*MS,* 225). This is the Apollonian significance of his name; like Florian Deleal's name, Emerald's also reflects the Dionysus-Apollo combination. The last part of Emerald's surname, *wart,* is significant, too. In military colloquial use the word refers to a very young subaltern—obviously suitable, for Emerald as a subaltern reminds us of Pater's other military heroes: the knightly Cornelius, the soldier-Emperor Aurelius, Sebastian van Storck's saintly namesake, and the masculine youth of Lacedaemonia whose disciplined lives reflect the Apollonian order.[10]

Before we turn to the career of the "young subaltern" in the army, one more point should be noted: Emerald's relation to his companion and senior at school, James Stokes. The two become almost like brothers, are "bracketed together" (*MS,* 224), go always "side by side" (*MS,* 225). Pater tells us that James Stokes looks for "the Greek or the Latin model of their antique friendship" but that none "fits exactly" (*MS,* 214). Yet the general archetypal pattern of Demeter and Persephone seems strikingly close: "they are the *two* goddesses, the twin-named" (*GS,* 109) who go side by side in the great procession from Athens to Eleusis (*GS,* 45). And the particular version which this pattern takes in the "Lacedaemon" chapter in *Plato,* the background study for this portrait, is the myth of the Dioscuri, the twin brothers Polydeuces and Castor, who had an important cult in Sparta:

Brothers, comrades, who could not live without each other, they were the most fitting patrons of a place in which friendship, comradeship, like theirs, came to so much. Lovers of youth they remained, those enstarred types of it, arrested thus at that moment of miraculous good fortune as a consecration of the clean, youthful friendship, "passing even the love of women," which, by system, and under the sanction of their founder's name, elaborated into a kind of art, became an elementary part of education. . . . The beloved and the lover, side by side through their long days of eager labour, and above all on the battlefield, became respectively, ἀΐτης, the hearer, and εἰσπνήλας, the inspirer; the elder inspiring the younger with his own strength and noble taste in things. (*PP,* 231–32)

The love of these two brothers provided the model of all true Spartan friendships and was fundamental to the whole Lacedaemonian scholastic and military structure.

---

[10] All of the elements in Emerald Uthwart's name suggest youth as well. The greenness of the emerald represents new life, while *uthe* is itself the obsolete form of the word *youth;* a *wart* is, by definition, youthful. One wonders if, with regard to Emerald's friend, James Stokes, his last name may not be another instance of characterization by nomenclature since *stoke* in Middle English means a thrust with a weapon, a stab—the army stoked poor Stokes. As to his first name, since Emerald and James were "brothers," perhaps we have a biblical reference to James, the brother of Christ.

This legend of the Dioscuri has its striking resemblances to the myths of both Demeter and Persephone and the two brothers Apollo and Dionysus, the elder god immortal, the younger one mortal. The Dioscuri myth, says Pater, tells of the twin-stars Gemini, of

> those two half-earthly, half-celestial brothers, one of whom, Polydeuces, was immortal. The other, Castor, the younger, subject to old age and death, had fallen in battle, was found breathing his last. Polydeuces thereupon, at his own prayer, was permitted to die: with undying fraternal affection, had forgone one moiety of his privilege, and lay in the grave for a day in his brother's stead, but shone out again on the morrow; the brothers thus ever coming and going, interchangeably, but both alike gifted now with immortal youth. (*PP*, 230–31)

Pater's description of Castor and Polydeuces is almost equally applicable to Emerald and James, whose friendship followed this Lacedaemonian ideal in every way. The two are so much like brothers that at the execution of Stokes Emerald felt as though "one half of himself had then descended" (*MS*, 240) into the grave. In *The Renaissance*, Pater had written that the friendship of Amis and Amile reflected "that curious interest of the *Doppelgänger* which begins among the stars with the Dioscuri, being entwined in and out through all the incidents of the story, like an outward token of the inward similitude of their souls" (*R*, 9). We are told that through love "Amis takes the place of Amile in a tournament for life or death" (*R*, 10), and that afterwards Amile, by the sacrifice of his children, redeemed Amis from leprosy. At the conclusion of the story even the children are restored, and there is great rejoicing. In this tale of Amis and Amile, as in the myth of the Gemini itself, we see life and death—or, more precisely, life-in-death—transformed into eternal life when the separated are reunited. So, too, in the portrait of Emerald and James. Neither alone is to be identified with Apollo; only in union do they rise above their individuality to join with the Absolute. But why, one inevitably asks, should these two, who are so obviously the military ideal of Sparta, come to such disgrace in the army?[11] In his ability to suppress emotion, in his tendency to shy away from the jarring disharmony of self-assertion, in his contentment with his own small

[11] Germain d'Hangest tells us (*Walter Pater*, II, 361) that "L'épisode militaire *d'Emerald Uthwart* ne paraît pas avoir de sources particulières, ce dont s'accommode fort bien sa nature extrêmement vague." Just like a Frenchman not to admit Napoleon's defeat! Pater carefully plants enough clues in the story so that we can definitely identify "the crowning victory" (*MS*, p. 239) as that at Waterloo in June, 1815.

place in the larger scheme—in all these aspects Emerald is a true member of the Platonic community, the perfect note in the great symphony of balanced forces. Again the typical pattern of Pater's fiction answers the question: it is a matter of the mean and its extremes. If Emerald's home was a formless world of disparate entities, so here we have a world without room for any individuality. The army is not the perfectly ordered Apollonian world, for the philosophy of the army, like the philosophy of Aurelius or Sebastian, does not recognize the fact that the universal order must be expressed in particular entities. In this portrait, the school comes closest to Pater's ideal Apollonian world, for the school, although it certainly demands a large measure of conformity from its students, nevertheless is willing to tolerate a certain variety within the unity. The army, on the other hand, insists on full conformity—or certainly Wellington's army did, says Pater. The British Army of 1814, a complete *tabula rasa*, fell seriously short of Plato's vision of what an army should be.

There are, in *Plato and Platonism*, two interesting references which, in passing, describe what an army ideally should be:

Plato's demand is for the limitation, the simplifying, of those constituent parts or units; that the unit should be indeed no more than a part, it might be a very small part, in a community, which needs, if it is still to subsist, the wholeness of an army in motion, of the stars in their courses, of well-concerted music, if you prefer that figure, or, as the modern reader might perhaps object, of a machine. (*PP*, 241)

We are to become—like little pieces in a machine! you may complain.—No, like performers rather, individually, it may be, of more or less importance, but each with a necessary and inalienable part, in a perfect musical exercise which is well worth while, or in some sacred liturgy; or like soldiers in an invincible army, invincible because it moves as one man. (*PP*, 273)

From these quotations we learn what two characteristics an army should have: it must have an organic co-ordination, not that of a machine the parts of which have no true individual being, and it must also combine motion with unity. Unfortunately, the army in which Emerald finds himself is not like the Platonic army. First, the British Army operates much more like a machine: "They come in sight at last of the army in motion, like machines moving" (*MS*, 230), Pater writes. Secondly, in short order the machine stops moving altogether: "It was like a calm at sea, delaying one's passage, one's purpose in being on board at all, a dead calm, yet with an awful feeling of tension, intolerable at last for those who were still all athirst for action" (*MS*, 232). Does Emerald's gesture of insubordination, then, break "*l'enchantement d'une parfaite musique*," as d'Hangest says it does?[12] Surely not, for music without movement, music which has stopped, does not exist at all. Plato's ideal army transcends the British machine because it blends the whole and the part in harmonious, purposeful motion. It is this awareness of the necessity of movement which gives to the Platonic vision its necessary centrifugal counterbalance.

The seizure of the enemy's flag by Stokes and Uthwart, then, differs not in its heroism from the act which had inspired it (*MS*, 223); rather, it differs in that it ran against the enforced unity of the army, like the act of the unfortunate colonel (*MS*, 233). The monstrous punishment of the offenders testifies to the inhumanity of the machine, to its total inability to comprehend the value of individual life or of a deed which is later declared by all to be unquestionably heroic. This complete unconcern with individual suffering or death recalls Sebastian's indifference toward the death of the individual and Aurelius' impassivity toward the pain of animals, Gauls, and Christians. James Stokes, intelligent and kind, lying there, his body riddled by the firing squad, his head shattered by the *coup de grâce* of the musket—Stokes becomes here, in effect, a year-daimon—presents a striking contrast to the way in which the Platonic society would treat the man who did not fit: " 'We should tell him,' says Socrates, 'that there neither is, nor may be, any one like that among us, and so send him on his way to some other city, having anointed his head with myrrh and crowned him with a garland of wool, as something in himself half-divine' " (*PP*, 276). The contrast tells us all we need to know: the British Army has been weighed and found wanting.

At the close of the portrait of Emerald, Pater probes the significance of Emerald's "good-fortune, its terrible withdrawal, the long agony" (*MS*, 243). Pater had closed his portrait of the visitor to Sparta with much the same question directed at some hypothetical Lacedaemonian:

Why this strenuous task-work, day after day; why this loyalty to a system, so costly to you individually, though it may be thought to have survived its original purpose; this laborious, endless, education, which does not propose to give you anything very useful or enjoyable in itself? . . . Why, with no prospect of Israel's reward, are you as scrupulous, minute, self-taxing, as he? (*PP*, 232–33)

[12] *Ibid.*, n. 44.

In *Plato* Pater does not answer the question directly; he says only that, like Saint Paul, we are puzzled by the Greeks:

It is because they make us ask that question; puzzle us by a paradoxical idealism in life; are thus distinguished from their neighbours; that, like some of our old English places of education, though we might not care to live always at school there, it is good to visit them on occasion; as some philosophic Athenians, as we have now seen, loved to do, at least in thought. (*PP*, 234)

The question does, however, have an answer. It is implied in the image of the English school and of the Dorian community. The vision of the "City of the Perfect, *The Republic*, Καλλίπολις, *Uranopolis, Utopia, Civitas Dei, The Kingdom of Heaven*" (*PP*, 266), is one of those constant traditions in history, an idea "which *will* recur" (*PP*, 73), as is amply testified to by its plurality of names throughout history. Plato, says Pater, "would not be surprised if no eyes actually see it. Like his master Socrates, as you know, he is something of a humorist; and if he sometimes surprises us with paradox or hazardous theory, will sometimes also give us to understand that he is after all not quite serious" (*PP*, 266). But the significance of all those who, like Emerald and James, strive after Spartan perfection is that by the very existence of their self-discipline, love, and suffering, their lives seem to testify visibly to that Apollonian ideal which orders all chaos and is the essence of that Perfect City toward which all humanity is moving.

The strongest guarantee of the reality of this ideal is seen in the heroic sort of love which conquers death, as in the myth of the Dioscuri the love of Polydeuces resulted in the immortality of Castor. But it is not the abstract love of an Aurelius which will provide the foundation for the perfect society. Like the army of Wellington, such love is a *tabula rasa* wholly indifferent to individual values. Only the love of one individual for another, the love of a Marius for a Cornelius, of an Amis for an Amile, of an Emerald for a James, can create the Ideal City. Emerald characteristically refuses to be swept into abstractions: "In fact, as the breath of the infinite world came about him, he clung all the faster to the beloved finite things still in contact with him; he had successfully hidden from his eyes all beside" (*MS*, 241–42). This is the reason that the "saintly vicar" wonders "what kind of place there might be, in any possible scheme of another world, for so absolutely unspiritual a subject" (*MS*, 241).

Yet for all his seeming unspirituality (indeed, at first he had even wanted to be buried in the animal graveyard), Emerald attains to the very highest state of grace. We recall that curious postscript from the diary of a surgeon who had been summoned to remove the bullet from Emerald's old gun-shot wound. What most impressed the surgeon about the body was its almost unearthly perfection:

> I was struck by the great beauty of the organic developments, in
> the strictly anatomic sense; those of the throat and diaphragm in
> particular might have been modelled for a teacher of normal physi-
> ology, or a professor of design. The flesh was still almost as firm
> as that of a living person; as happens when, as in this case, death
> comes to all intents and purposes as gradually as in old age. (MS, 245)

There is in the corpse, strangely, a very real sense of "health and life" (MS, 245). The significance of this becomes quite clear when we recall from *Appreciations* a similar circumstance described by another medical doctor:

> The leading motive of Browne's letter is the deep impression he has
> received during those visits, of a sort of physical beauty in the coming
> of death, with which he still surprises and moves his reader. There
> had been, in this case, a tardiness and reluctancy in the circumstances
> of dissolution, which had permitted him, in the character of a physi-
> cian, as it were to assist at the spiritualising of the bodily frame
> by natural process; a wonderful new type of a kind of mortified grace
> being evolved by the way. The spiritual body had anticipated the
> formal moment of death; the alert soul, in that tardy decay, changing
> its vesture gradually, and as if piece by piece. The infinite future
> had invaded this life perceptibly to the senses, like the ocean felt
> far inland up a tidal river. (Ap, 152–53)

This kind of death is not really death at all and may better be described as a "translation." It contrasts rather obviously with James Stokes' death. Stokes died of his bullet wounds suddenly, violently, like the typical year-daimon. Emerald, as the surgeon's autopsy reveals, was shot in the heart, yet, contrary to usual experience, his wound seemingly heals.

If we invoke the Polydeuces-Castor myth here, we may perhaps be justified in assuming that Emerald, as his name implies, is the immortal Polydeuces and that Stokes is the mortal Castor. Stokes, like Castor, moves by an abrupt transition from the mortal to the immortal state, whereas Emerald, who does not die but is like the immortal Polydeuces, carried the presence of death in his heart for a time. In his year of aimless wandering, looking for the grave he cannot find, Emerald certainly resembles Demeter searching for her lost Persephone, Demeter in her sorrow, the winter Dionysus. His shining immortality is in eclipse, veiled like the face of Demeter, until that which is lost and dead can be restored again. The two coffins, one filled and the other empty—we are reminded of the coffins in "Denys" and "Duke Carl"—symbolize that state of life-in-death through which the questing soul must move looking for the life beyond mortality. For Emerald, as for Demeter or Semele or the others, "one half of himself" (*MS*, 240) had gone down into the jaws of death, and he, too, felt that coldness in his heart.

Certainly the only possible objection to seeing Emerald as Polydeuces and Stokes as Castor is that Emerald is the younger of the two friends, whereas in the myth Castor was younger. But this difficulty is resolved if we recall the mythic pattern in which the year-daimon is awakened by the *Magna Mater*, who is then herself fructified and recreated by his death. Emerald and Stokes are each in relation to the other creator and created; we recall how the two mutually caught fire in school and war. And perhaps Emerald's age-in-youth is not without its overtones also of Browne's letter to his friend. In it, Browne had commented upon the young man who, by his exemplary life, had at his early death "already fulfilled the prime and longest intention of his being":

> Though age had set no seal upon his face, yet a dim eye might clearly discover fifty in his actions; and therefore, since wisdom is the grey hair, and an unspotted life old age; although his years came short, he might have been said to have held up with longer lives.[13]

Thus Emerald, who is closest to that half-ideal childhood "full of the fruits of old age" (*Ap*, 55) celebrated by Wordsworth and Vaughan, is also the one who has lived the longest since a return to child-like innocence is the whole aim of the circle of life. Perhaps this is the reason that the sense of immortality is so strong when death comes to the young.

"APOLLO IN PICARDY" (1893)

In his essay on "Pico della Mirandola," in *The Renaissance*, Pater noted that certain of the Italian scholars of the fifteenth century had made an attempt "to reconcile Christianity with the religion of ancient Greece" (*R*, 30). He wrote that "an earlier and simpler generation had seen in the gods of Greece so many malignant spirits, the defeated but still living centres of the religion

[13] *The Works of Sir Thomas Browne*, ed. Simon Wilkin (Bohn's Antiquarian Library, London, 1852), III, 79. Could Emerald's nickname, Aldy, be significant? *Ald* is an obsolete form of the word *old*.

of darkness, struggling, not always in vain, against the kingdom of light" (*R*, 30). "Apollo in Picardy," as we shall see, is a study of the struggle of one such mind in an "earlier and simpler generation" to reconcile the seemingly incompatible forms of sentiment in the religion of Greece and the religion of Christ. It is not Apollo who is the subject of this portrait, but Prior Saint-Jean, and in this respect "Apollo in Picardy" differs from the portrait so often considered its companion piece, "Denys L'Auxerrois." Denys can be the central subject of his portrait because, however much his behavior approximates that of the god Dionysus, Denys is still human. Apollyon, on the other hand, is actually the god Apollo, though disguised in human form, and presumably the "sensations and ideas" of a god are not for human conceiving. However, as we shall see, there is very little difference between Apollyon and Denys. Like all of Pater's heroes, they both proclaim a romanticism in which the beauty and light of the summer world of Dionysus are discovered anew and are again enjoyed for their own sakes.

The struggle within the Prior's mind had its roots in the historical development of the church. In *Marius the Epicurean*, Pater had written that the barbarian invasion, though it could not kill the church, did suppress the culture of the pagan world with the lamentable result that "the kingdom of Christ was to grow up in a somewhat false alienation from the light and beauty of the kingdom of nature, of the natural man, with a partly mistaken tradition concerning it, and an incapacity, as it might almost seem at times, for eventual reconciliation thereto" (*ME*, II, 29). Pater expands this idea later in the novel when he writes:

The sword in the world, the right eye plucked out, the right hand cut off, the spirit of reproach which those images express, and of which monasticism is the fulfilment, reflect one side only of the nature of the divine missionary of the New Testament. Opposed to, yet blent with, this ascetic or militant character, is the function of the Good Shepherd, serene, blithe and debonair, beyond the gentlest shepherd of Greek mythology; of a king under whom the beatific vision is realised of a reign of peace—peace of heart— among men. Such aspect of the divine character of Christ, rightly understood, is indeed the final consummation of that bold and brilliant hopefulness in man's nature, which had sustained him so far through his immense labours, his immense sorrows, and of which pagan gaiety in the handling of life, is but a minor achievement. Sometimes one, sometimes the other, of those two contrasted aspects of its Founder, have, in different ages and under the urgency of different human needs, been at work also in the Christian Church. (*ME*, II, 114–15)

It is evident that the ideal of the church in Prior Saint-Jean's day was asceticism. Anything associated with the world, with the darkness of matter, was despised with an almost Gnostic fierceness.

Apollo, then, is appropriately called by the name of "a malignant one in Scripture, Apollyon" (*MS*, 152), the angel of the bottomless pit (Rev. 9:11). Heine's theme of the gods in exile exactly fits Pater's purposes here. Heine had written that at the triumph of Christianity the old temples and statues could not be spared,

> for in these still lived the old Greek joyousness which seemed to the Christian as devildom. In these temples he saw not merely the subjects of a strange cultus and a worthless and erroneous faith which wanted all reality, but the citadels of actual devils, while the gods whom the statues represented existed for him in reality, but as the devils themselves.[14]

Apollo, under his Bunyanesque appellation, becomes one of the sinister gods in exile. He is, with his "titanic revolt" (*MS*, 143) and his ability to change size at will, with his preference for darkness and his malign powers, not without a certain likeness to the Miltonic Satan. Indeed, Pater often seems at pains to make the *vallis monachorum* seem a nightmarish place, and at first the idea is never far from the reader's mind that this enchanted valley may resemble Milton's hell, a kind of symmetrical but inverted lens-image of the normal. At any rate, the Prior feels uneasy in his new environment: "these creatures of rule, these 'regulars,' the Prior and his companion, were come in contact for the first time in their lives with the power of untutored natural impulse, of natural inspiration" (*MS*, 156). The Prior is quite convinced of Apollyon's evil, believing him "immersed in, or actually a part of, that irredeemable natural world he had dreaded so greatly ere he came hither." He seemed to have "an air of unfathomable evil about him as from a distant but ineffaceable past, and a sort of heathen understanding with the dark realm of matter" (*MS*, 158–59).

Yet the strange thing about Apollyon is his irresistible attractiveness despite his obvious involvement with the natural order. The Prior is drawn to Apollyon against his will, and the reader soon begins to perceive that the distorting element here in the valley of the monks is the Prior's mind itself. Monasticism, described in *Marius*, represents the extreme result of the tendency to regard the moral life "as essentially a sacrifice, the sacrifice of one part

[14] *The Works of Heinrich Heine*, trans. Charles G. Leland (London, 1892–93), XII, 306.

of human nature to another, that it may live the more completely in what survives" (*ME*, II, 121). This attempt to find God by a quite literal self-annihilation, in which the objective focal point of the One in the here-and-now is ignored for the sake of some disembodied universal, is a philosophy not unlike that of the Emperor Aurelius, "a despiser of the body" (*ME*, II, 53), whose asceticism required "a sacrifice of the body to the soul" (*ME*, I, 191).

Another ideal, however, competes with asceticism, that of culture. The ideal of culture, actually attained to a high degree by the early Christian church, represents the moral life "as a harmonious development of all the parts of human nature, in just proportion to each other" (*ME*, II, 121). This cultural ideal of harmony and proportion is Apollonian, and in the Pythagoreanism of antiquity we can find its clearest philosophic expression. Indeed, Apollyon may be fully as much a reincarnation of Pythagoras as Apollo, for as Pater tells us in *Plato and Platonism*, many thought that Pythagoras was

a son of Apollo, nay, Apollo himself—the twilight, attempered, Hyperborean Apollo, like the sun in Lapland: that his person gleamed at times with a supernatural brightness: that he had exposed to those who loved him a golden thigh. . . . He had been, in the secondary sense, various persons in the course of ages, . . . showing out all along only by hints and flashes the abysses of divine knowledge within him, sometimes by miracle. (*PP*, 53–54)

One of the central tenets of the Pythagoreans was that the material world is a kind of perfect "musical instrument" (*PP*, 54) upon which the true philosopher can miraculously play. And so we learn without surprise that music seems to be everywhere in the valley of the monks. The strange sound of thunder late in November, we are told, "seemed to break away into musical notes. And the lightning lingered along with it, but glancing softly; was in truth an aurora, such as persisted month after month on the northern sky as they sojourned here. Like Prospero's enchanted island, the whole place was 'full of noises.' The wind it might have been, passing over metallic strings, but that they were audible even when the night was breathless" (*MS*, 148). The lyre and presence of Apollo, the source of this Pythagorean music, are included in the portrait to symbolize for us the perfect harmony between the physical and spiritual aspects of life.

Only to the apprehensive medieval mind is this world at all sinister. The twilight in which Apollyon lives is, of course, that of the world of the Hyperborean Apollo, but it is also that enchanted darkness of "Hippolytus Veiled," the twilight in the first moments of promise just before the dawn. Here is no evil magic; it is, rather, the white magic of Prospero or that of the enchanted storm in Beethoven's *Sixth Symphony*. The valley of the monks reminds the reader of the harmony and perfection embodied in another quaint figure of Pythagorean thought, the circle, an image which is used at least a half-dozen times in this portrait. The valley itself, like "hollow Sparta" (*PP*, 207), comes as close as is possible in an imperfect world to the perfect circle of the original garden, for it is an "immense oval cup sunken in the grassy upland" (*MS*, 147). The air, says Pater, "might have been that of a veritable paradise, still unspoiled" (*MS*, 150), and Apollyon is the unfallen man, "the old Adam fresh from his Maker's hand" (*MS*, 149). This is the reason that both Prior and novice grow younger, the influence of the place seeming to bring out a certain "boyish delight" (*MS*, 150) in both of them. Indeed, that the visitors are aware of the music in the valley at all is an indication that their primal innocence is beginning to return, since it was with the Fall that man lost the ability to hear the music of the spheres (*PP*, 70).

But the impact of the natural order on the cold and repressive medieval world becomes almost disastrous. The twelfth and final volume of the Prior's epic work, "a dry enough treatise on mathematics, applied, still with no relaxation of strict method, to astronomy and music" (*MS*, 143), presented "a strange example of a cold and very reasonable spirit disturbed suddenly, thrown off its balance, as by a violent beam, a blaze of new light, revealing, as it glanced here and there a hundred truths unguessed at before, yet a curse, as it turned out, to its receiver, in dividing hopelessly against itself the well-ordered kingdom of his thought" (*MS*, 143).[15] Apollyon, who, as god of the sun, has a certain stake in the matter, teaches the Prior the truth of what the Greeks, Pythagoras' disciples, knew many years before—the nature of the heliocentric

---

[15] The famous biblical passage from Luke 11:14–26, in which Christ answered those who said He cast out devils by the power of Beelzebub, has several verbal echoes in the portrait and casts into high relief the struggle between the "religion of light" and the "world of darkness." The idea of the kingdom divided against itself is found in this passage on devils, as is that description used by the monks when the Prior desires to return to the *vallis monachorum*: "He is like the damned spirit, think some of the brethren, saying, 'I will return to the house whence I came out'" (*MS*, p. 170). There is perhaps another biblical reference in Prior Saint-Jean's name. Did not the Prior at the end of his life, like St. John, have a vision of the ideal City or world?

(or pyrocentric) planetary system. Under Apollyon's tuition, the Prior eventually begins to hear the old Pythagorean singing of the planets. However, his attempts to arrest "this beam of insight, or of inspiration" (*MS*, 164) on the written page is not wholly satisfactory. The Prior's capacities as a writer are seemingly not commensurate with the demand, and as a result, his dissertation is not in conformity with the requirements:

The very shape of Volume Twelve, pieced together of quite irregularly formed pages, was a solecism. It could never be bound. . . . Soft wintry auroras seemed to play behind whole pages of crabbed textual writing, line and figure bending, breathing, flaming, into lovely "arrangements" that were like music made visible; . . . winged flowers, or stars with human limbs and faces, still intruding themselves, or mere notes of light and darkness from the actual horizon. There it all is still in the faded gold and colours of the ancient volume—"Prior Saint-Jean's folly." (*MS*, 144–45; 165)

It is as though William Blake had been anticipated in the twelfth century, and the perceptive reader wonders if the Prior really does lose his mind, as all seem to think, or whether under the influence of Apollo he becomes sane, healthy, for the first time. If the Prior seems out of step with the rest of the world, it may be that he is marching to a music no one else hears.

The second project the Prior undertakes has an almost equally bizarre outcome. Having written so learnedly on architecture, he is given, as an interim task, the supervision of the erection of a barn which under the influence of Apollo turns into a kind of Greek temple. At the very top of the temple Apollo sits,

on the gable which looks northward, though much weather-worn, and with an ugly gap between the shoulder and the fingers on the harp, as if, literally, he had cut off his right hand and put it from him:— King David or an angel? guesses the careless tourist. The space below has been lettered. After a little puzzling you recognise there the relics of a familiar verse from a Latin psalm: *Nisi Dominus aedificaverit domum*, and the rest: inscribed as well as may be in Greek characters. Prior Saint-Jean caused it to be so inscribed, absurdly, during his last days there. (*MS*, 154)

Like the Prior, the writer of the psalm quoted was also a temple builder, for the verses are from one of Solomon's psalms, Number 126 (Vulgate): "Unless the Lord build the house, they labour in vain that build it. Unless the Lord guard the city, in vain does the guard keep vigil. It is vain for you to rise early, or to put off your rest [the Prior writing his treatise?], you that eat hard-earned bread, for he gives to his beloved in sleep." It is entirely clear that the "Lord" who built this house is the one perched on its gable. He is, however, a lord in eclipse. The gap where the right hand should be recalls another familiar scriptural passage: "If thy right hand offend thee, cut it off, and cast it from thee: for it is profitable for thee that one of thy members should perish, and not that thy whole body should be cast into hell" (Matt. 5: 30). The ascetic ideal, the "spirit of reproach" (*ME*, II, 114), as Pater calls it, has maimed the perfect form of the god, yet even in the hostile environment of the Middle Ages he is able to exert his old power. It is Apollo with his harp who in fact builds "the house":

Almost suddenly tie-beam and rafter knit themselves together into the stone, and the dark, dry, roomy place was closed in securely to this day. Mere audible music, certainly, had counted for something in the operations of an art, held at its best (as we know) to be a sort of music made visible. That idle singer, one might fancy, by an art beyond art, had attracted beams and stones into their fit places. (*MS*, 154)

Pater is echoing here the old fable which tells how Apollo helped Poseidon, who was building the walls of the city for the king of Troy, how by his marvelous musical powers Apollo was able to move the huge blocks of stone into the places designed for them. The secret of the power of Apollo's music lay in its Pythagorean harmony. In *Plato and Platonism*, Pater had written that

κόσμος; order; reasonable, delightful order; is a word that became very dear as we know, to the Greek soul, to what was perhaps most essentially Greek in it, to the Dorian element there. Apollo, the Dorian god, was but its visible consecration. It was what, under his blessing, art superinduced upon the rough stone, the yielding clay, the jarring metallic strings, the common speech of every day. (*PP*, 36)

Prior Saint-Jean felt the influence of Apollyon not only in his scholarly and practical pursuits, but also in the performance of his religious duties. He was forced to break off unconsummated the Midnight Mass of the Feast of the Nativity because of the disruptive influence of Apollyon, who had seemingly become the officiating priest. This is hardly surprising, for as has always been known, indeed as Prior Saint-Jean himself must have known, Christmas Day is observed at the winter solstice when the Mithraic festival of the *Dies Natalis Solis Invicti* was formerly commemorated. The Feast of the Nativity proclaiming the rising of the Sun of righteousness "with healing in his wings" (Mal. 4:2) is not entirely without its echoes of the old pagan celebration of the victory of light over darkness.[16] Apollyon, then, need not remain a purely pagan god; rather, it is perfectly appropriate that he identity himself with the object of Christian worship, Christ Himself:

Apollyon, who entered the chapel just then, as if quite naturally, though with a bleating lamb in his bosom ("dropped" thus early in that wonderful season) by way of an offering, took his place at the altar's very foot, and drawing forth his harp, now restrung, at the right moment, turned to real silvery music the hoarse *Gloria in Excelsis* of those rude worshippers, still shrinking from him, while they listened in a little circle, as he stood there in his outlandish attire of skins strangely spotted and striped. (*MS*, 161–62)

The humble role of the Good Shepherd was not unknown to the exiled god who, in olden days, had tended the sheep of Admetus, King of Thessaly. So now in the valley of the monks, he kept the sheep, "was an 'affectionate shepherd;' cured their diseases; brought them easily to birth, and if they strayed afar would bring them back tenderly upon his shoulders. Monastic persons would have seen that image many times before" (*MS*, 158). Such an image had stood in the church in Cecilia's house, and it expressed a religious ideal not ascetic, but "serene, blithe and debonair" (*ME*, II, 114). The perfect harmony of this blithe religion is obviously Apollonian, and the "little circle"—the Pythagorean figure again—around Apollyon during the Christmas singing of the *Gloria* is, in effect, an image drawn from the ancient worship of Apollo. K. O. Müller writes in one of his chapters devoted to the Dorian Apollo:

One of the important parts of the Pythagorean worship was the *paean*, which was sung to the lyre, in spring time, by a person sitting in the midst of a circle of listeners: this was called the καθαρσις, or purification. This is evidently an application of ancient rites of the worship of Apollo. The Pythian oracle likewise commanded the Greeks of Lower Italy to sing paeans in the spring as a means of atonement.[17]

In the paradoxical religious symbolism, suffering and death are identified with birth, and the song which commemorates the atonement of Christ, the reconciliation of man and God, serves as a prelude to the denouement of the portrait.

[16] James, *Mother Goddess*, p. 220. See also Chambers, *Medieval Stage*, I, 242.
[17] Müller, *Die Dorier*, II, 384.

Like so many of Pater's portraits, "Apollo in Picardy" reaches its climax in a violent death. In *Plato and Platonism*, Pater tells his readers that the great Lacedaemonian religious festival of the *Hyacinthia* occurred

at the season between spring and summer when under the first fierce heat of the year the abundant hyacinths fade from the fields. Blue flowers, you remember, are the rarest, to many eyes the loveliest; and the Lacedaemonians with their guests were met together to celebrate the death of the hapless lad who had lent his name to them, Hyacinthus, son of Apollo, or son of an ancient mortal king who had reigned in this very place; in either case, greatly beloved of the god, who had slain him by sad accident as they played at quoits together delightfully, to his immense sorrow. That Boreas (the north-wind) had maliciously miscarried the discus, is a circumstance we hardly need to remind us that we have here, of course, only one of many transparent, unmistakable, parables or symbols of the great solar change, so sudden in the south, like the story of Proserpine, Adonis, and the like. (*PP*, 228–29)

The death of Hyacinth, then, is that of a year-daimon, and the "immense cry, as from the very heart of ancient tragedy, . . . like the sound of some natural catastrophe" (*MS*, 168), which Apollyon utters at the death of Hyacinth has its biblical overtones. In the great cry, as in the storm which follows, we sense something of the crucifixion agony of Christ Himself. But the hope of resurrection also is implied in the various images of circularity which reflect the elemental cycle over which Apollo is the sovereign lord: in the trees "moaning in wild circular motion" (*MS*, 168); in the instrument of death itself, the discus; and in the figure of the thrower, with his round, halo-like tonsure, "the disk in his right hand, his whole body, in that moment of rest, full of the circular motion he is about to commit to it" (*MS*, 167).[18] Apollyon the next day departs northward, carrying the awakening of nature to a winter land, and the Prior, who takes his place, is accused of the murder of Hyacinth. Just as the shock of the exhumation of the saint threw Denys into a subdued and melancholy mood in which joy and sorrow were both present, so the Prior finds hope in the midst of desolation. He, like Denys, reminds us of

[18] It is appropriate that Apollo, as patron of the muses, should be the inspiration of many diverse works of art. Apollyon's form here duplicates exactly the statue of Myron's Discobolus, which for Pater united perfectly the opposites of rest and motion (*GS*, p. 287). The sleeping Apollyon discovered by the Prior is a description of the well-known Apollo Belvedere. Finally, Apollyon is also seen in the form of the famous Christian image of the Good Shepherd.

Demeter at the return of Kore, "chastened by sorrow, . . . blessing the earth" (*GS*, 136).

The movement of the Prior away from his self-annihilating world of the winter Dionysus to an entrance upon the larger centripetal world, where the spirit of God endows the sensuous beauty of nature with life, is symbolized by his relation to the monastary:

> The structure of a fortified medieval town barred in those who be-longed to it very effectively. High monastic walls intrenched the monk still further. From the summit of the tower you looked straight down into the deep narrow streets, upon the houses (in one of which Prior Saint-Jean was born) climbing as high as they dared for breathing space within that narrow compass. (*MS*, 145)

This monastary which Prior Saint-Jean loved is simply Pater's description of the narrow prison of the self. Its solipsism is in sharp contrast to the world lying around about which could be seen from the summit of the tower: "you saw . . . the green breadth of Normandy and Picardy, this way and that; felt on your face the free air of a still wider realm beyond what was seen" (*MS*, 145). But the Prior does not like the view; he prefers the narrow walls of his cell. It is not difficult to see how such radical subjectivity would render his attempt to grasp Apollyon's beam of insight a near disaster. His brain is a narrow, centrifugal thing, and the new wine stretches it to bursting:

> If he set hand to the page, the firm halo, here a moment since, was gone, had flitted capriciously to the wall; passed next through the window, to the wall of the garden; was dancing back in another mo-ment upon the innermost walls of one's own miserable brain, to swell there—that astounding white light!—rising steadily in the cup, the mental receptacle, till it overflowed, and he lay faint and drowning in it. Or he rose above it, as above a great liquid surface, and hung giddily over it—light, simple, and absolute—ere he fell. Or there was a battle between light and darkness around him, with no way of escape from the baffling strokes, the lightning flashes; flashes of blind-ness one might rather call them. (*MS*, 164–65)

The description of the Prior's delirium resembles Pater's comments on William Morris' poetry in its portrayal of that "beautiful disease or disorder of the senses" which was so characteristic of the medieval mind, infusing all nature with "the maddening white glare of the sun, and tyranny of the moon, not tender and far-off, but close down—the sorcerer's moon, large and feverish." The medieval world, says Pater, had a deep sense of the things of nature, "but its sense of them was not objective, no real escape to the world without us" (*Ap*[1889], 218–19).

Clearly much of what Pater says in "Aesthetic Poetry" concerning the psychology of the Middle Ages is applicable to his portrait of Prior Saint-Jean. We are immediately reminded not merely of such explicit parallels as the Prior's deal with Apollyon to draw "the moon from the sky, for some shameful price, known to the magicians of that day" (*MS*, 166), but also of that transition which Pater perceived generally from what may be called a medieval subjectivity to a Renaissance objectivity. Morris' later poetry represents "almost a revolt," says Pater:

> Here there is no delirium or illusion, no experiences of mere soul
> while the body and the bodily senses sleep, or wake with convulsed
> intensity at the prompting of imaginative love; but rather the great
> primary passions under broad daylight as of the pagan Veronese. This
> simplification interests us, not merely for the sake of an individual
> poet—full of charm as he is—but chiefly because it explains through
> him a transition which, under many forms, is one law of the life
> of the human spirit, and of which what we call the Renaissance is
> only a supreme instance. (*Ap*[1889], 221)

Pater continues this passage with an example which is so apropos of the Prior that one can hardly refrain from noting how characteristic it is that one of Pater's very earliest essays should provide so clear a comment upon his last finished portrait, undeniable proof of the life-long consistency of his thought:

> Just so the monk in his cloister, through the "open vision," open only
> to the spirit, divined, aspired to, and at last apprehended, a better
> daylight, but earthly, open only to the senses. Complex and subtle
> interests, which the mind spins for itself may occupy art and poetry
> or our own spirits for a time; but sooner or later they come back
> with a sharp rebound to the simple elementary passions—anger, desire,
> regret, pity, and fear: and what corresponds to them in the sensuous
> world—bare, abstract fire, water, air, tears, sleep, silence, and what
> De Quincey has called the "glory of motion." (*Ap*[1889], 221–22)

At the close of the portrait, the Prior's attitude has undergone a radical change. He, too, has been thrown back upon "the simple elementary passions"—the greatest of them all, tragic sorrow over the death of the lad Hyacinth.

We see him last confined in a room from which he can still see the *vallis monachorum* to which he desires to return. No longer does the Prior shudder at the view:

Gazing thither daily for many hours, he would mistake mere blue
distance, when that was visible, for blue flowers, for hyacinths, and
wept at the sight; though blue, as he observed, was the colour of
Holy Mary's gown on the illuminated page, the colour of hope, of
merciful omnipresent deity. The necessary permission came with difficulty, just too late. Brother Saint-Jean died, standing upright with
an effort to gaze forth once more, amid the preparations for his departure. (*MS*, 170–71)

For the Prior, salvation was not easy. Only the pain of Hyacinth's
death could break through that narrow subjectivity which barred
his consciousness from the elemental passions and sensations of
the natural world. Hyacinth is irrevocably dead, yet Prior Saint-
Jean still retains what Hyacinth has come to mean for him in
terms of "the desire of beauty quickened by the sense of death"
(*Ap*[1889], 227). It does not reduce the terror or the pity, but
this is what is impervious to being taken away. The Emperor
Aurelius, sorrowing over the death of his child, somehow failed
to make the Prior's discovery that natural beauty holds within
itself the hope of an eventual resurrection. The coincidence of the
necessary permission arriving on the day of the Prior's death tells
us what the nature of his death is: the completion of the circle
of life and his entering into the infinite circle of glory. Having
begun with a quotation from Pater's essay on Pico, let us close
with another one:

The Renaissance of the fifteenth century was, in many things, great
rather by what it designed than by what it achieved. Much which
it aspired to do, and did but imperfectly or mistakenly, was accom-
plished in what is called the *éclaircissement* of the eighteenth century,
or in our own generation; and what really belongs to the revival
of the fifteenth century is but the leading instinct, the curiosity, the
initiatory idea. It is so with this very question of the reconciliation
of the religion of antiquity with the religion of Christ. (*R*, 33)

Obviously, Prior Saint-Jean was a precursor of this fifteenth-century Renaissance, but the work which the fifteenth century took
up so vigorously was not completed, says Pater, until "our own
generation." Yet the visions of these earlier children of Apollo
pointed the way. Just as the Prior's dream of "a low circlet of
soundless flame" (*MS*, 147) presaged the nature of his eventual
discovery, so also Pico's mother at the time of his birth saw "a
circular flame which suddenly vanished away, on the wall of the
chamber where she lay" (*R*, 39). The ultimate reconciliation of
the sensuous world of Greece with the inwardness of Christianity
has for its symbol the "firm halo" (*MS*, 164) of the sun itself,

the promise of a new Age of Gold ruled by "a king under whom the beatific vision is realised of a reign of peace—peace of heart—among men" (*ME*, II, 114). This is the Renaissance which the Prior bequeathed to those who came after him.

"TIBALT THE ALBIGENSE" AND "GAUDIOSO, THE SECOND"

Like *Gaston de Latour* or "An English Poet," "Tibalt the Albigense" and "Gaudioso, the Second" are incomplete,[19] and so, again, any thorough-going structural analysis of the works is precluded. "Tibalt" is roughly 2500 words long, and "Gaudioso" runs to almost the same length. These two are probably, judging from the length of Pater's finished portraits, between a quarter and a third complete. They are long enough, however, to give us a good idea of what the theme of each is, and they attest unequivocally to the fact that Pater is again working with his usual subject of Renaissance, in one case the early French Renaissance and in the other and high Italian Renaissance. The commentator on these two incomplete portraits is fortunate in that in both cases Pater is obviously reworking the subject matter of his criticism into fiction, as is so often his custom. I shall first make a few remarks on "Tibalt" since its historical period antedates "Gaudioso," though it may very well be that "Gaudioso" is the earlier, Pater having already conceived its subject by 1890 at the latest.

Pater's *Renaissance* opens with the essay "Two Early French Stories." In this essay Pater reminds us that the Renaissance began in France. French historians, says Pater, "have often dwelt on this notion of a Renaissance in the end of the twelfth and the beginning of the thirteenth century, a Renaissance within the limits of the middle age itself—a brilliant, but in part abortive effort to do for human life and the human mind what was afterwards done in the fifteenth" (*R*, 1). The stories which Pater translates in the essay are, in their illustration of "the ideal intensity of love" (*R*, 23), examples of "this medieval Renaissance" (*R*, 3). For, says Pater,

One of the strongest characteristics of that outbreak of the reason
and the imagination, of that assertion of the liberty of the heart,
in the middle age, which I have termed a medieval Renaissance, was
its antinomianism, its spirit of rebellion and revolt against the moral
and religious ideas of the time. . . . More and more, as we come
to mark changes and distinctions of temper in what is often in one
all-embracing confusion called the middle age, that rebellion, that

[19] See Chap. V, n. 9.

sinister claim for liberty of heart and thought, comes to the surface. The Albigensian movement, connected so strangely with the history of the Provençal poetry, is deeply tinged with it. (*R*, 24–25)

"Tibalt the Albigense" is, then, a story of one such "revolt against the moral and religious ideas of the time."

Introducing his portrait of Tibalt, Pater points out that in Languedoc at the close of the twelfth century the harshness of the early Reformation was not unallied with the gaiety of the beginnings of the Renaissance. The common ground between Renaissance and Reformation, says Pater, was the old Manichean doctrine of the eternity of matter and its unalterable opposition to spirit. That this single belief should be the common source of conflicting movements is, for Pater, proof that metaphysical doctrine is too abstract to embody reality. As he had remarked similarly in *Marius*, such divergence demonstrates that,

> in the reception of metaphysical *formulae*, all depends, as regards their actual and ulterior result, on the pre-existent qualities of that soil of human nature into which they fall—the company they find already present there, on their admission into the house of thought; there being at least so much truth as this involves in the theological maxim, that the reception of this or that speculative conclusion is really a matter of will. (*ME*, I, 135–36)

In Tibalt's people, the belief in the eternity of matter created an excessive spirituality and asceticism. In Count Raymond's court, the doctrine issued in an excessive sensuality. As is obvious, the one is the world of the summer Dionysus, the other of the winter Dionysus. Neither of the Dionysian extremes induced by the old Manichaean doctrine are satisfactory, for the doctrine has set up an opposition which violates Apollonian harmony. Paralleling a passage in the Rossetti essay (*Ap*, 212), Pater writes in this portrait of Tibalt that the spirit and matter of the metaphysicians are but the creations of the philosophers themselves and can only be roughly distinguished from each other in actual experience, since soul and body are fused into each other with the unity of the human personality itself.

Tibalt's people rejected the bodily, physical side of existence entirely; their religion embodied that "spirit of reproach" so evident in the foregoing portrait. Indeed, it is not without reason that we are reminded of the way in which Prior Saint-Jean looked upon "that irredeemable natural world" (*MS*, 158). The natural world and the human body were seen as a prison of the spirit by those fanatical vassals of the Court of Toulouse. Like that of

Aurelius or Sebastian, their desire to free the caged bird of the soul took the form of a rejection of all phenomena. Tibalt, to be sure, shared none of this with his progenitors. He was a truer reflection of his period, of that moment at the end of the twelfth century when, as Pater says in *The Renaissance*, "the rude strength of the middle age turns to sweetness" (*R*, 2). Tibalt, we can be certain, was intended to represent the harmony between the summer and winter Dionysus, court and country. He, more than either extreme, would reflect the real Albigensian spirit, and, as a true representative of the Renaissance, would "refuse to be classified" (*R*, 27).

There is much in the portrait of Pater's "English Poet" reflected in "Tibalt." The environment, the stern mountains, the exotic flowers, the gentle women and children—all of these had their counterpart in the English world of the young poet. And Tibalt, like the English poet, rises above his milieu and fuses the spiritual with the material world. In him, as in the Renaissance generally, "all breathes of that unity of culture in which 'whatsoever things are comely' are reconciled for the elevation and adorning of our spirits" (*R*, 27). His vocation, that of a physician, is the direct fruit of his innate concern with the material side of life, for the harshness of his environment seemed to accentuate the suffering of the children, the aged, and the infirm. Such suffering inspired in him a great tenderness, a tenderness in which, as Pater said in "The Child in the House," "the concentrated sorrow of the world seemed suddenly to lie heavy upon him" (*MS*, 182).

The portrait of Tibalt breaks off at this point, but the remainder of his story can almost be sketched from the general pattern of Pater's fiction. Tibalt goes to Albi, or perhaps to Toulouse as court physician, and probably is violently killed in the 1209 persecutions, the terrible series of events which terminated the Albigensian movement. But, typically, Tibalt has stood, like so many of Pater's heroes, in the vanguard of the coming Renaissance. What Pater wrote of Abelard in "Two Early French Stories" is equally applicable to Tibalt: "he prefigures the character of the Renaissance, that movement in which, in various ways, the human mind wins for itself a new kingdom of feeling and sensation and thought, not opposed to but only beyond and independent of the spiritual system then actually realised" (*R*, 6–7). On this note we turn to Gaudioso, who embodies perfectly that culture for which Tibalt struggled.

On October 18, 1890, Pater wrote to Arthur Symons the following: "I never got to Italy after all, this summer: instead, finished a paper of Art-Notes in North Italy, by way of prologue to an Imaginary Portrait with Brescia for background."[20] This portrait is undoubtedly the fragmentary "Gaudioso, the Second." Fortunately, the essay tells us a great deal about the unfinished portrait. Pater begins his portrait with a discussion of the rare picture by Romanino, now hanging in the British National Gallery, which had been painted for the high altar of one of the Brescian churches. A consideration of this very same picture closes the art-notes essay. The story, then, seems almost to be the imaginative continuation of the essay, a rather clear reflection of Walter Pater, the leisurely and educated traveler in North Italy, although, ironically, that summer he "never got to Italy after all" because he wrote the essay instead. "Art Notes," like so much of Pater's criticism, reaches its climax in the last paragraph; it begins with North Italian art generally and seems to focus downward—through specific towns, then Brescia, then a church—until it finally concentrates on a single figure, that of Gaudioso II, whose features were used by Romanino in his picture for the fifth-century Gaudioso I, "saint and bishop." The point of transition between criticism and fiction lies in the following sentences:

The face, of remarkable beauty after a type which all feel though
it is actually rare in art, is probably a portrait of some distinguished
churchman of Romanino's own day; a second Gaudioso, perhaps, setting
that later Brescian church to rights after the terrible French occupation
in the painter's own time, as his saintly predecessor, the Gaudioso
of the earlier century here commemorated, had done after the invasion
of the Goths. The eloquent eyes are open upon some glorious vision.
"He hath made us kings and priests!" they seem to say for him, as
the clean, sensitive lips might do so eloquently. Beauty and Holiness
had "kissed each other," as in Borgognone's imperial deacons at the
Certosa. At the Renaissance the world might seem to have parted
them again. But here certainly, once more, Catholicism and the Renaissance, religion and culture, holiness and beauty, might seem reconciled,
by one who had conceived neither after any feeble way, in a gifted
person. Here at least, by the skill of Romanino's hand, the obscure
martyr of the crypts shines as a saint of the later Renaissance, with
a sanctity of which the elegant world itself would hardly escape the
fascination, and which reminds one how the great Apostle Saint Paul
has made courtesy part of the content of the divine charity itself.
(MS, 107–8)

The key phrase here is, characteristically, "reconciled . . . in a gifted person," for "Gaudioso, the Second" is, again, a study of

[20] IPB, p. 1.

the Dionysian priest in whom the two worlds of soul and matter, winter and summer, fuse to create the Apollonian synthesis.

Gaudioso the Second, who was Bishop of Brescia toward the end of the sixteenth century, is fictionally Domenico Averoldi, a handsome young man of the select social world, who met a young lady, fell in love, and became engaged. But when difficulties about the dowry arose and the lady also proved to be indifferent to his love, he renounced the world and became a priest, his action designating him as yet another chaste consort of Apollo. The old bishop, who ordained Domenico, appointed him, on the basis of Matthew 18:9, as a curator of relics, and he thereafter spends his days searching for the remains of early martyrs in the dark, mouldering crypts beneath the Brescian churches. The ascetic world which in "Apollo in Picardy" had demanded the right hand here demands the eye: "if thine eye offend thee, pluck it out." And Domenico's detestable task is meant to pluck out that "lust of the eye" so antithetic to the ascetic temperment. But the old bishop's plan fails. There is a curious fusion of Christian doctrine with that idea of which Pater speaks in "Two Early French Stories"; namely, "the return of that ancient Venus, not dead, but only hidden for a time" (*R*, 24). As Domenico works, he occasionally stumbles on the beautiful temple-corner of some ancient building buried with the relics beneath the city. He may even have found, says Pater invoking the gods-in-exile theme explicitly, the statue of Venus lying beneath the dust for fifteen hundred years—Venus Victrix, not dead but only hidden, who seems to touch him with her finger, asking that he should bring her, as well as the relics, to the light of day.

And so, on the dank, subterranean walls, young Domenico inscribes those biblical verses which attest to the resurrection of the material world in all its physical beauty, such as the verse from David's psalm, "My flesh shall rest in hope, for thou wilt not leave my soul in hell; neither wilt thou suffer thine Holy One to see corruption" (16:9–10), and also the words of Job expressing his intense awareness of the resurrected body: "Oh that my words were now written! oh that they were printed in a book! That they were graven with an iron pen and lead in the rock for ever! For I know that my redeemer liveth, and that he shall stand at the latter day upon the earth: And though after my skin worms destroy this body, yet in my flesh shall I see God: Whom I shall see for myself and mine eyes shall behold, and not another; though my reins be consumed within me" (19:23–27). Domenico seems purposefully to select these Old Testament passages which prophesy the Messiah and the individual's resurrection in Christ, for he quite literally took the doctrine of the resurrection of the carnal body, a doctrine which became with him the essence of Revelation itself.[21]

Thus, out of the dead world of the winter Dionysus, which recalls so vividly the exhumation scene in "Denys" and the burial vaults in "Duke Carl," comes the artistic impulse. Domenico, unlike so many of Pater's heroes, does not die until he has reached an advanced age in which his features assume the beauty of the child again. He had made his descent into hell, into the Chthonian world, as he toiled among the charnel houses and the dark Brescian crypts. Here, in the ashes, he discovered the tomb of the pagan world and the beauty of sensuous nature, the ancient green flask in the coffin, so to speak. The very fact of Christ's Incarnation, flesh made God, is for Domenico proof of the sanctification of all visible beauty, and he becomes, after the manner of the old Greek artists and artisans, a spiritual materialist. Like Apollo, he is for his century an important patron of the Italian arts. Perhaps, in his first renunciation of his fiancée and the world, Domenico may have resembled Sebastian in his rejection of the arts and sensuous life. But to Domenico, the truth comes very quickly; knowledge and love of the visible world need not take one out of the presence of God, he declares. Regaining that first Dionysian world of summer, but on a higher artistic-religious level, Domenico fulfills the description of the epigraph from Crashaw which prefaced his portrait: "A happy soul, that all the way / To heaven hath a summer day."

[21] These Old Testament phrases also have their counterpart in Peter's Pentecostal speech in Acts 2. The epigraph from Joel about "vision," which Pater had employed in *Marius*, is also found here. Evidently this speech on the resurrection of Christ is one of the loci of Pater's religious thought.

VII

𝒢𝒮 MYTH AND METAPHOR

In the opening chapter, "Art and the Gods of Art," an attempt was made to show how the subject of Pater's first book, *The Renaissance*, served as the leading idea in all his later fiction. Renaissance, an artistic and cultural awakening, is the subject of historical and imaginary portraits alike. Such an awakening occurs whenever the static forms of classicism are charged with the fluid power of romanticism. "Spirit and matter," says Pater in his essay on Rossetti, "have been for the most part opposed, with a false contrast or antagonism by schoolmen, whose artificial creation those abstractions really are. In our actual concrete experience, the two trains of phenomena which the words *matter* and *spirit* do but roughly distinguish, play inextricably into each other" (*Ap*, 212). In the world of the summer Dionysus, which is the world of childhood, a perfect rapport exists between the soul and physical nature. But as the young soul grows, as its spirituality becomes more and more a reflection of that spirit which is God, it needs must expand into an objectivity larger than the narrow world of the summer Dionysus. As with the schoolmen, so here a "false contrast or antagonism" has appeared. Soul and matter are no longer harmonized. The external world has become the trap of the winter god; the disembodied dreams of the soul have become delirium.

The world of Apollo, more inclusive, yet sensuous and visible, offers the mature soul a larger form. Apollo embodies that harmony of spirit and matter which Dionysus and his *"Doppelgänger"* (*GS*, 44.) lack. Although Pater never explicitly uses the figure of the circle, it is, nevertheless, the image which best explains the relation between the two gods. In terms of his metaphor of the subject-object relation—"the centrifugal and centripetal tendencies, as we may perhaps not too fancifully call them" (*GS*, 252)—Dionysus is the god of the circumference, of the centrifugal tendency, and Apollo is the god of the center, the centripetal tendency. The centrifugal, we recall, is the principle of individuation, variety, and formlessness, whereas the centripetal is that of proportion, centrality, and simplicity. In youth the child-soul easily enough finds sensuous form in a physical nature which is not really Apollonian, only the summer of Dionysus. But the characteristic of the growing soul is to spread itself out from this objective focal point of nature; in a number of places, Pater speaks of "the gradual expansion of the soul" (*MS*, 173; *ME*, II, 93) in describing this process of maturation.

As the soul grows, it moves outward from the center of its childhood form and often finds itself trapped at a particular point on the circumference, unable to synthesize the larger world of temporal and spatial particulars. In his essay, "Style," Pater has designated the presence of romanticism in literature as "soul," and it was characterized, he said, by its "infinite" (*Ap*, 27) quality. Soul is, then, non-finite; it is uncircumscribed by that limiting classical form which Pater called "mind" (*Ap*, 25), that ideality within the sensuousness of the centripetal form. Without mind, the soul cannot find its objective counterpart in the formless entities of the "perpetual flux," for the greater the expansion of the soul, the farther the points on the circumference lie from each other, and, hence, the more individual they are. On the periphery, all connection with the central One is lost by extreme expansion; it is the wintry world of the Dionysian god of unharmonized opposition. Pater has used numerous images to describe this condition: prison, isolation, dream, illusion, delirium, fever, plague, poison, intoxication, the macabre, the grotesque, shame, loss, bereavement, death, and so on. In the religion of the Middle Ages, for example, the object of love, the ideal but sensuous form of God, "was absent or veiled, not limited to one supreme plastic form like Zeus at Olympia or Athena in the Acropolis, but distracted, as in a fever dream, into a thousand symbols and reflections" (*Ap*[1889], 216). Because the visible object toward which emotions would naturally be directed was gone, the sentiments were turned toward an imaginary object instead. But this gave rise to a "passion of which the outlets are sealed," so that the emotions redound upon the mind, and "the things of nature begin to play a strange delirious part" (*Ap*[1889], 218). Prior Saint-Jean is Pater's best fictional example of this medieval delirium. On the level of secular love, Pater has depicted this state in the sexual license of Phaedra, Flavian, Manon Lescaut, and the erotic poets of Provençal. They all lack an objective counterpart toward which their sentiments can be directed; each is a solitary prisoner locked within the echoing walls of his own soul. Here, in such a culture, says Pater, "as in some medicated air, exotic flowers of sentiment expand, among people of a remote and unaccustomed beauty, somnambulistic, frail, androgynous, the light almost shining through them, as the flame of a little taper shows through the Host."[1]

But this faint light of the taper, shining through the body of the crucified God, reminds us of the brighter image of the Apollonian hero. That light, growing clearer and clearer in the character of the hero, leads us to the center. As the objects on the circumference contract, the scattered rays, those "distracted reflections," finally unite like the spot of a burning glass into the "hard gemlike flame" (*R*, 236) of the absolute center. This is the locus of the flaming sun-god Apollo, and as any hermetic or astrological treatise of the Renaissance would have told Pater, the standard symbol for the sun was the circle with a dot at the center: the solar disk with its central point of perfect proportion and harmony. Here multiplicity is reduced to true unity, the substance and its "qualities" are one, matter and form have coalesced, and the androgynous soul without a mate has found its sensuous counterpart. When Pater describes the Apollonian character in "Diaphaneitè" as "that fine edge of light, where the elements of our moral nature refine themselves to the burning point" (*MS*, 248), one may quite reasonably see in this halo-image of the "fine edge of light"—Prior Saint-Jean and Pico's mother had seen the halo—a Dionysian circumference refining itself of its space-time qualities until it reaches the hard gem-like flame of the central moment. The function of the artist-hero, says Pater in a later essay, is "to define, in a chill and empty atmosphere, the focus where rays, in themselves pale and impotent, unite and begin to burn" (*R*, 214).

To perceive the ideal form within the visible world allows the hero, in the chill and barren atmosphere of the winter god, to define the focus of Apollo. But how does the hero grasp this elusive form of the burning divinity? This is essentially the question posed in the Conclusion to *The Renaissance:* "How shall we pass most swiftly from point to point, and be present always at the focus where the greatest number of vital forces unite in their purest energy?" (*R*, 236) Often Pater's heroes find themselves trapped on the circumference in some particular moment of space and time, out of contact with the central point of the universe. For them, the Dionysian cycle has become the "issueless circle" (*IP*, 14) of the bird-soul which Marie-Marguerite observed in the

[1] *Westminster Review*, XXXIV, 302.

stone church. The bloom of physical nature itself does not offer the mature hero a stable resting place, for, as Pater says in *Marius*, while beautiful things "might indeed be the burning of the divine fire," they "pass away like a devouring flame, or like the race of water in mid-stream" (*ME*, I, 131). And the hero's life, too, dissolves in the perpetual flux: "This at least of flamelike our life has, that it is but the concurrence, renewed from moment to moment, of forces parting sooner or later on their ways" (*R*, 234). Only art, or some visible moral order such as the Church, can give permanent form to the fragile, adventurous, disembodied intuitions of the soul.

It is not without significance, then, that Pater's Conclusion to *The Renaissance* should culminate in a discussion of art. The Conclusion was, we recall, a paean of praise to that fire—Apollonian, Heraclitean, Pythagorean, perhaps even Hebraic—which the diverse schools of antiquity had by common consent placed at the center of the universe. Art is the supreme visible embodiment of this central fire, for the aesthetic object condenses the random movements of the circumference to the hard, gem-like permanence of central form, a hardness like that of the metal-worker (*IPB*, 46; *ME*, I, 104, 115, 167–68; *PP*, 127) whose craft shapes the visionary intuitions of the soul and gives to them the solidity of brass or iron. Just as the "perpetual flux" of the infinite, uncircumscribed world of soul is metaphorically represented by water or the ocean, as in "Sebastian van Storck" and "The Chant of the Celestial Sailors," so the beauty of sensuous form is often represented by the flame-like flower: the red hawthorn and honeysuckle of Florian's and the English poet's childhood or the roses in "Duke Carl" and *Marius*, for example. Like the work of art, the person of the hero himself represents a transformation of the infinite fluidity of the soul to the fire of sensuous color. He is, like Dionysus, "the spiritual form of fire and dew" (*GS*, 9), a creation of that imaginative power which unifies and brings together "things naturally asunder, making, as it were, for the human body a soul of waters, for the human soul a body of flowers" (*GS*, 29). But the figure of the hero, even in his moments of greatest joy, reflects merely the sensuous form of the summer Dionysus. Only by dying does he reveal, in a single supreme moment of tragic joy, that greater Apollonian light within himself and call forth the permanent flower of art.

Pater's choice of the circle-center metaphor to describe this relation between Dionysus and Apollo is essentially an adaptation of a symbol whose possibilities had already been well explored by medieval and Renaissance theologians as a description for a divine Being other than Apollo. "God," says the pseudo-hermetic *Book of the XXIV Philosophers*, "is a circle whose center is everywhere and whose circumference is nowhere."[2] And Saint Bonaventura combined this definition with Boethius' definition of eternity as a perfect and simultaneous possession of eternal life:

> If one says that eternity signifies an existence without end, it is necessary to reply that one does not exhaust by this the sense of the word eternity, because it means not only interminability, but also simultaneity; and as by the mode of interminability it is necessary to conceive an intelligible circumference without beginning and end, so by the mode of simultaneity it is necessary to conceive the simplicity and indivisibility that are the modes of the center; and these two things are affirmed at the same time in the divine Being, because It is at the same time simple and infinite; and it is thus that it is necessary to conceive circularity in eternity.[3]

Within the divine sphere, every point and every moment is identical with every other point and moment, so that the circumference which embraces all duration and extension is identified with the central point which excludes all duration and extension. When Pater, in "Diaphaneitè," defines the Apollonian character as cutting across the flux and linking opposites, we should see it in terms of this medieval circle-center paradox in which the breadth and generality of the circumference is refined by the hero's character

> to the burning point. It crosses rather than follows the main current of the world's life. The world has no sense fine enough for those evanescent shades, which fill up the blanks between contrasted types of character—delicate provision in the organisation of the moral world for the transmission to every part of it of the life quickened at single points! For this nature there is no place ready in its affections. This colourless, unclassified purity of life it can neither use for its service, nor contemplate as an ideal. *"Sibi unitus et simplificatus esse,"* that is the long struggle of the Imitatio Christi. (*MS*, 248)

This passage, it seems, is strongly reminiscent of the way in which Thomas Aquinas, drawing on the medieval tradition, described the divine character:

[2] Proposition II. Pater quotes this definition of God in *ME*, II, 42. In my discussion of the circle-center as a medieval image of God, I am in debt to Georges Poulet's *Les Métamorphoses du cercle* (Paris, 1961), Introduction. I think, however, that the tradition of the circle may be older than Poulet suggests and may actually have its origin in Pythagorean speculations in antiquity.

[3] Poulet, *Métamorphoses du cercle*, p. v.

Eternity is always present in the time or instant which is. One is able to see an example in the circle: a given point of the circumference, which is indivisible, certainly does not coexist with all the other points, because the order of succession constitutes the circumference; but the center, which is outside of the circumference, is in immediate rapport with any given point of the circumference.[4]

Pater's conception of the Apollonian center, then, has much in common with traditional Christian thought.

But although for Pater the pure form of God is indeed "outside" the spatial-temporal order of sense, all those traditional forms of Christian mysticism advocating a direct intuition of God in a way differing from ordinary sense perception he regarded as of only limited value. Certainly Marius' mystic experience in the inn garden or Pascal's sense of the divine companion were of value, but only because those intuitions led them out into the visible world in an attempt to find their concrete embodiment. The center of the circle is not reached by the turning of one's back upon the visible world, as Sebastian or Aurelius or, in a measure, even Coleridge had done. Instead of desiring to concentrate all energy like the spot of burning glass and so find God in the totality of phenomena, the mystical temperament prefers to diffuse the gem-like flame by a reverse process so that life becomes a mere *tabula rasa*. In his portrait of Sebastian, Pater specifically invokes this circle-center image when he writes that the Absolute mind need not inspire a cold rejection of the sensuous world:

There might have been found, within the circumference of that one infinite creative thinker, some scope for the joy and love of . . . finite interests around and within us. Centre of heat and light, truly nothing has seemed to lie beyond the touch of its perpetual summer. It has allied itself to the poetical or artistic sympathy, which feels challenged to acquaint itself with and explore the various forms of finite existence all the more intimately, just because of that sense of one lively spirit circulating through all things—a tiny particle of that one soul, in the sunbeam, or the leaf. (*IP*, 107–8)

The One, like the sun, endows the circumference with its life, and Sebastian's failure to perceive this led to his vain attempt to grasp the Absolute by a negation of the beauty and art of the finite world. But the utterly transcendent center at which Sebastian supposes himself to have arrived is nothing at all. There can be no rapport between it and the circumference, for it is a spirit cut off from matter, a pure abstraction without content. One must,

---

[4] *Ibid.*, pp. vi–vii.

Pater insists, always reach the noumenal by taking the path down through the phenomenal. Hence, the center of Pater's circle is visible, sensuous, and concrete form, the visible vesture and expression of God, not the pure form of God as He is.

This centripetal form represents a harmony related to the "cosmos" of the universe itself. Pater's equation of the center of the circle with the sun reveals the dramatic basis of his artistic-religious metaphor, the solar system. Dionysus, the god of the circumference, is a seasonal god, his cycle of summer and winter being a function of the orbital cycle of the earth itself. At the center of the seasonal circle is Apollo, the sun-god. The sun, which accounts for the Dionysian alternations of the seasons, is the true principle of rebirth on the purely physical level, as it is metaphorically the quickening force on the artistic plane. We recall how Apollyon taught the Prior the wicked, unscriptural truth that the sun lay at the center of the solar system. Here, in the mythic figure of Apollo, the grey and formless spirituality of the Prior is reconciled with the fire of color. The void of Aurelius, the nihilism of Sebastian, the abyss of Pascal—all these modes of the indefinitely expanded circle are given concrete form at the center, a form which is a reflection of the all-pervasive order of the universe itself. Moreover, Pater invests his metaphoric cosmos with the significance of old Pythagorean lore. The Pythagoreans supposed that the movement of the heavenly spheres around the central fire, the principle which governs the universe, produces a musical harmony. For Pater, this ancient Pythagorean music of the spheres is a metaphor of the harmony between circumference and center. Harmony, Pater reasons, transcends melody, for melody belongs entirely to the circumference. Melody is merely "the opposition of successive sounds," but harmony is "the richer music generated by opposition of sounds in one and the same moment" (*MS*, 114)—the *totum simul*.

Again and again, Pater returns to the metaphor of musical harmony to describe the central fire. The Heraclitean fire of the Logos, which like the Pythagorean fire is the universal reason in things, is described by Pater as a "harmony of musical notes" (*ME*, I, 131), an "antiphonal rhythm" (*PP*, 17). In "Diaphaneitè," Pater writes that the Apollonian hero, who is a reflection of this intellectual fire, is one in whom "no single gift, or virtue, or idea, has an unmusical predominance" (*MS*, 252). And in *Marius* Pater describes morality as "one mode of comeliness in things—as it were music, or a kind of artistic order, in life . . . —such a music as no one who had once caught its harmonies would willingly jar"

(*ME, II,* 4, 10, 23). It is artistic creation, however, which is most often characterized by Pater in terms of music. "Music," says Pater, in the wider Platonic sense "comprehends all those matters over which the Muses of Greek mythology preside" (*ME,* I, 147; *PP,* 200). That is, music symbolizes the arts themselves, and Apollo with his lyre was the "creator of that music" (*PP,* 203). We are not surprised, then, when Pater says in the essay on Giorgione that "all art constantly aspires towards the condition of music" (*R,* 135), for he naturally conceives of music as the most perfect expression of the fusion of form and matter:

> It is the art of music which most completely realises this artistic ideal, this perfect identification of matter and form. In its consummate moments, the end is not distinct from the means, the form from the matter, the subject from the expression; they inhere in and completely saturate each other; and to it, therefore, to the condition of its perfect moments, all the arts may be supposed constantly to tend and aspire.
> (*R,* 138–39)

As a child, especially, Pater found the romantic and unharmonized sides of Dionysus' joy and sadness united by Apollo's lyre. He was aware not only of "the visible, tangible, audible loveliness of things" but also of "the sorrow of the world," and it was "in music sometimes the two sorts of impressions came together, and he would weep, to the surprise of older people" (*MS,* 181). Thus, music is more than a pleasing simile in Pater's writings; and when, for example, we are told by Marie-Marguerite in her journal that a work of Watteau's is "like a piece of 'chamber-music' " (*IP,* 22) or when we read that Denys' organ "expanded to the full compass of his nature, in its sorrow and delight" and "was the triumph of all the various modes of the power of the pipe, tamed, ruled, united" (*IP,* 72) or when we hear of the "musical notes" (*MS,* 148) which mysteriously pervade the *vallis monachorum,* we should sense Pater's underlying image of the circumference harmonized at the center.

For the medieval theologians, the paradox of the *totum simul* was spanned by the Incarnation when, in a single divine personality, the center and circumference were identified, infinity manifesting itself in the finite. Certainly Pater did no violence to tradition when he transferred the circle-center image from Christ to Apollo; we are reminded of that old pun son-sun, linking Apollo with the Christian tradition in which God is *Pater Luminum* and Christ is *Lux Mundi.* More specifically, the day sacred to *Sol Invictus* is also, as we saw in "Apollo in Picardy," the day when the birth of *Sol Iustitiae* was celebrated. Further, Apollo is in his function the most Christ-like of the ancient gods. He is the god who accepts repentance as an atonement for sin, who pardons the contrite sinner, and who acts as the special protector of those who, like Orestes, have committed a crime which requires long years of expiation. And, of course, having once tended the flocks and herds of Admetus, Apollo is also the Good Shepherd. But neither Christ nor the Paterian hero is, in the mortal state, wholly God. The hero is the servant of God. His life takes the form of a quest for unity, but the gap is successfully spanned only at the moment of his death.

In Pater's fiction this quest for Christ-like mediation between circle and center is dramatically rendered as a search by the hero for the object of his love. The attainment of his love is identical with his possession of the center. In the very first essay in *The Renaissance*, "Two Early French Stories," Pater speaks of the Middle Ages and its "ideal intensity of love" (*R*, 23), a love which is flawless and ideal because it embodies the spiritual element as well as physical passion and because in its ultimate tendency soul and matter are perfectly blended in ideal sensuous form. Pater gives the examples of Amis and Amile, Tannhäuser and Venus, Abelard and Heloïse, Aucassin and Nicolette, Dante and Beatrice, among others. Later, in his essay on Rossetti, Pater singles out Dante as the "central representative" of the true medieval spirit which "had set itself against that Manichean opposition of spirit and matter." In the "vehement and impassioned heat" of Dante's vision, "the material and the spiritual are fused and blent; if the spiritual attains the definite visibility of a crystal, what is material loses its earthiness and impurity" (*Ap*, 212; *PP*, 135). In the "ideal intensity" (*Ap*, 212) of Dante's love for Beatrice, so like the "perfect imaginative love" (*ME*, I, 92) of Psyche's passion for Cupid, we observe the power which forges the broken world of the lovers into the single intense flame of the center.

But throughout Pater's fiction this ideal love is brushed with sadness; it waits upon death for its complete realization. In every love there is some sense of separation, some longing for union, some element of the untiring quest for completion and fulfillment. The love quests of Psyche for Cupid or of Demeter for Persephone are perhaps the archetypal patterns. Other illustrations are numerous in Pater's writings. Besides the examples of the quest found in "Two Early French Stories," one can cite at random those of Dionysus for Semele (*GS*, 45), of Semele for Zeus (*GS*, 24), of Apollo for Hyacinthus (*PP*, 229), of Polydeuces for Castor

(*PP*, 230), of the Halcyon for Ceyx (*ME*, II, 81), of Hercules for Alcestis (*ME*, II, 103), of Menelaus for Helen (*GS*, 129), of Prior Saint-Jean for Hyacinth (*MS*, 170), of Emerald for James (*MS*, 239), of Hippolytus for Artemis (*GS*, 169), of Gaston for Colombe (*GdL*, 129), of Duke Carl for Gretchen (*IP*, 149), of Mademoiselle van Westrheene for Sebastian (*IP*, 102), of Marie-Marguerite for Watteau (*IP*, 9), of Winckelmann for Friedrich von Berg (*R*, 191), of Leonardo for Mona Lisa (*R*, 124), of Michelangelo for Vittoria Colonna (*R*, 83). Some examples more obvious and many less obvious are scattered throughout the pages of Pater's writings. These loves are not in the ordinary sense sexual; there is no distinction of male and female, no physical union; indeed, in every case the object of the love is absent or unattainable. Such loves are allegories of the quest of the soul for the visible form of the Logos in the flux of the circumference and of the quest of the circumference for the central resting place of the Logos in the soul-point.

When the soul separates from the Logos, it descends into the sensuous world, and like Persephone, it takes up a life-in-death existence, yearning for reunion with the divine form from which it came. Because it is mortal, it cannot apprehend the divine form of the Logos as it is, only its sensuous embodiment. But on the fractured Dionysian circumference, even this visible object of its love is broken into "a thousand symbols and reflections." Only through his death can the hero bring the circumference back to the form at the center. At the moment of death, the divine dwells in the whole circle at the soul-center, for the soul is the representative of humanity and, purified of the dross of its mortality, is the channel of Revelation to the whole community. The virgin and sterile circumference—Demeter, humanity, the *Mater Ecclesia*—is fructified by the death of the hero and travails in birth. The relation between center and circumference, soul and humanity, is, therefore, that of being mutually creator and created. Just as the exiled soul seeks to identify within the flux of the circumference some coherent form toward which its emotions can be directed, so the circumference struggles to find some particular soul-point which will serve as the center of its unification. Or, to cast it in mythical and fictional terms, the search of Persephone for Demeter is also the search of the *Magna Mater* for the daughter. For just as the year-daimon is awakened by the *Magna Mater*, who is then renewed by the daimon's death, so, for example, the soul of Marius is sustained and carried forward by the Church, which is then fructified by his martyrdom.

The tombs and catacombs in *Marius*, the exhumation of the saint in "Denys," the burial vaults in "Duke Carl," the subterranean exile of Domenico—all reflect that Chthonian world which is mortality itself. Caught in the grave of mortal life, the hero finds his escape in death. For him, the veil of sleep, of mortality, is pierced by those rays of Apollo's love stronger than death. The dawn, then, represents that moment of hope when the dark night of the soul, shrouded in the shadows of the wintry god of death, begins to yield to the "mixed lights" of the new age. Demeter, veiled by sorrow, or Hippolytus, veiled by exile, searches for the light of the divine countenance. "He who is ever looking for the breaking of a light he knows not whence about him, notes with a strange heedfulness the faintest paleness in the sky" (*MS*, 251), says Pater of the Apollonian hero. It is just this sort of "strange heedfulness," an almost heliotropic nature, which, by anticipating the new era, actually calls forth that "reaction from dreamlight to daylight" (*Ap*[1889], 222). Speaking of Leonardo's "strange veil of sight," Pater says that "things reach him . . . in no ordinary night or day, but as in the faint light of eclipse, or in some brief interval of falling rain at daybreak, or through deep water" (*R*, 111). The translucence of Leonardo's vision is the veil of mortality through which the light of immortality is already perceived—like the shining of the taper through the Host. And so also in *Marius* the rain at dawn is a prelude to sacrificial death and unobstructed vision. We recall the morning when Marius first witnessed the celebration of the Mass, how on that day "he awoke with a sharp flash of lightning in the earliest twilight," how "the heavy rain had filtered the air," and how "under the clear but immature light of winter morning after a storm, all the details of form and colour in the old marbles were distinctly visible, and with a kind of severity or sadness—so it struck him—amid their beauty" (*ME*, II, 129).

Exile, pilgrimage, vision—these are the three stages in which victory is wrung from suffering. Childhood, perhaps, is the only time in the life of the soul that it does not feel the sting of its mortality, the curse of its alienation from God. Pater, like Wordsworth, felt keenly the passing of a childhood in which "the relics of Paradise still clung about the soul—a childhood, as it seemed, full of the fruits of old age, lost for all, in a degree, in the passing away of the youth of the world, lost for each one, over again, in the passing away of actual youth" (*Ap*, 55). "Our birth is but a sleep and a forgetting," says Wordsworth in his famous ode, and though "heaven lies about us in our infancy," the "shades of the prison-house" soon close about the soul.[5] Maturity, for Pater as for Wordsworth, then, is regarded as a kind of fall. But it is not all somber. As Pater wrote in *The Renaissance* in speaking of the passing of civilization's youth:

The longer we contemplate that Hellenic ideal, in which man is at unity with himself, with his physical nature, with the outward world, the more we may be inclined to regret that he should ever have passed beyond it, to contend for a perfection that makes the blood turbid, and frets the flesh, and discredits the actual world about us. But if he was to be saved from the *ennui* which ever attaches itself to realisation, even the realisation of the perfect life, it was necessary that a conflict should come, that some sharper note should grieve the existing harmony, and the spirit chafed by it beat out at last only a larger and profounder music. (*R*, 222)

Maturity for the soul is, so to speak, a fortunate fall, for the loss of a first Eden brings "at last only a larger and profounder music." Insofar as there is original sin in Pater's theology, its consequence is "the lust of the eye" (*MS*, 181), for sin creates mortality and mortality gives rise to the need to perceive the ideal in visible form. But vision is not negative as it was for Augustine; rather, vision is what the fallen soul craves as the surest way back to its state of grace. "Our pilgrimage is meant indeed to end in nothing less than the *vision* of what we seek" (*PP*, 192), Pater writes in *Plato*. And so an individual such as Florian Deleal leaves his paradise to wander, like the exiled gods of Heine's myth, through space and time in search of the visible form of the ideal. Florian remembers "gratefully how the Christian religion, hardly less than the religion of the ancient Greeks, translating so much of its spiritual verity into things that may be seen, condescends in part to sanction this infirmity, if so it be, of our human existence, wherein the world of sense is so much with us" (*MS*, 187).

Pater's heroes, though wandering like the ghostly gods, are not really exiles without a goal. They are pilgrims—those who will eventually find the lost form of the center after traveling the circumference. Stopping at one of the inns of life, Marius can see himself moving as on a distant road, as if he were another person, "through all his fortunes and misfortunes, passing from point to point, weeping, delighted, escaping from various dangers" (*ME*, II, 66). He then has a vision, albeit mystical and without visual content. But later that content is supplied in a "single form, like the *Zeus* of Olympia," by the Mass, with its "unity of a single

[5] Wordsworth's "Intimations" ode seems to be the immediate source of much of Pater's dream, sun, and circle imagery.

appeal to eye and ear" (*ME*, II, 128) so that the "absent or veiled" (*Ap*[1889], 216) form is once again central and seen. In *Plato* Pater had spoken of the "dialectic" method of the dialogues as "a circuitous journey" (*PP*, 178), an image which fuses the pilgrimage motif with that of the circle-center. He visualizes Plato's quest for truth as spiraling around a mountain, upward toward the central and highest point. Only on the summit, at the center, with the last step, does the hero complete the circle of truth, observing of the world "that, next to that final intuition, the first view, the first impression, had been truest about it" (*PP*, 180). One is reminded of Florian Deleal's agony of homesickness and Vaughan's wistful longing for backward steps; for this final intuition is a discovery of the indwelling form of God of which the harmony of childhood had been a handsel. For those like Sebastian, sensuous form seemed a trap, and his bodily malady was a symptom of his self-imposed exile. The early poetry of Morris, faint and spectral, represented just such a delirious desire to escape sense; the secret of its enjoyment, says Pater, "is that inversion of home-sickness known to some, that incurable thirst for the sense of escape, which no actual form of life satisfies, no poetry even, if it be merely simple and spontaneous" (*Ap*[1889], 213–14). But it is only in sensuous form that the exile can again find home and turn to his rest; thus, Pater's typical hero traces out a sort of "mental pilgrimage through time and space" (*PP*, 165), returning, indeed, physically as well as spiritually to that first home which he had been "ever seeking to regain" (*ME*, I, 22).

That vision of home at which the hero finally arrives is depicted in Pater's thought as the Perfect City—Olympus, *Civitas Dei*, the Kingdom of Heaven, Utopia, the Personalistic Community of Selves. The Apollonian hero, by recovering this spirit of God and possessing that harmonious world within himself, points the way which humanity must take to reach the Perfect City. "A majority of such," says Pater of the hero, "would be the regeneration of the world" (*MS*, 254). It is especially appropriate that the Paterian hero, as a reflection of the god Apollo, should be the creator of this City, this expression of Love on earth, for Apollo himself was the greatest patron of the founding of cities, and the Greeks built no cities without first consulting the Delphic oracle. This Apollonian city is pre-eminently a city of harmony, and Pater reminds us in his portrait of Prior Saint-Jean that Apollo's city-building in antiquity had been done to the harmonious music of his lyre, as, for example, when he helped Poseidon with the walls of Troy. Pater properly stresses the musical qualities which Plato had associated with his Perfect City. In the Pythagorean system, the planetary motions were taken to

produce, naturally enough, sounds, that famous "music of the spheres." . . . Now the harmonious order of the whole universe was what souls had heard of old; found echoes of here; might recover in its entirety, amid the influences of the melodious colour, sounds, manners, the enforced modulating discipline, which would make the whole life of a citizen of the Perfect City an education in music. (*PP*, 70)

Pythagoras, who was the first to perceive the real importance of harmony, was himself considered by the "fantastic masters of Neo-Platonism, or Neo-Pythagoreanism" to be "a son of Apollo, nay, Apollo himself" (*PP*, 53):

As his fellow-citizens had all but identified Pythagoras with him, so Apollo remained the peculiar patron of the Pythagoreans; and we may note, in connexion with their influence on Plato, that as Apollo was the chosen ancestral deity, so Pythagoreanism became especially the philosophy, of the severely musical Dorian Greeks. (*PP*, 55)

The Apollonian city of the future, then, is pervaded by the music of the spheres, the most fitting expression of its centrally balanced harmony of parts.

But part of the power of Pater's vision is that the future is not excluded from already pre-existing in the present. In the Conclusion to *The Renaissance,* he had said that to "a single sharp impression, with a sense in it, a relic more or less fleeting, of such moments gone by, what is real in our life fines itself down" (*R*, 236). Yet in that moment of epiphany we can embrace a wider realm of experience and can make a single point on the circumference become, for an instant, the center. The distinction of time and eternity is owing only to our finite standpoint, but at the summit of the mountain all things are beheld, in Spinoza's phrase, *sub specie aeternitatis.* What had existed for the human consciousness as a time-development, now exists, as it does for the Divine consciousness itself, as an eternally complete whole. The center of the circle, the "*nunc*" of eternity, as the Scholastics termed it, corresponds to what Pater called "the mystic *now*" (*ME*, I, 154), which Marius and Prior Saint-Jean, among others, struggled to grasp and describe in language. In his description of the Platonic mountaintop, Pater implies, in the circle-center image of the horizon and the central point, that all the varied determinations of the circumference stand before the mind in simultaneous reality:

"Persevere," Plato might say, "and a step may be made, upon which, again, the whole world around may change, the entire horizon and its relation to the point you stand on—a change from the half-light of conjecture to the full light of indefectible certitude." That, of course, can only happen by a *summary* act of intuition upon the entire perspective, wherein all those partial apprehensions, which one by one may have seemed inconsistent with each other, find their due place, . . . in which the mind attains a hold, as if by a single imaginative act, through all the transitions of a long conversation, upon all the seemingly opposite contentions of all the various speakers at once. (*PP*, 181)

Poetry, such as the sort the English poet must have written, also often arrests these "perfect moments:"

It is part of the ideality of the highest sort of dramatic poetry, that it presents us with a kind of profoundly significant and animated instants, a mere gesture, a look, a smile, perhaps—some brief and wholly concrete moment—into which, however, all the motives, all the interests and effects of a long history, have condensed themselves, and which seem to absorb past and future in an intense consciousness of the present. [They are] ideal instants, . . . exquisite pauses in time, in which, arrested thus, we seem to be spectators of all the fulness of existence, and which are like some consummate extract or quintessence of life. (*R*, 150)

Even the humble objects of the natural world, the gem, the flower, or the seashell—three of Pater's favorite objects of beauty—are at times enriched by the "colour and expression of the whole circumjacent world, concentrated upon, or as it were at focus in, it. By a kind of short-hand now, and as if in a single moment of vision, all that, which only a long experience, moving patiently from part to part, could exhaust, its manifold alliance with the entire world of nature, is legible upon it, as it lies there in one's hand" (*PP*, 158).

Such power of imagination is unfortunately what Lucian lacked, and the centerlessness of his skeptical circle is sufficient comment upon such as he. But for Pater and his heroes, however, to see in any meaningful sense at all is to see imaginatively. If Pater borrowed the word *imaginary* from Landor to characterize his portraits, it carried for him the added significance given it by the *Biographia Literaria*—a perception or intuition of the divine within the flux. Coleridge himself, Pater felt, all too often hoped to grasp the Spirit permeating the visible world without duly valuing natural objects themselves, and so at times his imaginative visions were but the delirium, the narcotic dream, of the imprisoned mind. But if one uses imagination rightly, the delirium becomes the vision of the burning center. It is the divine and poetic madness of the Platonic tradition, or in Christian terms it is the inspiration of the Holy Spirit. To burn with the hard gem-like flame surely finds its most literal equivalent in the tongues of fire, and the storm at dawn, which Pater mentions in a number of places, is not unlike the mighty rushing wind. But the coming of this storm, as at the end of "Sebastian," "Duke Carl, or "Apollo," has the power of an inspiration which literally destroys the beholder, for the awakening of the vision and the sight of the face of God are death in Hebraic and Greek tradition alike. We recall the lightning in which the divine form of Zeus appeared to Semele and struck her dead, for "not without loss of sight, or life itself can man look upon it" (GS, 24). But if Semele's death symbolizes the mortality which her son Dionysus undergoes, just as the opening of Marius' eyes at Pisa began his long exile, nevertheless, that first death and its mortality contain within them the seeds of the second death and its awakening to immortality. Certainly there is a sad "fatality which seems to haunt any signal beauty" (ME, I, 93), for the gaining of the center of the circle is a martyr's death. But yet that death is not without the sort of quiet joy with which the Christians buried Marius, for while the ultimate of the religious quest is only penultimate, yet the vision at the center is the hope of an awakening from mortality.

INDEX

PATER'S PORTRAITS
Mythic Pattern in the Fiction of Walter Pater
by Gerald Cornelius Monsman

Designer: *Gerard Valerio*
Typesetter: *The Maple Press Company*
Typeface: *Waverly Linotype and Forum Display*
Printer: *The Maple Press Company*
Paper: *Mohawk Tosca*
Binder: *The Maple Press Company*